New Knowledge in Human Values

HARPER & ROW, PUBLISHERS
New York and Evanston

NEW KNOWLEDGE IN HUMAN VALUES

VALUES

EDITED BY ABRAHAM H. MASLOW

Professor of Psychology, Brandeis University

FOREWORD BY PITIRIM A. SOROKIN

Professor of Sociology, Emeritus, Harvard University

NEW KNOWLEDGE IN HUMAN VALUES

Library of Congress catalog card number: 58–11051

Contents

v

PART II. *COMMENT AND REPLIES*

Preface

THIS volume springs from the belief, first, that the ultimate disease of our time is valuelessness; second, that this state is more crucially dangerous than ever before in history; and finally, that something can be done about it by man's own rational efforts.

The state of valuelessness has been variously described as anomie, amorality, anhedonia, rootlessness, emptiness, hopelessness, the lack of something to believe in and to be devoted to. It has come to its present dangerous point because all the traditional value systems ever offered to mankind have in effect proved to be failures (our present state proves this to be so). Furthermore, wealth and prosperity, technological advance, widespread education, democratic political forms, even honestly good intentions and avowals of good will have, by their failure to produce peace, brotherhood, serenity, and happiness, confronted us even more nakedly and unavoidably with the profundities that mankind has been avoiding by its busy-ness with the superficial.

We are reminded here of the "neurosis of success." People can struggle on hopefully, and even happily, for false panaceas so long as these are not attained. Once attained, however, they are soon discovered to be false hopes. Collapse and hopelessness ensue and continue until new hopes become possible.

We too are in an interregnum between old value systems that have not worked and new ones not yet born, an empty period which could be borne more patiently were it not for the great and unique dangers that beset mankind. We are faced with the real possibility of annihilation, and with the certainty of "small" wars, of racial hostilities, and of widespread exploitation. Specieshood is far in the future.

The cure for this disease is obvious. We need a validated, usable system of human values, values that we can believe in and devote ourselves to because they are true rather than because we are *exhorted* to "believe and have faith."

And for the first time in history, many of us feel, such a system —based squarely upon valid knowledge of the nature of man, of his society, and of his works—may be possible.

This is not to maintain that this knowledge is *now* available in the final form necessary for breeding conviction and action. It is not. What *is* available, however, is enough to give us confidence that we know the kinds of work that have to be done in order to progress toward such a goal. It appears possible for man, by his own philosophical and scientific efforts, to move toward self-improvement and social improvement.

The Conference on "New Knowledge in Human Values" was conceived as a first organizing step in this direction. The following letter of invitation was sent to representative scholars from various disciplines, who had already made significant contributions to the study of values. The letter of invitation read as follows:

Dear ——:

We, the undersigned, have been appointed by the Research Society for Creative Altruism as a Program Committee to organize a conference on New Knowledge in Human Values to be held October 4 and 5, 1957, at the Kresge Auditorium, Massachusetts Institute of Technology, Cambridge, Massachusetts.

This is the first conference sponsored by the Research Society for Creative Altruism, incorporated in April, 1956. In accordance with the aims of the Society, the conference is designed to form a report to the public by objective, deeply concerned, hopeful scholars of work in the broad field of human values—moral, spiritual, aesthetic, economic—and their application to the affairs and institutions of mankind. The speakers to be invited, representing a cross-section of academic disciplines and human endeavor, symbolize the growing convergence towards a common framework of attack on the chief intellectual challenge to twentieth-century man.

We hope the conference will make an impressive demonstration of (a) the general concern of thoughtful people with this problem; (b) the convergence of conclusions by people working independently in different fields; and (c) the increasing hope that a "science" of values is possible, and that we need no longer be content only with exhortation, with authoritarian statements, or with "a priori" thinking.

This letter is an invitation to you to be one of the speakers on this program; to tell us how your work and your field might contribute to the general theme of the conference.

We hope very much that you share with us our belief that such a conference could be the beginning of fruitful collaborations.

> Sincerely yours,
> Abraham H. Maslow, *Chairman*

Swami Akhilananda	Gyorgy Kepes
Gordon W. Allport	James H. Shrader
E. Francis Bowditch	Pitirim A. Sorokin
Ralph W. Burhoe	Victor F. Weisskopf

These statements were elaborated in a later letter which asked each speaker "to address himself to the problem 'What do we know about human values?'" He was told that this could be interpreted variously as "What can we know about human values?" or "What new developments—theoretical, experiential, empirical—in your field of study are important for the future study of human values?" or "Is a science of human values possible?"

That there eventuated a heartening amount of convergence and agreement can easily be seen by the reader. These, as well as the divergences in basic point of view, are brilliantly set forth in Dr. Weisskopf's summary chapter. It was also hoped that the Conference would open up new lines of research, and this expectation has been amply fulfilled. Many such suggestions will be found throughout this volume, either implicitly or explicitly stated. Finally, many of the speakers have presented potent criticisms of extant value theories which serve also as prolegomena to any future value theory. These must be taken seriously not only by professional thinkers on the subject but also by all thoughtful people everywhere.

It is our hope that this volume will be a stimulus to widespread individual and organized work toward the end that the possibilities here presented may be progressively actualized.

Mr. E. Francis Bowditch was the moving spirit in the organization of the M.I.T. Conference on "New Knowledge In Human Values," and therefore of this book. His unusual devotion, capacity and hard work in arranging and administering the Conference in all its details are very gratefully acknowledged.

ABRAHAM H. MASLOW

Foreword from the Society

_____ PITIRIM A. SOROKIN

THIS volume is the result of the First Scientific Conference on New Knowledge in Human Values organized by the Research Society for Creative Altruism at the Kresge Auditorium, Massachusetts Institute of Technology, October 4 and 5, 1957. The Research Society itself is a cultural child and successor of the Harvard Research Center in Creative Altruism. And the existence of the Harvard Research Center, in its turn, is due to the spontaneous concordance of the ideas and ideals of Eli Lilly and my own, plus a lucky, or perhaps providential, combination of circumstances.

The mass exterminations and the horrors of the First World War, and especially of the Russian Revolution—in both of which I participated as an observer and actor—had led me to the conclusion summed up in my *Leaves From a Russian Diary* (1924)—that "cruelty, hatred, and injustice never can and never will be able to create a mental, moral, or material millennium," and that "the creative, unselfish work of love for humanity at large is the key to the reconstruction of the world."

Subsequently, my studies of social and cultural dynamics and of the nature of the epochal crisis of our age (published in my *Sociology of Revolution* [1924], *Social Mobility* [1927], *Social and Cultural Dynamics* [1937], and *Crisis of Our Age* [1941]) reinforced the conclusion that, without a transformation of modern sensate man and of the dominant sensate culture, this crisis could develop into an Apocalyptic war capable of terminating mankind's creative history. A few years later these conclusions were to be tragically confirmed by the Second World War, by a multitude of hot and cold wars, and by a legion of bloody revolutions and disorders. The unprecedented destructiveness, bestiality, and moral insanity of these convulsions—and the millions victimized by them —led me, in February 1946, to the decision to devote my free time from then on to the study of unselfish, creative love, and of effective techniques for transforming the motivational systems of man— and thus transforming his sociocultural universe.

My previous studies, published in some eight volumes, were made without any grants for research assistantships in my work, and I expected to carry on this exploration also by my personal efforts. This plan was altered by the generous interference of Eli Lilly. In his first letter to me, dated April 20, 1942, he wrote kindly: "Your book, 'Crisis of Our Age' has created a most favorable impression and influence among my friends and practically all are certain that your theories are right. Our main interest now is what can we do about it. . . . If you can answer this question, it will be greatly appreciated."

At that time I did not know Mr. Lilly personally, nor did I know anything about his cultural activities; nor had I any knowledge about Lilly Endowment, Inc. For this reason I did not ask for, or expect, any help from him in my studies.

This explains my surprise at receiving a letter, April 17, 1946, in which he informed me: "I shall be very glad to give a sum of $10,000 or $20,000 [for a research assistantship in my studies of unselfish creative love] as soon as you feel a practical plan has been made. Later I hope additional and more substantial sums could be forthcoming."

After consulting with President Conant of Harvard, I informed Mr. Lilly that I was gratefully accepting his generous grant and that it could formally be given to Harvard University for the research assistantship. In this way the cornerstone for the Harvard

Research Center was laid. The continuing interest and support of the Lilly Endowment later made possible the establishment of the Center, in February 1949.

Thanks to the generous cooperation of some thirty scholars— American, European, Asiatic, and African—leading in the strategic fields of the study, the Center has been able to publish, so far, ten substantial volumes of its investigations. Some of these volumes have already been translated and published in German, Spanish, Japanese, Norwegian, Swedish, and French. Despite a modest annual budget, the studies of the Center have attracted worldwide attention and have been instrumental in the establishment, under diverse names, of several similar research centers in various countries.

With the development of this research, my conviction that its goal—fostering the spirit of altruism in man—is indeed the paramount business on today's agenda of history has been increasingly reinforced and confirmed. This logically suggested the next step in the development of scientific study of this "mysterious, powerful grace," namely, the establishment of a national and even international research society in this field, which could be an independent institution and could do the research and educational work of the Center on a larger and deeper scale.

In accordance with this idea, I organized a meeting, on October 29, 1955, at Emerson Hall, Harvard University, of an initiatory group for discussion of this problem. The group consisted of Melvin Arnold, Dean E. F. Bowditch, Dean Walter H. Clark, Senator Ralph E. Flanders, The Rev. Duncan Howlett, Dr. F. Kunz, Professor H. Margenau, Chancellor Daniel Marsh, Professors A. Maslow, F. S. C. Northrop, J. H. Shrader, R. Ulich, Dr. I. I. Sikorsky, and Swami Akhilananda. After a careful discussion the group unanimously voted that the Research Society for Creative Altruism should be established and incorporated in the State of Massachusetts. At the next meeting of the initiatory group, November 19, 1955, in the presence of Professor Hunting, Notary Public, the constitution of the Society was discussed and approved; all the members of the initiatory group were voted to be the members of the

Council of the Society. Dr. I. I. Sikorsky was elected President of the Society, F. S. C. Northrop, Vice President, Dr. P. A. Sorokin, Director and Secretary, and E. F. Bowditch, Treasurer. In April of 1956 the Society was officially incorporated in the State of Massachusetts. In January of 1957 E. F. Bowditch was voted in as Administrative Director for one year. Later on, Mr. Harry Culbreth, Mr. Thomas R. Reid, and Mr. Moorhead Wright were added to the Council.

The Society is prepared to move steadfastly ahead in carrying out a program which may be described briefly as organizing high-level research in "moral phenomena and values" and methods of application and dissemination of the results of such research in the most efficient manner possible. Most existing organizations which are pursuing somewhat similar purposes are doing so on the basis of existing knowledge and techniques. It is the determination of this Society to concentrate first and foremost on the development of *new knowledge* and *new methods* for its application.

In organizing the First Scientific Conference on New Knowledge in Human Values, it was the Society's belief that only by bringing together scholars who have made, and are making, major creative contributions could it be made clear to the public what may be accomplished if men and women have but the courage and faith to back a realistic program.

PART I. ADDRESSES

The Powers of Creative Unselfish Love

————————————————— PITIRIM A. SOROKIN

MORAL TRANSFORMATION IS PARAMOUNT TASK OF OUR TIME

THE CENTRAL reason for the establishment of the Harvard Research Center in Creative Altruism and of the Center's progeny—this Research Society—has been the idea that the *moral transformation of man and the man-made universe is the most important item on today's agenda of history*. Without moral transformation in altruistic directions, neither new world wars and other catastrophes can be prevented nor a new—better and nobler—social order be built in the human universe. Without a notable increase of what we call creative unselfish love in man and in the human universe, all fashionable prescriptions for prevention of wars and for building of a new order cannot achieve their purpose.

For instance, one such fashionable prescription is a political reconstruction of all nations along the lines of American democracy. Despite the popularity of this belief, it is questionable. Tomorrow, hypothetically, you could have all nations reconstructed politically along the lines of the American brand of democracy; and yet such a reconstruction would neither prevent nor decrease the chances of new world wars or of bloody internal revolutions. Why? Because study of all the wars and important internal disturbances from 600 B.C. to the present time reveals that democracies are no less belligerent, no less militant, and no more orderly than autocracies.[1]

[1] See the detailed data in P. Sorokin, *Social and Cultural Dynamics*, American

This conclusion is unpleasant. Nevertheless, it is true.

Another favorite prescription against wars and bloody strife is more education and more schooling. Again, hypothetically, tomorrow you could have all men and women at the age of sixteen and over miraculously transformed into Ph.D.'s and super-Ph.D.'s. And yet, such a miraculous increase of education would not decrease the chances of either civil or international wars. Why? Because the prevailing forms of education and the growth of science and technology do not curb or even decrease wars and bloody revolutions. From the tenth century up to the present time, the number of schools, beginning with kindergartens and ending with universities, the percentage of literacy, the number of scientific discoveries and technological inventions, have been continuously increasing, especially during the last two centuries. Despite this enormous educational, scientific, and technological progress the curve of wars (measured either by frequency of wars or by the size of armies or by the amount of casualties per million population) has not gone down during these centuries. If anything, with great fluctuations, it has also gone up. The same is true of revolutions and revolts.[2] We are living in the most scientific, most technological, and most schooled century; and the same century happens to be the bloodiest of all the preceding recorded twenty-five centuries.

The same is true of other popular prescriptions against world wars and internal disturbances—such panaceas as the establishment of a universal capitalistic or communistic or socialistic economic organization. Even the so-called religious factor has failed to alter the pattern—if, by religion, we mean just a set of beliefs, dogmas, and rituals. Among the proofs for this statement we mention here our study of seventy-three converts of popular American and English evangelists. We wanted to know if the conversion of

Book Company, 1937, vol. 3, Chaps. 9–14; in abridged edition of this work, see *ibid.*, Porter Sargent, 1957, Chaps. 32–35.

[2] See the figures in P. Sorokin, *Reconstruction of Humanity*, Beacon Press, 1948, Chap. 3.

these seventy-three persons had changed their minds and, particularly, their overt behavior in altruistic directions, by making it nearer to the sublime precepts of the Sermon on the Mount? The result was not cheerful. Out of these seventy-three persons, only one has shown a tangible change of his personality and overt behavior. About one-half of the converts changed somewhat their speech reactions: instead of profanities they more frequently began to pronounce the name of "Our Lord Jesus Christ" and so on, but their outward behavior did not change at all; and the remaining half of the converts did not change even their speech reactions.

Evidence of this sort, I believe, makes it clear why prevention of future catastrophes is hardly possible without some fundamental change of man's motivations in the direction of altruism. Still less possible becomes the building of a more harmonious and more creative social and cultural order.

THE GIGANTIC POTENTIAL POWER OF LOVE

There is a second reason for the paramount importance of the moral transformation of man. Recent studies have shown that what we tentatively call "unselfish creative love" is not only one of the highest values of the Trinity of value, Truth, Goodness, Beauty, but it is also one of the three most sublime forms of energy, having gigantic potential power for the modification of man and man's universe. The last few decades have been marked in many disciplines—biology, sociology, psychology, anthropology, and others—by an emergence and growth of a *remarkable convergence toward one central point. All these disciplines have been increasingly emphasizing the all-important role of this mysterious power of love.* In recent decades rapidly growing scientific evidence tends to confirm the age-old discovery: God is Love and Love is God. Whereas the biology of the nineteenth century emphasized the role of the struggle for existence, the biology of our time more and more emphasizes—whether in evolution of species or in survival of separate species, or in maintenance of health, vitality, and longevity—the factor of mutual aid, cooperation, or friendship, all these terms being but different words designating diverse aspects of the same creative unselfish love.

Today's biology tells us that this factor has been playing at least as important a role as the factor of struggle for existence; and as time goes on the emphasis upon the power and role of love increases progressively. Among other things, contemporary biologists show clearly that, for survival and multiplication of unicellular or multicellular organisms, cooperation between parental and progeny organisms is absolutely necessary, especially in such species as homo sapiens, in which the newborn baby is helpless and, in order to survive, needs several years of help and love.[3]

The biological, the psychological, the anthropological, and the sociological disciplines are bringing an ever-increasing body of evidence that demonstrates the vitalizing and ennobling power of unselfish love. A few examples well illustrate this point. For instance, studies of suicide show that so-called egotistic suicide (the act of anomie) is caused mainly by loneliness and psychosocial isolation of an individual, especially when it is caused by a sudden disruption of his social ties. *The best antidote against suicide is therefore a transcendence of this isolation by unselfish creative love for other human beings.*[4] A number of studies, including those done by the Harvard Research Center, have shown that *love is a factor which seems to increase the duration of life.*

We have taken something like 4500 Christian saints about whom more or less reliable data could be collected. They lived in various periods beginning with the first century of our era and ending with the present time. Among other things, we investigated the duration of their lives. More than 98 per cent of these saints lived before the nineteenth century. As we approach our time, "the production of saints" rapidly decreases. Now, the average life expectation in the centuries from the first to the eighteenth was much lower than it is in the United States at the present time. Many of these saints in-

[3] Cf. Ashley Montagu, *On Being Human,* Schumann, 1950; P. Sorokin (ed.), *Explorations in Altruistic Love and Behavior,* Beacon Press, 1950.
[4] Durkheim, *Suicide,* Free Press, 1954.

tentionally tortured their bodies and deprived them of satisfaction of their elementary needs. About 37 per cent of these saints died prematurely by martyrdom. In spite of all these adverse conditions, a rough average of life-duration of these saints happened to be at least as long as that of the contemporary American. What is the cause of this? Since most of the saints have been extraordinary apostles of unselfish love, this factor of love has possibly been the most important cause of their longevity.[5]

A number of psychological, psychiatric, sociological, and educational researches have proved that a *minimum of this love is absolutely necessary for survival of newborn babies and for their healthy growth*. Among several studies of this kind, Dr. René A. Spitz's investigation can be mentioned. He reported and filmed the death of thirty-four foundlings in a foundling house. In the foundling home these babies had all the necessities and care except motherly love. After three months of separation from their parents the babies lost appetite, could not sleep, and became shrunken, whimpering, and trembling. After an additional two months they began to look like idiots. Twenty-seven foundlings died in their first year of life, seven in the second. Twenty-one lived longer but were so altered that thereafter they could be classified as idiots.

The curative and integrating power of love shows itself in many other forms. The grace of love—in both forms of loving and being loved—is the most important condition for babies to grow into morally and mentally sound human beings. Many sociological studies show that the *bulk of juvenile delinquents are recruited from the children who in their early life did not have the necessary minimum of love. Deficiency of "the vitamin of love" is also responsible for many mental disorders*. On the other hand, in our age of psychoneuroses and juvenile delinquency, the Mennonite, the Hutterite, some Quaker, and even the Chinese communities in the United States yield either none or the lowest quota of delinquents, mentally sick persons, and drug addicts. The main reason for this is that these

[5] Cf. P. Sorokin, *Altruistic Love: A Study of American Good Neighbors and Christian Saints*, Beacon Press, 1950.

communities not only preach love but realize it in their daily life; they are united into a sort of a real brotherhood.

The curative power of love is also increasingly emphasized by the recent studies in psychiatry. The investigations of K. E. Appel, F. E. Fiedler, C. Rogers, V. E. Frankl, H. J. Eysenck, G. W. Allport, R. Assagioli, E. Straus, and other psychiatrists and psychologists show that the *main curative agent in the treatment of mental disorders* is not so much the specific technique used by various schools of psychiatry as the establishment of the rapport of *empathy, sympathy, kindness, and mutual trust between the patient and the therapist and the placing of the patient in a "social climate" free from inner and interhuman conflicts.*

The studies of the Harvard Research Center in Creative Altruism and of other scholars disclose other manifestations of the power of love. Despite our meager knowledge of the mysterious and sublime energy of love, its revitalizing, curative, ameliorative, and creative functions are already demonstrated by numerous converging studies of love. For instance, our experimental transformation of formerly inimical relationships between the members of each of five pairs of Harvard and Radcliffe students into amicable ones (within the period of three months, by the method of "good deeds" rendered by one of the partners of each pair to the other partner) demonstrates well the *power of love in mitigation of interhuman hatred and in elimination of interhuman strife.*

Likewise our experimental and clinical investigations of the friendly and inimical approaches and responses among the students of Harvard and Radcliffe and among the patients of the Boston Psychopathic Hospital clearly confirm the truth of the old motto that *"love begets love and hate begets hate."* Roughly from 65 to 80 per cent of the responses to the friendly (or the aggressive) approaches were respectively friendly (or inimical). Similarly, our detailed study of how and why each of some five hundred Harvard and Radcliffe students happened to feel and regard a certain individual as his or her "best friend" and another individual as "the worst enemy" disclosed the fact that *in all cases of "the best friend" the friendship was started by some friendly action of the person who, continuing to be friendly, eventually became "the best friend," and in all cases of "the worst enemy" the animosity was started by an aggressive action of the person who gradually became "the worst enemy."*

I wish these experimentally tested truths could be deeply implanted into the minds and hearts of contemporary American and Soviet politicians. They seem to be trying to achieve a lasting peace by following the old method of mutual hate and vituperation, by mutual aggressive and harmful actions, and by cold and hot wars. They seem to believe in the policy of "hate begets love, and love begets hate" and "cold and hot wars beget peace." No wonder their policies have not brought peace, despite hundreds of billions of dollars spent, hundreds of thousands of lives sacrificed, and an untold amount of energy, time, health, security, and happiness of millions wasted in these absurd policies.

The constructive efficacy of love clearly manifests itself also in the life history of various societies and in the national and international life of mankind. *Creative love increases not only the longevity of individuals but also of societies and organizations.* Social organizations built by hate, conquest, and coercion, such as the empires of Alexander the Great, Caesar, Genghis-Khan, Tamerlane, Napoleon, or Hitler, have, as a rule, a short life—years, decades, or rarely, a few centuries. Often they crumble before the death of their builders. The average duration of various social organizations in which unselfish love plays an unimportant part is also comparatively modest. Thus, the average longevity of small economic establishments such as drug-grocery-hardware stores in the United States is only about four years; of big business firms (listed on English, Swiss, American stock exchanges), only about 27 years. Even the longevity of most of the states rarely goes beyond one or two hundred years. *The longest existing organizations are the great ethico-religious organizations—Taoism, Confucianism, Hinduism, Buddhism, Jainism, Christianity, Mohammedanism, and the like.* They have already lived more than one or two or even three millennia. And these organizations are motivated by, and dedicated to, the altruistic education of millions in unselfish love.[6]

The case of Emperor Asoka gives an example of *the power of love in taming war and other bloody forms of interhuman strife*. Horrified by the disastrous results of his victorious wars, Asoka, in the second half of his life, under the influence of Buddhism radically replaced his policies of war by the policies of peace, friendship, and constructive reforms; building highways, orphanages, schools, museums, temples, planting trees, digging wells; eliminating injustice, alleviating misery, and in all possible ways helping his own population as well as that of neighboring states. By this friendly policy Asoka secured peace for a period of some seventy-two years. Considering that, on the average, war occurred once in every two years in the history of Greece, Rome, and nine other main European countries in the period beginning with 600 B.C. and ending with the present time; and that a seventy-two-year-long period of peace occurred only twice in the Graeco-Roman and the Western worlds during some twenty-five centuries of their history, Asoka's realization of lasting peace is most instructive: it suggests that the policy of friendship and mutual aid can secure a lasting peace more successfully than that of hate, destructive rivalry, and war.

Finally, the gigantic power of love has manifested itself also in *the greatest and longest influence exerted by the highest apostles of love upon human beings and human history*. If we ask ourselves what sort of individuals have been most influential in human history, the answer is such individuals as Lao-Tze, Confucius, Moses, Gautama Buddha, Mahavira, Jesus, St. Paul, St. Francis of Assisi, Mahatma Gandhi and other founders of great religions, discoverers of eternal moral principles, and living incarnations of sublime, unselfish love. In contrast to the short-lived and mainly destructive influence of autocratic monarchs, military conquerers, revolutionary dictators, potentates of wealth, and other historical persons, these great apostles of spirituality and love have most tangibly affected

[6] Cf. the typical longevity of various social organizations in P. Sorokin, *Society, Culture, and Personality*, Harper, 1947, Chap. 34.

the lives, minds, and bodies of untold millions, of many generations, during millennia of human history; and they are tangibly influencing us at the present time. They had neither army and arms nor physical force nor wealth nor any of the worldly means of influencing the historical destinies of nations. Nor, to obtain their power, did they appeal to hate, envy, greed, and other lusts of human beings. Even their physical organism was not of the strongest kind. And yet, together with a handful of their followers, they morally transformed millions of men and women, reshaped cultures and social institutions, and conditioned the course of history. They did all this by the mere power of their sublime, pure, and overabundant love, by their unselfish spirituality and supreme wisdom.

Summing up the outlined powers of unselfish love, we can say that unselfish creative love can stop aggressive interindividual and intergroup strife and can transform inimical relationships between persons and groups into amicable ones; that love begets love, and hate begets hate (in about 70 to 85 per cent of the cases studied); that love can tangibly influence international relationships and pacify international conflicts. In addition, unselfish and wise love is a life-giving force, necessary for physical, mental, and moral health; altruistic persons live longer than egotistic individuals; children deprived of love tend to become morally, socially, and mentally defective; love is a powerful antidote against criminal, morbid, and suicidal tendencies; love is the loftiest educational force for enlightenment and moral ennoblement of mankind; love performs important cognitive and aesthetic functions; love is the heart and soul of freedom and of all moral and religious values; a minimum of love is necessary for a durable, creative, and harmonious society and its progress; finally, in this catastrophic moment of human history an increased "production, accumulation, and circulation of love-energy" in the whole human universe is a necessary condition for the prevention of new wars and for the alleviation of enormously increased interindividual and intergroup strife.[7]

7 See for the evidential data, detailed analysis, and the literature in P. Sorokin, *The Ways and Power of Love*, Beacon Press, 1954; P. Sorokin (ed.),

Fyodor Dostoievski wrote prophetic words: "Seeing the sins of men, one sometimes wonders whether one should react to them by force or by humble love. Always decide to fight them by humble love. If it is carried through, the whole world can be conquered. Humble love is the most effective force, the most terrific, the most powerful, unequaled by any other force in the world."

Symposium: Forms and Techniques of Altruistic and Spiritual Growth, Beacon Press, 1954; P. Sorokin, *Studies of Harvard Research Center in Creative Altruism,* Beacon Press, 1956.

The Science of Value

ROBERT S. HARTMAN

ALTHOUGH the subject of this essay is the science of value, it deals with value only indirectly. The *science* of value is to value as the science of botany, for example, is to a rose: it does not smell; or as the symbols of Einstein are to the atomic bomb: they do not explode. There are no big blasts in a science, no excitement, no drama—except, perhaps, the excitement that comes from precise thinking and the drama that comes from intellectual discovery. The science of value is an intellectual, not a valuational, enterprise. The value analyst does not value but analyzes value, just as the analyst of motion does not move but analyzes motion.

Thus the science of value is primarily a matter of science, of precise and exact knowledge, the object of which happens to be value. In this respect the science of value is like any other science: it has its axioms, its definitions, its rules of deduction, and its dimensions, its measurements and its calculations; what is measured, however, is value, and what is calculated is the value content of situations. Thus the science of value is potentially as precise, exact, and powerful as the science of nature; but, whereas the precision and exactness of the science of nature is quantitative, the precision and exactness of the science of value is qualitative. The science of nature measures spatiotemporal being; the science of value measures meaning. To be sure, the science of value will change the world as did the science of nature. Its result will be the abundant life that is mankind's promise

—provided we do not fail. Thus the science of value is potentially as powerful as is the science of nature. And just as the *essence* of the science of nature, and that of nuclear power, is nothing but a formula of five little symbols—$E=mc^2$—with all that this implies from Riemannian geometry to Oak Ridge, so the *essence* of the science of value is nothing but a formula of five little symbols— $(\psi)\psi\omega\Phi$, if we choose to express it in symbolic language. Both of these formulae are equally valid; the one represents a measurement of physical qualities, the other a measurement of value qualities. But, whereas one formula is omnipotent, sucking up the wealth of nations, ruling their budgets, and dominating their thought, the value formula is all but unknown. Once the two formulae are of equal social importance—as they are of equal logical validity—value will acquire energy and energy value: the disequilibrium from which we suffer will be overcome and both value and energy will be combined in the harmony of a new age.

THE SCIENCE OF NATURE AND THE SCIENCE OF VALUE

For the time being we seem to be far from such a goal. Yet, the development of modern philosophy has been converging toward it. It has been recognized for a long time that what we suffer from is a disequilibrium between our intellectual and our moral insight. Whereas the natural sciences have developed the methods that have brought us control of the cosmic powers, the moral sciences—ethics, the so-called social sciences, and the humanities—have not developed correspondingly. Philosophers have recognized for some time that the only way to bring order into the present chaos of these sciences—and hence the world of human relations—is to make the same kind of systematic analysis of moral phenomena and moral philosophy that has been made by the founders of natural science in the field of natural phenomena and natural philosophy. As the natural philosophers developed mathematics as a tool for understanding nature, the moral philosophers are now developing a tool for understanding moral nature. This tool is called *axiology*, from the Greek word *axios*, valuable.

There are two ways in which to bring about this new science, the naturalistic and the nonnaturalistic. This means, one can either try to use the apparatus of the natural sciences, the mathematical and empirical method, or try to develop a new method which has nothing to do with that of natural science but is original to moral science. Both methods have been tried in the history of philosophy; the former by the founders of natural science itself. Descartes intended not only a mathematical *natural* science but also such a *moral* science. "Mathematical morality; that was the bold program! Nothing in the development and the system of Descartes can be rightly understood unless this is understood," says one of his biographers. For Leibniz, the inventor of the differential calculus, this calculus was only part of a large calculus of universal logic applicable to all the sciences and humanities, so that "two philosophers who disagree about a particular point, instead of arguing fruitlessly, could take their pencils and calculate." Spinoza, of course, applied the geometrical method to the whole of ethics in an "Ethica ordine geometrico demonstrata." Locke wrote his *Essay on Human Understanding* as prolegomena to "a subject very remote from this," namely, morality and revealed religion, and showed "that moral knowledge is as capable of real certainty as mathematics." The full title of Hume's *Treatise* is: "A Treatise on Human Nature, Being an Attempt to Introduce the Experimental Method of Reasoning into Moral Subjects." And even Berkeley used epistemology only as a tool for theological ethics, the rules of which "have the same immutable universal truth with the propositions of geometry."

Thus, the greatest philosophers of the modern age have attempted to found a science of ethics on the method of natural science—and failed. The reason is that the world of value is of such a nature that mathematical and empirical methods cannot be applied to it. If they are, ethics turns into a natural science, such as naturalistic psychology or sociology or anthropology, and disappears. Ethics thus is elusive game; unless you approach her just right she will change in your hands and vanish—like the princess in the fairy tale who, when "caught," appears as a deer.

This autonomous nature of ethics, which we call nonnaturalistic, was seen by Plato, but the philosopher who established it in modern times was Kant. Unfortunately, at the same time he deepened the confusion between naturalists and non-naturalists. As a result, by the thirties of this century, value theory as a going concern, with a modicum of agreement among its devotees, had all but disappeared. Some naturalists said that valuation was nothing but a psychosomatic noise, others that it was nothing but a sociological or anthropological phenomenon; and the nonnaturalists said that it was neither, even though, unfortunately, they could never say what it was. The confusion between the naturalists and the nonnaturalists was at its height in the twenties—the naturalists hunting the elusive game—"value"—with sharp, but improper tools—the method of empirical science—and proclaiming their catch, which was nothing but psychology, or sociology, or anthropology, as ethics; the nonnaturalists hunting with proper but blunt tools, no method at all, and never catching anything. Thus, the naturalists were good hunters of the wrong prey and the nonnaturalists bad hunters of the right prey. Moral philosophers either got the right thing and didn't know what they had when they had it, or else knew what they had, but it was not the right thing! It was almost like the Uncertainty Principle in physics, where you can never determine with equal precision the position and the impulse of a particle. When you look at an electron it is not there, and when it is there you cannot look. Thus, we may call the naturalist-nonnaturalist split in ethics the Uncertainty Principle in Ethics. Whenever you can reach the good it isn't there, and whenever it is there you cannot reach it. But, just as the Uncertainty Principle in physics has been exactly defined and methods have been developed, or are being developed, either to reach separately what cannot be reached simultaneously or to overcome the split in quantum physics by a new theory, so in ethics the split between naturalists and nonnaturalists is not necessary, and an exact theory of value which does tell us exactly what is Value is possible.

G. E. Moore's "Prolegomena" to the Science of Value

The new course begins with G. E. Moore's *Principia Ethica* in 1903. The title is, of course, patterned after Newton's *Principia*

Mathematica Philosophiae Naturalis in 1687, the basis of all future natural science. So G. E. Moore, in 1903, wrote that his *Principia Ethica* would serve "as Prolegomena to any future ethics that can possibly pretend to be scientific."

The thesis of the book is simple: there is Good, and it is not naturalistic but *sui generis*. What it is, unfortunately, Moore does not know. Like all non-naturalists he has good smell—philosophically called "intuition" (hence he is called an intuitionist)—but bad hunting skill. This is a literal—and the central—quote from the book: "Good is good, and that is the end of the matter." Good, says Moore, is indefinable. And the motto of the book, by Bishop Butler, is: "Everything is what it is, and not another thing." Thus the book is short. It is, in spite of this, the classic of a new age.

It is so for two reasons: its positive and its negative content. Positively, the book says, very simply, that good is good and not another thing. But this is a most important thesis, because most of the philosophers between Plato and Moore (which is the whole history of philosophy) had mixed up goodness with things that *are* good. They have said goodness is pleasure, goodness is satisfaction, goodness is the good life, goodness is God, goodness is being, or evolution, and the like. But pleasure, satisfaction, the good life, God, being, evolution, etc., are things that *are* good; they are not goodness itself. Pleasure *is* good, but pleasure is not goodness. If pleasure were goodness, then to say, *Pleasure is good* would mean the very same thing as *Pleasure is pleasure*. Moore calls this mix-up of goodness with good things the *naturalistic fallacy*. And the negative content of the book is: to trace this fallacy throughout the history of ethics and to show that all moral philosophy before Moore had been wrong, and thus to open the door at last to the right question, namely—What is Goodness itself? Although Moore did not answer this question, he made clear that goodness itself is that which all good things have in common, and that this itself is not a good thing. If one speaks of a good button, a good airline, oneself as a good person, or God—the question is, what have all these goodnesses in common? What has the goodness of a good button, or a good airline, to

do, say, with the goodness of oneself as a moral person, or the goodness of God? That is the question, and, as far as Moore is concerned, Goodness only knows!

This then was the situation when I was a student: Moore had
shown that there was goodness, but that it was indefinable, and that
what the naturalists defined was not goodness. The naturalists, on
the other hand, went on defining as goodness whatever they liked
best or was their specialty, perhaps with a footnote saying: "What
I am doing here is called by G. E. Moore the naturalistic fallacy. I
am committing it." In this sense, Moore has never been taken
seriously by moral philosophers.

The question then for us, as students, was: Where to go from
here? If Moore was wrong, then there was no goodness in itself; if
he was right, then it was not definable. In neither case would it be
worth while to give one's life to the quest for the good. Thus we had
to make up our minds that both Moore and his critics were partly
right and partly wrong. The naturalists were right in insisting on the
rationality of the quest and wrong in their commission of the naturalistic fallacy. Moore was right in insisting on the uniqueness of
good and wrong in saying that it was indefinable. In other words,
one had to combine the uniqueness of good with its definability and
reject its naturalistic character and its indefinability.

What then is Good in itself and how is it to be defined?

Moore's first book appeared in 1903. Although there he said that
"good" is indefinable, he spent the rest of his life in determining it
more and more closely. Twenty years later he wrote and forty years
later he clarified—and this became the basis of what I call formal
axiology—that "two different propositions are both true of *goodness*":
(1) that it is not a natural property but (2) *though* this is so, it
depends entirely on the natural properties of that which has it. By a
natural property he has been interpreted to mean—probably rightly—
a sense property, anything which we can see, hear, smell, touch,
such as "yellow" or "tall." Although good is not a sense property,
he says, it depends entirely on the sense properties of the thing that
is called good. I want to explain this briefly.

If one says to a person, "I have a good car," what does he know of the car? He knows a great deal. He knows it has an engine that runs, an accelerator that accelerates, brakes that brake, tires, doors, seats, etc. But he knows absolutely nothing of the car itself. He does not know what make of car, whether Ford, Chevrolet, Oldsmobile; what type of car, convertible or sedan; whether it has two doors or four; whether it has white or dark tires; whether it has eight cylinders, six, four. He knows nothing about the car, yet, "though this is so," as Moore says, he knows a great deal of it. He knows nothing of the actual natural properties of the car, the sense qualities; if one tells him, "I have a good car; go outside and find it for me," he will, of course, never find it. Thus, good is not a natural property. Yet, it depends entirely on the natural properties of the thing that has it; the goodness of the car depends entirely on the sense properties of the car; for if the car were to brake when one accelerated, or accelerate when one braked, if it were to have no doors, no motor, no tires, it would certainly not be a good car.

This, then, is Moore's result: good is not a natural property, yet it depends entirely on the natural properties of that which is said to be good. If only I knew, he said, in which way "it depends," I would know what good is. At this point formal axiology sets in and defines exactly this "depending." The result is the Axiom or Fundamental Definition of Scientific Value Theory.

THE AXIOM OF VALUE SCIENCE

Moore's result was a life-long puzzle to him. "What in the world" one of his favorite expressions—could it mean that good is not a natural property yet depends entirely on the natural properties of the thing that is good? The solution of the puzzle is as follows: *Good is a property not of objects but of concepts.* When a person understands that a thing "is good," it is not necessary that he know anything of the thing in question; but he must know something of the *concept* of which the thing *is an instance*. In the case of the automobile, he does not have to know anything of the particular automobile in question, but he must know something of the concept "automobile" of which one *particular* automobile is an instance. He must know *what is an* automobile, but he does not have to know what is *this* automobile. The word "good" applies *not* to the knowledge of the *particular* automobile but to the knowledge of the *concept* "automobile." Thus, whenever the word "good" is used, a logical operation is performed: we combine the properties of the *concept* of the thing with the idea of the particular thing that is said to be good. When we hear of a *good automobile,* we combine the properties of the concept "automobile," which we have in our minds, with the idea of the particular automobile in question. We give to the particular automobile, of which we may know nothing, the properties of automobile in general, of which we must know something. And this we do whenever we hear that a thing is "good"; we combine the properties of the *concept* of the thing with the idea of the thing itself. This logical operation is the *meaning* of the word "good." It is expressed in the *definition* of good, that is, of that which all good things have in common: *A thing is good when it fulfills the definition of its concept.* This is the axiom or fundamental principle of formal axiology, and it is the meaning of the symbols mentioned earlier.[1] From the formula follows the theorem that a thing is not good, or bad, when it does *not* fulfill the definition of its concept. A chair is a good chair if it actually and sensibly has the properties that define the concept "chair." If the definition of the concept "chair" is "a knee-high structure with a seat and a back," then anything that is called "chair" and is a knee-high structure with a seat and a back is *a good chair;* whereas a thing called "chair" that is not knee-high and/or has no seat and/or no back is not *a good chair,* whatever else it may be (for example a *good stool*).

The axiom of value—that a thing is good if it has the qualities that define its concept—has four properties which make it *scientific.* The first is that it opens up a new field, that of value, by defining the central term of the field—value—in terms of a formal system, namely, logic itself. For the relation between a concept, its definition, and its referents is the fundamental relation of logic. Since logic is an exact

---

[1] *(ψ)ψω⁴* —see Robert S. Hartman, "Value Propositions," *The Language of Value,* Ray Lepley, ed., Columbia University Press, 1957, p. 202.

and elaborate system, this system can now be used for the explication of value.

This procedure is analogous to the procedure in the natural sciences, except that there mathematics and not logic is used to explain nature. Thus, in optics, a ray of light is defined as a straight line, that is to say, in terms of geometry. Hence, the system of geometry can be used to explain the path of a ray of light in a homogeneous medium—and this kind of explication is precisely what we call the science of optics. In the same way, the explication of *value* in terms of the system of *logic* is what we call scientific *axiology*. Thus, axiology is the framework for the explication of value phenomena, just as mathematics is the framework for the explication of natural phenomena.

The second scientific characteristic of formal axiology is the fact that the axiom of axiology is parallel to that of mathematics. The recognition that value predicates apply to concepts rather than to objects corresponds to the exactly analogous recognition that arithmetical predicates—such as "four"—apply to concepts rather than to objects. This was the fundamental insight of Frege, in the last century, on which Russell and Whitehead based the logical theory of mathematics.

Connected with this is the third scientific characteristic of the axiom: its formal nature. It consists of variables: not of specific values but of a form which determines the specifications of all possible values. It is, in other words, a formula. The term "good" in the axiom is a purely formal term, applicable to anything whatever. This universal and formal nature of "good" has been observed throughout philosophical history. Aristotle called it the homonymity of the term, the scholastics its transcendental nature, modern value theoreticians its "polyguity" or its "punning meaning." Formal axiology recognizes in it the logical nature of "good" as a variable.

The fourth scientific characteristic of formal axiology is the most interesting of all, for it shows that axiology follows the exact method of Galileo. As Galileo had to find a standard for the measurement of motion, so axiology had to find a standard for the measurement of value. Galileo found the standard of measurement of motion by disregarding the secondary qualities of the phenomenon and concentrating on its primary qualities—that is, qualities amenable to measurement—centimeters, grams, seconds—so that what was measured was not the sense phenomenon of ordinary life with its secondary properties but a construct consisting of primary properties. In value measurement, what is to be measured is precisely what Galileo had to disregard, the ordinary sense object—and this object not only as *possessing* its secondary properties, but rather this very possession as what measures its value. Hence for value measurement the *secondary properties must be used as primary properties.* The question thus was to find the standard which is to the secondary properties as primary standards—of length, weight, etc.—are to primary properties. What, in other words, is it that contains the secondary properties as, say, the meter contains the centimeter? The answer is: *The definition of a concept.* The concept serves as the standard for value measurement: a thing has value in the degree that it fulfills the definition of its concept—the same result as the deduction from Moore. Value measurement, in a word, is measurement of conceptual qualities.

The science of value is built up on the basis of this axiom in three stages: first, the axiom itself, which has several implications; then the categories or dimensions of value which follow from the axiom; and thirdly the logic and the calculus of value, which arise from the combination of the dimensions of value. Let me shortly explain each of these stages.

IMPLICATIONS OF THE AXIOM

First the axiom itself. It has certain implications which explain a multitude of problems that have plagued value theory for two thousand years. I shall mention seven: the relationship between fact and value, the absoluteness or relativity of value, the rationality or irrationality of value, the objectivity or subjectivity of value, the normativity or descriptivity of value, the nature of optimism and pessimism, and the goodness or badness of the world.

The relationship between fact and value is that between the frame of reference of mathematics and the frame of reference of formal axiology. A fact is a mental content to which mathematical categories are applied and a value is a mental content to which axiological categories are applied. Thus, when the *Enola Gay*, the plane that carried the atomic bomb, sped toward Hiroshima, its speed, the wind velocity, engine revolutions etc., were facts; but the pilot's entry in the log book when he saw the city disappear—"My God, what have we done!"—was a value, and it can be analyzed in exact terms in formal axiology—indeed, in a formula. It reads, if you want to hear it, $(I_S)_I$, signifying a high value, and is one of thousands of possible formulae systematicaly developed and to be developed in this new science.

The absoluteness or relativity of value is an age-old question. Its resolution is simple. The question is whether there is an absolute norm of value, that is, a universal measure in terms of which every other value is determined. The answer, as we have seen, is, yes, there is. The universal norm of value for each thing is the thing's own concept or name. *Norm equals name.* Whenever I judge a thing as to its value, I compare the meaning of its name with the properties of the thing itself. Just as I can value things, I can value value. The concept "value" is defined in formal axiology as we just did: the degree of a thing's fulfillment of its concept. Hence, the value of value is the fulfillment of the concept of value; and axiology, as defining this concept, is the absolute standard of value. It is based on the logic of the human mind itself.

This means, thirdly, that *value is rational.* One can value a thing only if one knows it, that is, if one knows its name and its properties. That this is true is confirmed by the fact that when we want to value something precisely we call in an expert. The difference between him and us is simply that he *knows* the thing better than we do.

Is value objective or subjective? The answer is simple: the axiom of value is *objective.* It is valid for every rational being whatsoever; but its *application* is *subjective.* It may be possible that what one calls good, another calls bad, and what the second calls good, the first calls bad. But this is a matter of application of axiology and not of axiology itself. The same is true of mathematics. If you walk down the street with a friend and you see two people coming, and your friend, who is a little drunk, sees four, then, for that matter, he is not invalidating mathematics, he is only applying it wrongly. His mistake is in seeing, not in adding. "Two and two is four" is true for him as for you. So in axiology: anyone calls "good" what he thinks fulfills its concept and "bad" what he thinks does not. Whether or not it does is a question of application, not of axiology.

Thus axiology is no more and no less *normative* than mathematics or physics. Anyone is free to try to break the laws of arithmetic and say that two and two are five or to defy the law of gravitation and walk out of the window. So anyone is free to try to break the law of axiology and call good what is bad and bad what is good. But the sanction in all three cases is the self-assertion of these laws: the arithmetical blunderer will go bankrupt, the gravitational blunderer break his neck, and the axiological blunderer be caught between the stones of the mills which grind slowly but exceedingly fine. The normativity of value judgments is thus a consequence of the validity of the axiological laws, and, unless these are determined, the emphasis of value theoreticians on normativity, commands, etc., lacks basis.

The difference between the *pessimist and the optimist* also explains itself simply. Anything which under one concept is good because it fulfills the concept may under another concept be bad because it does not fulfill *that* concept. Thus, as Spinoza has already observed, a good ruin is a bad house, and a good house is a bad ruin. A good jalopy is a bad automobile, and a good automobile is a bad jalopy; a good chair is a bad stool and a good stool is a bad chair, and so on *ad infinitum*. It is the art of the optimist always to find that concept in terms of which the thing appears good, and that of the pessimist always to find that concept in terms of which the thing appears bad. The pessimist suffers from incorrectness of thought and is, as the philosopher Peirce has said, "a little insane." He is out of tune with the world, and the world, as we shall see now, is good.

This is another consequence of the axiological axiom. A thing is good if it has all the properties of its concept. The proper concept of the world must contain all the natural properties there are, have been, or will be. The world is that which has all these properties and thus always fulfills its concept. Therefore it is good. The *goodness of the world* is, of course, not ethical, but axiological, goodness. Although the world as such is good, the things in it may and indeed must be both good and bad for, as we have just seen, anything that is good under one concept may be bad under another. Badness thus is the transposition of concepts or the incompatibility of things which in themselves are good. The world thus, axiologically good as it is, contains the maximum variety of both good and bad things—it is the best possible world because it contains the maximum of axiological variety, the maximum of concepts fulfilled or not fulfilled. Thus we get an axiological version of Leibnizian metaphysics.—So much for the first level of formal axiology, the axiom of value.

THE DIMENSIONS OF VALUE

The second level of axiology deals with the *dimensions of value* which are derived from the combination of standards of value measurements, just as physical dimensions are derived from combinations of physical standards. There are three standards of value measurements, just as there are three standards of physical measurements—centimeter, gram, second—but the three kinds of value standards are three kinds of concepts, namely, analytic, synthetic, and singular concepts; the first being abstractions from empirical reality, the second mental constructs, the third proper names. Without going into details, it is sufficient to say that the fulfillment of each kind of concept gives a different kind of value: the fulfillment of the synthetic concept gives systemic or mental value, the fulfillment of the analytic concept gives extrinsic or classificatory value, and the fulfillment of the singular concept gives intrinsic or singular value. These value dimensions interplay all the time in our valuation. Usually, values grow from systemic to extrinsic to intrinsic.

Take love. As children we know there are girls, but, as we say, they do not *mean* much to us. Their meaning is systemic, merely a difference in shape and form. As we become adolescent we value girls extrinsically, as members of the class of girls, whom we like to sample as to their possession of the class properties. And as we mature there occurs the incredible and irrational event that only axiology can explain: we forget all the girls in the world and indeed, all the world for one single unitary woman. This is intrinsic valuation. We marry this one-and-only—and after some months or years, the process may go in reverse. We value her extrinsically in comparison with other women, systemically as our housekeeper, and get cross—transposition of frames of reference!—when dinner is not on time or she squeezes the toothpaste tube at the top instead of the bottom; and when she cries our heart melts and we see her again as the one-and-only in the world—and so life goes from one valuation to the next.

Everything in the world can be valued in these three dimensions—a button, Eastern Airlines, myself, or God. A button is valued systemically in a button factory, extrinsically in its function on my coat, intrinsically by a button fetishist. Eastern Airlines is valued systemically by the Civil Aeronautics Board, extrinsically by the passengers, and intrinsically, we hope, by Capt. Rickenbacker and his pilots, I value myself systemically if I pretend I am what I would like to be, extrinsically in my social role, intrinsically in being what I am. God is valued systemically in theology, extrinsically in comparative religion, intrinsically in the mystic experience, and so on.

The third level of axiology is the logic and the *calculus of value.* It arises as the combination of the value dimensions and their logical analysis and enables us to analyze any situation or text in detail axiologically, as in the formula of the *Enola Gay's* pilot.

The logical analysis of the value dimensions shows that the intensions, or connotations, of the three kinds of concepts have each a characteristic number of terms. The number of terms of a systemic connotation is finite; this finiteness, or definiteness, is what makes the systemic concept systemic. The number of terms of an extrinsic connotation is potentially infinite but denumerable—for these terms arise from abstraction and represent common properties of at least two things. Being abstracted and in common, these properties must be discrete and the corresponding intensions discursive; but there is no reason why they may not, theoretically, contain as many terms as possible, even the whole language. Thus, "the world" may be regarded as an extension, the intension of which is the totality of all possible terms of all possible ordinary languages. The number of terms, or meaning(s), of this intension then is that of a denumerable infinity, or $\aleph_0$. The number of terms of an intrinsic intension is different. Intrinsic intension connotes an experience of total representation, that is to say, each object intrinsically experienced represents the whole world. Linguistically this means that *each term* denoting such an object connotes the world, or the meaning(s) $\aleph_0$. Terms of this kind are metaphors; a metaphor is a term which may, theoretically, connote any other term in the language: we may speak of a peach of a dog as well as a doggone peach. If the number of meanings in all possible ordinary languages is denumerably infinite or $\aleph_0$, then the number of all possible meanings in all possible metaphorical languages is $\aleph_0{}^{\aleph_0} = \aleph_1$, or nondenumerably infinite. A metaphor, then, as part of a metaphorical language, is a continuum containing the meanings of all other meanings of the language.

The logical analysis of the value categories shows that to each of them—systemic, extrinsic, intrinsic—belongs a specific language, the technical, the ordinary, and the metaphorical, respectively, and that each meaning or connotation of the language shares the characteristic number of the language. Thus, a systemic connotation has the characteristic number n, an extrinsic connotation the characteristic number $\aleph_0$, and an intrinsic connotation the characteristic number $\aleph_1$. Since value is the fulfillment of these respective connotations, systemic, extrinsic, and intrinsic value can be characterized by these same respective numbers.

Again, since value is defined as the fulfillment of a connotation, the more of a connotation there is to be fulfilled the higher is the value. A systemic value fulfills a connotation of only n terms, an extrinsic value one of at most $\aleph_0$ terms, and an intrinsic value one of $\aleph_1$ terms.

Thus, the logic of value applies the calculus of transfinite numbers to value theory, through the analysis of the structure of intension, and shows the isomorphism between this calculus and the statements of value philosophers on intrinsic and extrinsic value.[2]

In addition to this molecular analysis of connotations, value logic analyzes value concepts atomically, examining the relations between value terms, value relations, and value propositions. The basic value terms are "good," "fair," "bad," and "no good." They have definite logical interrelationships.[3] The value relations are "better," "worse"; "good for," "bad for," "better for," "worse for"; "it is good that," "it is bad that," "it is better that," "it is worse that"; and "ought." The latter is the relation between a nonfulfillment and a fulfillment of an intension or connotation. A thing that is a member of a class C but does not fulfill the connotation of C ought to fulfill this connotation, that is, be a good C. This is the positive sense of "ought." A thing that is a member of C and does fulfill C ought not not to fulfill it, that is, ought not to be a bad C. This is the negative sense of "ought." Thus what is bad ought to be good and what is good ought not to be bad. "Ought" thus is defined in terms of "good" and "bad." (It also turns out to be equivalent to "it is better that.")

THE CALCULUS OF VALUE

The *calculus of value* arises by combining the three value dimensions—or modes—S (systemic), E (extrinsic), and I (intrinsic) and their respective values n, $\aleph_0$, and $\aleph_1$. Combinations of these three value dimensions can be either *compositions* or *transpositions*. A *composition* of values is a positive valuation of one mode of value by another, whereas a *transposition* is a negative such valuation. The terms "positive" and "negative" are defined by means of the term "ought." The positive value of a thing is that which the valued thing ought to be, and the corollary negative value is that which it ought not to be. As we have seen, a thing always ought to be good and ought not to be bad; it ought always to fulfill and never not to fulfill the intension of its concept: it ought, in other words, always to be as

---

[2] Cf. Edwin T. Mitchell, *A System of Ethics*, Scribner, 1950, pp. 127ff.
[3] For details on this and the following see Robert S. Hartman, *op. cit.*

valuable as possible. The same is true when the "thing" in question is a value. The most valuable value, that is, the value that fulfills the concept "value" most fully, is intrinsic value. Any value, thus, ought to be intrinsic value. Intrinsic value is the positive value of a value, that which the value ought to be. Any direction away from intrinsic value is negative, any direction toward it, positive.

There are nine compositions and nine transpositions of the three value categories; that is to say, the positive and the negative permutations of the three modes of value are together eighteen. Thus, the valuation of a systemic value in terms of another systemic value is a composition of value—it upgrades value in the direction of intrinsic value—and so is the valuation of a systemic value in terms of an extrinsic or an intrinsic value; or of an extrinsic value in terms of another extrinsic, intrinsic, or systemic value. Value compositions, in other words, are potentiations of value, raising value to a higher power. The transpositions are the corresponding disvaluations, or negative potentiations, raising value to a negative power. Thus, the systemic valuation of a systemic value is a composition consisting of two systemic values, a potentiation of one systemic value by another, or the raising of a systemic value to the power of a systemic value, similar to the arithmetical operation a^a; which we write "S^S". This signifies, for example, the writing of a systematic treatise about mathematical logic, or jurisprudence, or, for that matter, value theory. Again it is a composition of two extrinsic values—E^E—if one extrinsic value is valued in terms of another; for example, the mixing of chocolate with whipped cream. On the other hand, it is a transposition or disvaluation of one extrinsic value by another—E^{-E} or E_E—if the chocolate is mixed with sawdust.

The compositions and transpositions of value can be systematized and symbolized. As we have seen, the symbol of a systemic-systemic composition is "S^S", that of an extrinsic-extrinsic transposition E^{-E} or E_E, as we write, in order to make clear the devaluation or downgrading of valuation, which appears in the fact that $E^{-E} = \dfrac{1}{E^E}$. In other words, composition and transposition are inversely proportional value quantities; one proportional to the reciprocal of the other. This implies that the product of a composition and its corresponding transposition cancel each other, that is, cancel their respective value elements. The result is a situation without value which we call a fact, and its symbol is 1. The *value of fact* thus is exactly between value and disvalue. Fact is value with the exponent 0.

The axiological rank or value of each composition or transposition arises from the values of each of the values which make it up, as deduced from the nature of the systemic, extrinsic, or intrinsic intension or connotation, respectively. Since systemic value—that is, the fulfillment by an object of the systemic intension or connotation of its concept—has the axiological value n, being the fulfillment of a minimum number of connotational attributes, while extrinsic value has the value $\aleph_0$ and intrinsic value the value $\aleph_1$, the compositions and transpositions consisting of these values can in turn be exactly valued. Thus, for example, $S^E = n^{\aleph_0} = \aleph_1 = I$. The extrinsic valuation of a systemic value is an intrinsic value. In this way the hierarchy of values, which originally only comprises the three dimensions S, E, and I, can now be expanded into one of combinations of the three: whereas the former hierarchy is atomic, the latter is molecular.

As is obvious, the combinations of value can in turn be combined. Thus, there arise secondary, tertiary, quaternary, etc., compositions and transpositions of value. A secondary composition, for example, is $(S^S)^E$, which would be, for example, the empirical value—or price— of a treatise on axiology; a secondary transposition $(I_S)I$, the intrinsic disvaluation of the systemic disvaluation of intrinsic value, *e.g.*, of the atomic bombing of human life—the formula of the *Enola Gay's* pilot.

Just as primary value combinations have their exact axiological values so do secondary, tertiary, quarternary, etc. combinations. Thus,

if $E^E = \aleph_0 \aleph_0 = \aleph_1$, then $(E^E)I = \aleph_1 {}^{-\aleph_1} = \dfrac{1}{\aleph_2} = I_I$. In other words,

the value of the secondary value combination $(E^E)I$ is equal to that of the primary value combination I₁. To hate extrinsic valuation of extrinsic valuation is equal to hating intrinsic valuation.

The secondary value combinations arise by adding the exponents S, − S, E, − E, I, − I to each of the primary combinations. Since there are 18 primary combinations each of which can take the six exponents, we get $6 \times 18 = 108$ secondary value combinations. Again, each of these can take six exponents each, and thus we have $6 \times 108 = 648$ tertiary combinations, and so on. In general, the number of possible value combinations on a level n is 3×6^n, that is to say, on the primary level there are $3 \times 6^1 = 18$ combinations, on the secondary, $3 \times 6^2 = 108$, on the tertiary $3 \times 6^3 = 648$ combinations, and so on. The sum of all value forms on all levels is $3 \times (6^1 + 6^2 + \ldots 6^n)$. Thus, on the first through the third level there are $3 \times (6 + 36 + 216) = 774$ forms. The total of all forms in the first five levels is 27,990, in the first six levels 167,958, in the first seven levels 1,007,766.

The totality of all possible combinations of value constitutes the *calculus of value* or the *axiological calculus*. With the present automatic robots a table of the value forms, similar to a logarithmic or other mathematical table, could be produced within a relatively short time. This would give the axiological scientist an opportunity to apply the calculus to all possible kinds of situations, to create prototypical situations, and thus to create a catalogue of literary plots, metaphysical possibilities of thought, juridical cases, moral conflicts and solutions—in short, a genuine axiological science. As is clear from the little that has been said, even the most complicated axiological arguments and situations can be analyzed by means of this calculus.

THE APPLICATION OF VALUE SCIENCE

The *application of formal axiology* to value situations and arguments is the art of the axiologist—an art that has its own rules, as has the application of every formal system. Formal axiology has already been applied to many different situations, such as the critical analysis of poems and dramas, aesthetical productions, commercial organizations—*e.g.*, the valuation of the program of an insurance company, which analyzed the value of a "life" and of the class of persons which should "sell" insurance, etc.—and to the analysis of individual lives.

The application of the dimensions of value to the various fields of human activity originate the various social and moral sciences. Thus, the application of *intrinsic* value to persons produces ethics. A morally good person is one who fulfills his own singular definition of himself, who is, as we said, "genuine," "sincere," "honest," "has integrity," "self-respect" and so on—one who is who and what he is and does not pretend to be who and what he is not—a self-actualizing person, in Professor Maslow's terminology. Moral good must not be confused with axiological good. A murderer can be axiologically good if he murders well. But he cannot be morally good; for his definition of himself suffers from a self-contradiction: one cannot fulfill a self by extinguishing selves. The confusion between axiological good and moral good has been the bane of value theory for 2000 years. The application of *intrinsic* value to things produces aesthetics, to thoughts metaphysics; the application of *extrinsic* value to persons produces sociology, to things economics, to thoughts, epistemology; the application of *systemic* value to persons produces law, to things technology, to thoughts logic, and so on. There are libraries contained in each of the applications mentioned.

The structure and definition of axiological science is formal, hence not restrictive; on the contrary, it is creative of new insight, as was, and is, mathematics for nature. This new science already has had significant practical results and is changing the lives of those who have learned to use it. It has had results on the collective as well as the individual plane. I have been invited to teach it in Germany in order to help give our ideology a firm structure against the disciplined assaults of Communist ideologists who are talking circles around our German friends—and President Eisenhower himself has had some such difficulties with Marshal Zhukov. Axiology puts the spine into democratic ideology. It shows with crystal clarity the infinite and unique value of the human person. In my report to the

International Institute of Philosophy of UNESCO on the development of value theory for the last five years (1949–1955) I found that value theory all over the world—I reviewed some three hundred works written during that period—is developing in the direction of the formal axiology I described to you. Thus, what I have outlined—although in the barest terms—is a worldwide intellectual potentiality. It is the outline of the future science of moral humanity.

Naturally, there is a difference between the science of valuation and valuation itself. The *science* of valuation is not valuation; as reading the formula for TNT is not an explosion. Neither is *valuation* the *science of* valuation; a physicist falling downstairs is not an analysis of the law of gravitation. Yet both are interrelated. Hence it is not true, as many think, that a science of value diminishes the value experience. At the basis of this objection against such a science are three things, first, the suspicion of morally sensitive people against the kind of rationality that has brought about the atomic bomb and hence their escape into irrationality. Second, the common confusion of feeling with valuation. Valuation is no more nor less a matter of feeling than is, say, music. It is a matter of feeling *structured by laws*—feeling following definite laws. The laws of music are those of the theory of harmony, the laws of value are those of value theory. The feeling of value is nothing arbitrary. To quote the great German axiologist, Nicolai Hartmann, "the feeling of value is not free: once it has grasped the meaning of value it cannot feel differently. It cannot regard good faith as wicked, or cheating and deceit as honorable. It can be value-blind, but that is an entirely different matter: in this case it is not responsive to values at all and does not comprehend them"—like a person who is not musical or is color-blind. The third reason for the objection that value knowledge destroys the value experience is the naive tendency of the human mind to think that concrete problems must be solved by concrete ideas, whereas actually it is the most abstract ideas that give the most concrete solutions. "Nothing is more impressive," writes Whitehead in *Science and the Modern World*, "than the fact that as mathematics withdrew increasingly into the upper regions of ever greater extremes of abstract thought, it recurred back to earth with a corresponding importance for the analysis of concrete facts." The very essence of the concrete lies in the most abstract. So it is with value. Its essence lies in the most abstract thought, that is, in the symbols of axiology; and you can never reach the essence of value by dabbling in the concreteness of value phenomena.

Thus, the true knowledge of value lies in the *science* of value. From it will follow a world of valuation, just as the world of technology followed from the science of physics. And as natural science has changed the world, so moral science, once it is developed and fully known, is bound to change the world. There was no force that brought about the age of technology, other than the clarity of mind of people like Newton and Einstein. The only difference these men made in the world was that they gave us knowledge. All the rest followed by itself. Thus, all the difference that the new science is going to make to the world is that it gives us moral knowledge, and all the rest will follow by itself. There will come a time when the problems and conflicts that now plague us will be as forgotten as the tortures of the middle ages and the clubs of the cave men. There will be other problems, but they will differ from ours today as psychoanalysis differs from a witch trial. They will be less crude, more subtle, and more profound—in a word, more human.

BIBLIOGRAPHY

A survey of the entire field of present-day value theory, with extensive Bibliography, is:

Hartman, R. S., "General Theory of Value," *Philosophie: Chronique des Années 1949–1955, publiée par l'Institut International de Philosophie, sous les auspices de l'U.N.E.S.C.O.,* La Nuova Italia, 1958.

The general field of Formal Axiology is discussed in:

Hartman, R. S., *Axiologia Formal: La Ciencia de la Valoracion,* National University of Mexico, 1957.

————, Value, fact, and science, *Philosophy of Science,* 1958, 25, 97–108.

——, "Value Propositions," *The Language of Value*, Columbia University Press, 1957.

——, Value theory as a formal system, *Kant-Studien*, 1958–59, *50*, (forthcoming).

Specific problems in Formal Axiology are discussed in:

Hartman, R. S., "The Analytic and the Synthetic as Categories of Inquiry," *Perspectives in Philosophy*, Ohio State University, 1953.

——, The analytic, the synthetic, and the good: Kant and the paradoxes of G. E. Moore, *Kant-Studien*, 1953-1954, *45*, 67–82; 1954-1955, *46*, 3–18.

——, La creacion de una etica cientifica, *Dianoia: Anuario de Filosofia*, 1955, *1*, 205–235.

——, Group membership and class membership, *Philosophy and Phenomenological Research*, 1953, *13*, 353–370.

——, A logical definition of value, *Journal of Philosophy*, 1951, *68*, 413–420.

——, Niveles del lenguaje valorativo, *Dianoia: Anuario de Filosofia*, 1956, *2*, 254–269.

——, Research in the logic of value, *The Graduate School Record*, Ohio State University, 1952, *5*, 6–8.

——, Value analysis of legal decisions, *Ohio State Law Journal*, 1951, *12*, 23–35.

Some fundamental writings relevant to the relationship between natural science and moral science are:

Ayer, A. J., *Language, Truth and Logic*, Dover, 1946.

Blanshard, B., *The Impasse in Ethics and a Way Out*, University of California, 1955.

Braithwaite, R. B., *Theory of Games as a Tool for the Moral Philosopher*, University of Cambridge, 1955.

Casserley, J. V. Langmead, *Morals and Man in the Social Sciences*, Longmans, Green, 1951.

Christoff, D., Le fondement logique des valeurs, *Proceedings Xth International Congress of Philosophy*, North Holland, 1949, 454–455.

Dewey, J., *Reconstruction in Philosophy*, Beacon, 1948.

Edel, A., *Ethical Judgment*, Free Press, 1955.

Edwards, P., *The Logic of Moral Discourse*, Free Press, 1955.

Ewing, E. C., *The Definition of Good,* Macmillan, 1947.

Feigl, H., "Validation and vindication, an Analysis of the Nature and the Limits of Ethical Arguments, in W. Sellars and J. Hospers (eds.), *Readings in Ethical Theory,* Appleton, 1952.

Haezrahi, P., Some arguments against G. E. Moore's view of the function of "good" in ethics, *Mind,* 1948, 57, 322–340.

Hall, E. W., *Modern Science and Human Values,* Van Nostrand, 1956.

Hare, R. M., *The Language of Morals,* Oxford University, 1952.

Hill, T. E., *Contemporary Ethical Theories,* Macmillan, 1950.

Hilliard, A. L., *The Forms of Value,* Columbia University, 1950.

Kant, I., *Grundlegung zur Metaphysik der Sitten.*

Kecskemeti, P., *Meaning, Communication, and Value,* Chicago University, 1952.

Kneale, W., Objectivity and morals, *Readings in Ethical Theory,* W. Sellars and J. Hospers, ed., Appleton, 1952.

Langer, S., *The Practice of Philosophy,* Holt, 1930.

Lanz, H., *In Quest of Morals,* Stanford University, 1941.

Lepley, R., *Verifiability of Value,* Columbia University, 1944.

Lessing, T., *Studien zur Wertaxiomatik,* Meiner, 1914.

Margenau, H., "Remarks on Ethical Science," *The Nature of Concepts, Their Interrelation and Role in Social Structure,* Oklahoma A. and M., 1950.

——, Scientific ethics, *Scientific Monthly,* 1949, 69, 290–296.

McCracken, D. J., *Thinking and Valuing,* Macmillan, 1950.

Mitchell, E. T., *A System of Ethics,* Scribner, 1950.

Moore, G. E., *Philosophical Studies,* Routledge, 1922.

——, *The Philosophy of G. E. Moore,* Paul A Schilpp, Ed., Northwestern University, 1942.

——, *Principia Ethica,* Cambridge University, 1903.

Mora, J. F., Wittgenstein, a symbol of troubled times, *Philosophy and Phenomenological Research,* 1953, *14,* 89–96.

Northrop, F. S. C., *Logic of the Sciences and the Humanities,* New York, 1947.

——, "The Nature of Concepts and Conceptual Structure," *The Nature of Concepts, Their Interrelations and Role in Social Structure,* Oklahoma A. and M., 1950.

Ortega y Gasset, J., "Qué Son Los Valores?" *Obras Completas,* vol. VI, 315–335, Revista de Occidente, 1955.

Plato, *Philebos.*

Raphael, D. D., *Moral Judgment,* Allen and Unwin, 1955.

Rickert, H., *Kulturwissenschaft und Naturwissenschaft,* Mohr, 1915.

Rueff, J., *From the Physical to the Social Sciences,* Johns Hopkins, 1929.

Urmson, O., On grading, *Mind,* 1950, 59, 145–169. Also *Logic and Language,* II, A. G. N. Flew (ed.), Blackwell, 1953.

Waddington, C. H., *Science and Ethics,* Allen and Unwin, 1942.

Whitehead, A. N., "Mathematics and the Good," *The Philosophy of Alfred North Whitehead,* Paul A. Schilpp (ed.), Northwestern University, 1941. Also *Essays in Science and Philosophy,* Rider, 1948.

The Scientific Basis of Value Theory

HENRY MARGENAU

THE TWO KINDS OF VALUE

A VALUE is the measure of satisfaction of a human want. This brief definition, while seizing a central core of meaning, is inadequate to portray the fringes of significance that attach to the word value. It leaves aside, for example, what is often called intrinsic worth, a feature depending not so much on satisfaction achieved as on the difficulties encountered in procuring the object of value; it largely ignores elements of obvious, unreflective utility and therefore underrates the value of such things as the air we breathe. More importantly, it furnishes an awkward approach to the appraisal of abstract and ideal things such as honesty or friendship and of things such as life which are unique and incomparable with others.

A different light is cast upon the notion of value by an enumeration of the entities which carry values, to which value is said to adhere. There are, first, ordinary physical objects; second, processes and human activities designed to secure such objects; then follow, in the scale of increasing abstractness, actually experienced relations or conditions (fellowship, parenthood, freedom) and finally ideals such as truth, goodness, and beauty. All these are held together by one common bond: that they can be desired or spurned by man.

But it is not the purpose of this communication to establish unity among values, an attempt which would at best remain artificial and pedantic. Rather, it is to indicate at the outset that the loose com-

38

plex covered by our definition is pervaded by a deep fissure which separates beyond possibility of comparison two kinds of value, one called factual, the other normative. Crudely stated the difference is this: Factual values are observable preferences, appraisals, and desires of concrete people at a given time; normative values are the ratings, in some sense to be illuminated further on, which people *ought* to give to value objects. It might be that the second category is illusory, denotes a null class. At any rate, the conceptual difference is clear and present, and it is acknowledged by a large body of philosophic writing.[1] Normative value is more difficult to establish than factual value, and much of this paper is intended to show how this can be done. Suffice it to say at this point that factual values are neither right nor wrong but are facts of observation; they vary from place to place and from time to time; their claim is only with respect to prevalence and persistence. Normative value, however, makes a profounder claim of validity, presumes to have suasive force and regulative power. In this it is unique, notwithstanding a common error which mistakes what is prevalent for what is normative. One should do more than notice this error in passing, for too much of modern social theory is based on it. An act is not right because it is widely performed; a proposition is not true because it is widely believed; an object is not beautiful because it is widely desired—if the terms right, true, and beautiful are taken to denote normative values. The error, it seems to me, springs from the psychology of sinning: we somehow feel better about a lapse if we find ourselves in a large company of offenders, and the consciousness of blame is less intense.

In a vague way, a normative value is like a law of nature—idealized, lofty, and universal. A factual value is like an observation—primary, ubiquitous, and particular. The law of free fall sets a norm for the behavior of bodies. Actual observations differ greatly from

[1] As an example, let it be recalled that G. E. Moore, when he insists that experiences with certain "intrinsic properties are good in not an empirical but a necessary" sense (Schilpp, *The Philosophy of G. E. Moore*, p. 590), points specifically at the normative element which is above empirical verification.

this norm. If they are recorded and analyzed without theoretical preconception they are likely to lead to generalizations documented in Aristotle's physics, not to Galileo's law. Yet there is a sense in which these observations are relevant, crucially relevant to Galileo's law. We find here a clue in science which, when followed, may perhaps illuminate the important distinction between factual and normative values. Hence we carry the discourse temporarily into another field.

THE TWO KINDS OF SCIENCE

Geography and physics are both natural sciences; yet the methods they employ in their investigations differ widely in scope. Geography observes, describes, tabulates, and draws maps or graphs, physics does all of this but in addition predicts, predicts on the basis of carefully structured theoretical procedures. Collecting facts and adequately presenting them is the major business of geography, whereas in physics the emphasis shifts from description to theoretical understanding and thence prediction. To be sure, the geographer can also predict, but chiefly by induction from already observed materials; his typical method is statistical and it yields new results (*e.g.*, predictions of the topological features of an unexplored terrain) with probability only. The physicist, on the other hand, seems able to proceed deductively from general premises and to arrive at relatively certain knowledge by methods sometimes characterized as causal or dynamic. When his prediction fails, something is assumed to be wrong with his reasoning; when the geographer misjudges the topographical features of the South Pole, having studied the surrounding territory, his failure is not laid to his reasoning but considered as an acceptable departure from expectation.

Geography and physics are representatives of the descriptive or classificatory and the deductive or theoretical sciences, respectively. The former feature accurate description based on observation, the latter theoretical transcription also based on observation. Induction from facts is the ambition in the first, deduction from premises stabilized by facts that of the second category. For brevity, let me speak henceforth of the contrast between the *descriptive* and the *theoretical* sciences, with all that this implies, and ignore numerous other terms which have been used to label this distinction. Although the methodologies characteristic of the two kinds are quite distinct, the sciences themselves at times acquire components of both methodologies and therefore arrange themselves in a more or less continuous band from the descriptive pole to the theoretic. In fact, history shows that they move continually from one pole to the other. At present, the band stretches from geography, botany, zoology, through biology, sociology, economics, psychology, to chemistry, astronomy, and physics. Physics is at present remarkably theoretic, though its major phase was descriptive in Aristotle's day. Geography is today still descriptive, but it will transform itself by association with geology, astronomy, and nuclear physics into a theoretical science as it develops. Quite probably it will then change its name, as botany and zoology have become biology when they developed theoretical concerns, a circumstance which may be regarded as an unconscious tribute to our distinction.

The contrast between factual and normative values is parallel to the difference between descriptive and theoretical sciences, and, furthermore, the same methodological elements which transform a descriptive into a theoretical science are also capable of converting factual into normative values. Preliminary to this principal endeavor is the task of examining with greater care first the nature of normative value, then the nature of exact science.

VALUE AS DIRECTIVE OR COMMAND

Factual value has a fixed abode. It resides in the determinate specificity of human actions, of stated preferences, of opinion polls, and can be discovered by means both known and generally agreed upon. Hence it is an easy fallacy to suppose that normative value, too, has a static abode in human thought, a fixed basis in logic, an *a priori* origin. The search for values has therefore penetrated the length and breadth of philosophy, and there are reports alleging the discovery of values-in-themselves, reports too numerous to survey.

But the reports, though honest, turned out to be untrustworthy (I crave the reader's indulgence for this dogmatic assertion which is forced on me for lack of space). They were afflicted by the same misfortune that plagued the advocates of intrinsic, unalterable laws in mathematics and in logic, when it was shown convincingly how laws lack internal affidavits of truth and reduce upon careful inspection to mere consequences from postulates—and the postulates, though fundamental, are to some extent subject to choice. Values—and I speak henceforth of normative values—are likewise arbitrary as long as they stand by themselves. Life has or is a value and confers value on actions that preserve it, not as an isolated fact of experience, nor as an existential self-declaratory fact. Life has indeed no value in this sense for a person earnestly committed to the destruction of it. The life of an enemy is without value during war. But *if* you are committed to the prior maxim expressed in the decalogue, "Thou shalt not kill," then the value of life follows as a theorem follows from a postulate. And so it is with honesty, veracity, friendship, love of mankind, and all the rest: they point to and receive their value from a *command* or a *directive* to which a person is committed. Values are always relative to commands; value propositions are equivalent to exhortations to which one is committed. Removal of the commitment, reversal of the command, destroy or change the sign of a value.

The theory of value has remained a rather fruitless philosophic discipline because it tried to analyze the rainbow in substantial terms. It might have done better had it studied the sunlight of normative command of imperatives which shone into history on several blessed occasions and examined its refraction in the droplets of human behavior committed to the command. In this way it would surely have gained a better understanding of the rainbow of values.

Value propositions are sometimes expressed elliptically in a manner tending to obscure the reference to a commitment. We say: It is good to be honest, and thereby put the problem into the meaning of good, which is of course a value term, indeed, one of extreme vagueness. If we interpret it as "useful," then the statement is in-complete, for the sentence "It is useful to be honest" has no norma-tive content. To make it complete one must add: "I am committed to useful acts." This, coupled with "It is useful to be honest" makes honesty a value for me. Any other interpretation of good, *e.g.*, con-ducive to happiness, to some sort of perfection, to longevity, requires for completeness of the value sentence, "It is good to be honest," a similar dedication to happiness, perfection, or longevity, and this dedication is tantamount to the acceptance of what for brevity I have called a command; be happy! etc.

The situation becomes more confusing when for obscurity's sake an irrelevant reference is included in the hortative sentence. One hears: "Science shows that it is good to be honest." Now, science makes absolutely no normative appeal unless it is coupled with some sort of command. Alone, it can only show the results of a specified course of action; it allows the selection of means when the goal is set. It tells how to destroy as well as how to preserve life, how to ease misery as well as how to create it. Conceivably science might prove that honesty leads to collective human happiness, but never that happiness is desirable. Only if I commit myself to the proposition "Thou shalt be happy," and add this to the legitimate devices of science, does the sentence at the beginning of this para-graph become normatively meaningful.

But what about the sciences of life? Do they not contain vectors pointing in the direction of values? Much has been made of the theory of evolution which, in some forms of scientific humanism, is said to define values. "Desirable is all that toward which the process of evolution carries the human race." Value is then defined by a natural process, in apparent contradiction to the remarks just above. Notice, however, that this position still does not exempt us from agreeing that evolutionary progress confers value, since this is far from obvious and can be denied. The hidden commitment remains in the picture, the arrow is put on the vectors by a command. In this respect, then, the appeal to evolution profits us nothing. In another, it reveals an even more serious flaw, for the goal of evolution is not defined and suffers from an intolerable vagueness when considered as the basis of value theory. True, there are indications of human progress in some moral or aesthetic sense, and these could plausibly be taken as objects of commitments; but the motif of survival of the fittest, the tooth and claw doctrine of Darwinism, are equally eligible and lead to a subversal of all reasonable values.

Man's nature is occasionally said to define or imply values. His natural drives (longing for survival, love, striving for happiness) provide an obvious criterion for value judgments which is quite widely accepted. This view comes close to the theme of this paper, but it is not worth consideration in its present form. The commitment to a command proposition—"follow your drives"—is still required; human drives are often conflicting within a single person, and they vary from one person to another. Ways must be found (1) to make the commitment explicit and (2) to smooth out the inter- and intrapersonal fluctuations in man's natural desires.[2]

AUTHORSHIP OF THE COMMAND

If normative value rests upon a command, who is the author of that command, or what is its origin? These questions are crucially important if, for a functioning value theory, the commands must engage commitment. It is needful to stress here that the value theories favored historically with greatest success are precisely those in which the authorship of the commands is clearly known and unquestioningly accepted. They are, first, the various ethical systems stemming from divine revelation, where God is the author of the commands, secondly, systems of legislation, where a monarch, an appointed or an elected body—but always a known and specifiable origin—provides the commands. Commitment is then either auto-

---

[2] An approach to value theory which, though starting from an analysis of intrinsic meaning of value terms, is not subject to the foregoing criticism is that of R. S. Hartman (cf. "A Logical Definition of Good," *Journal of Philosophy*, June 21, 1951; "The Analytic, The Synthetic, and The Good," *Kant Studien*, Bd. 46, p. 67). He clearly recognizes the need for a normative definition and obtains it by logical analysis. Thus is generated what he carefully calls the axiological good. Now it seems to me that in the passage from this axiological good to the ethical good—or any other kind of applied value—considerations like those here presented are required.

matic or enforced, but it is known to be needed if the values imp
are to be effective.

A point of terminology should here be settled. One might say that
a command *defines* a value, whereas dedication to the command
makes it *effective*. I shall not belabor it, since in what follows
our interest will center upon values that are both defined and effective.

Today, religion seems to be outmoded as a source of values, and
legislation is too limited in its purview to establish the most em-
bracive moral, aesthetic, and logical values—not to speak of the
philosophic uncertainties which still becloud the scene of jurisprudence. In this predicament I suggest that we look once more at
science, not in a repetition of the futile attempt to wring values from
science but in an endeavor to understand how science, reared upon
its own premises, is able to define its conclusions (which because
of the nature of its premises are not values) convincingly, in the
hope of capturing, and perhaps transplanting into value theory, that
formal feature which imparts universal acceptance and persuasive
power to science. Indeed, I hope to show that the force of a command for action, recognized as the constitutor of value, arises in the
same methodological way as the force of a theoretical scientific
proposition.[3]

The Cogency of Scientific Judgments Contrasted
with the Suasion of Value Propositions

That task, however, meets a major obstacle at the very start, for
it must prevail against the inveterate belief that scientific propositions are universally valid, in principle, testable by everyone, "objective," unrelated to commands or commitments, while none of this
is true for values. Fortunately, that obstacle has been removed by
science itself. The developments of the last century, the advent of

---

[3] It will thus be seen that science can render an incomparable service to the
theory of values. But aside from this, our analysis, if it were sufficiently elaborated, would exhibit a close parallelism between the methodology of science
and the discipline of values. E. W. Hall's excellent recent book *Modern Science
and Human Values*, from which I have learned a great deal, misses the opportunity to show this connection.

many-valued logics, non-Euclidean geometries, non-commutative algebras even in an applied science like physics, clearly show the limitations, the conditioning by accepted postulates, of all scientific pronouncements that go beyond the statement of descriptive particulars. Nor are these qualities evident only in the esoteric reaches of science: they are apparent in the simplest circumstances to anyone willing to reflect.

Is "One plus one is two" to be taken as a fact beyond possible refutation? Doubtless, yes, insofar as the theorem follows from the postulates of arithmetic. As a hypothetical statement, "if certain axioms of arithmetic are accepted then $1 + 1 = 2$," it is clearly true, analytically true—but that is just the status of values relative to commands. Synthetically, $1 + 1 = 2$ fails to be true in most of our experience. It does not hold when one gallon of water is added to one gallon of alcohol; it is generally false when applied to clouds and to ideas. We then say, cagily, that the theorem does not apply, for instance, to the liquids as a whole, but that it does apply to the molecules which compose them. But sooner or later we learn quantum mechanics and with it new ways to modify the laws of arithmetic, and we are ultimately forced to realize that scientific theorems and values are, as a disparaging critic has put it, "in the same leaky boat." If this comes as a shock to the admirer of science, he should take comfort in a more important thought: what he did find admirable in science may occur in value theory as well.

ORIGIN OF THE FORCE OF SCIENTIFIC JUDGMENTS

A full exposition of the methodology of exact science is quite unnecessary for present purposes; we need here only an outline of its deductive movement, from postulate to verification. Let us review a well-established theory of natural science, Newton's theory of universal gravitation (acknowledging it to be slightly wrong in view of Einstein's general relativity; the latter would serve as well but it involves needless complications, yet nicely illustrates the temporal variability of scientific postulates).

Textbooks often make an unwarranted claim in alleging the inverse-square law of attraction between mass particles to be a generalization of direct observations. One sees the apple fall, one watches the parabola of a thrown object or a cannonball, one watches the motion of the moon and the planets and somehow comes forth with the certain conclusion: $F = G \frac{m.m.^2}{r^2}$ (where the letters have their usual significance). This is a logically impossible feat, not even accomplished by the genius of Newton. If it were possible it would be wrong because the answer for F is not unique. To put the matter succinctly, the formula for F cannot be derived from any finite set of observational data.

What Newton did was the reverse. He assumed ("committed himself to") the formula for F and *deduced* from it certain theorems which are uniquely entailed by it. These theorems included Kepler's laws of planetary motion, the law of free fall for bodies at the earth's surface, and innumerable others. Common to them is the following methodological trait. They contain parameters or variables which can be measured or observed, and, since the theorems represent a mathematical relation between these variables, the measurement of some leads to the predictions of others. When the prediction is checked by further observations the theory—*i.e.,* postulate and theorems—is said to be *verified.* Before verification postulate and theorems were neither true nor false; commitment to the postulate defined the theorems, to be sure, yet prior to verification there were many possible postulates to which dedication might have seemed reasonable—the truth, the force of the postulate arose through some sort of agreement between what it entails and what is observed. To collect the salient elements of the deductive process: it starts with a *postulate,* spins out by analytic means the consequences of the postulate into the form of *theorems* (sometimes called laws), and finally checks these against immediate experience through *verification.*

Verification is not a word ideally suited to describe the last phase of the process, since it suggests the conferral of truth in a final sense. Scientific truth is never final; later observations may disagree with the derived theorems and require a change of postulate. Perhaps one should therefore speak more modestly in terms of the contemporary strength of a postulate in the face of present observation, and replace verification by confirmation. However, having insured myself against such misunderstanding I shall drop this caution and continue to speak of verification.

But verification in science must never be regarded as something simple or obvious. Too many scientists ignore the intrinsic and difficult problems which that phase of the deductive process presents, ignore the fact that an element of choice enters at this point. If, for instance, one were to require exact agreement between prediction and observation, verification could never result. If we require agreement within the probable error of the measurement, an arbitrary measure which has come to be widely adopted, verification becomes possible but remains difficult; other conventions can be conceived to make it very easy and therefore less discriminating. Finally, there are sciences such as psychiatry and to some extent psychology where wholly different and much more subjective methods for verifying theories have been used. In honesty, we should therefore deny the frequent allegation that verification is an obvious and simple look-and-see procedure, should admit the intervention of choice and speak of an adopted *principle of verification.*

A MODEL FOR CONVERTING SUASION INTO COGENCY

The passage from postulate to theorems and their confrontation with observational experience has, I hold, a firm corollary in the theory of values. Here it is necessary to posit a command (postulate), to accept that command tentatively and investigate or spin out its consequences with respect to human actions. This procedure is not novel, although it has fallen into disfavor under the label of casuistry. And finally these consequences must be verified (if not disqualified) or, as I shall say in connection with values, *validated* (if not invalidated). The last phase, validation, again involves problems that are often overlooked.

For the sake of clarity, let me use a simple model in illustration of the value process, a model whose repulsive simplifying features the reader is asked to overlook. Essential to the theory here proposed are two initial choices which correspond to the postulates and the principle of verification in science. In a value system the postulate is a command, an imperative, an exhortation; the principle of verification becomes a principle of validation. In the model, we select the ten commandments for the one, survival of the group dedicated to them for the other. Within limits, we now have a working system. From the commandments, rules of conduct follow for practical situations, and these need to be spelled out like the theorems of science. The resulting value system, an ethic in this case because of the choice of ethical commands, becomes what I shudder to call a laboratory discipline, yet that is what it is. For we must, to follow through our model thinking, suppose a society to be established in which the code (Ten Commandments) has been tentatively adopted by all citizens and in which there is negligible interaction with the other societies; we must observe that society for a sufficient time (and this would, I am sure, mean centuries) and see whether it survives.

The model is one of many. Its most offensive element, the particularly simple choice of principle of validation, can be replaced by others such as maximum happiness for all members of the group, certain kinds of utilitarian requirements, the acquisition of material wealth, and so on; the command might be the golden rule, the calm of Taoism suitably explicated, the practical precepts of Confucius. Any of these can be coupled with any of the foregoing principles of validation, and a complete and workable system of ethics results.

Our model was of narrow range, capable only of generating ethical values. The methodology proposed, however, can, with suitable choice of codes and principles of validation, be extended to aesthetics. It needs no extension to the field of truth, for, as we have seen, it is there already being applied and successful.

In this paper, no choice is recommended, and attention is focused exclusively upon the formal elements of the necessary methodology of value theory. For it is the methodology that is controversial, and because of the universal dispute that continues to shake the foundations of values in a time when solidity and firmness are desperately required, few intracultural bonds have been established. Agreement on methodology and, even prior to that, on a clear statement of methodology are essential to the establishment of bonds.

But the philosophic gain accruing from this viewpoint is by no means small. The view brings order into a morass of traditional confusions. In exposing the *two* crucial requirements, commands and validation, and in clearly separating them, it shows why, for example, a system of ethics could never have been founded on the doctrines of hedonism, eudaimonism, or utility. For these are principles of validation that lack commands. Likewise, it explains why adherence to the ten commandments or to the golden rule—except by believers who renounce the full scope of value methodology—will never lead to a set of values that can be established with satisfying certainty—in other words, that is demonstrably normative. The view settles the historic argument as to the primacy of duty or expediency in ethics by embracing both, for duty enters through the command, expediency in some sense through the principle of validation. Finally, it shows how wrong Kant was when he endeavored to generate an ethic from his categorical imperative, a most unfortunate name for what in fact is nothing but a vaguely stated principle of validation. Values are not produced by parthenogenesis; they result from the fertilization of a principle of validation by a set of commands.

Human History as the Value Laboratory

The model introduced for discussion was odiously artificial. It called for the setting up of a social experiment, introduction of iron curtains, establishment of an international vacuum; it seemed to advocate social vivisection. None of this is intended. He who seeks values need no more acquire a social laboratory than the astronomer needs a special experimental universe. As the world is his laboratory, so is human history the proving ground of values. When this is realized the artificiality of our scheme vanishes at once, for is it not true that we have always looked, uncertainly it is true and without methodological conviction, at the teachings of anthropology, at the "nature of man as it reveals itself in history," for support of our choice of values? And furthermore, is the selection of commands and of a principle of validation really so arbitrary? I daresay there is greater unanimity with respect to these across the globe than there is regarding value methodology; golden rule and maximum happiness have, I think, been largely confirmed by history everywhere, and this combination, still incomplete, already suggests a basic set of values. Can we not go on from there? The critical issue at the moment is to secure agreement as to a method that can engender and test value content. Hence my plea for careful consideration of the lesson which value theory can learn from science.

The Values of Science

I HAVE one advantage over Dr. Robert Hartman, who seeks to derive a formal method of valuation from the informal philosophy of G. E. Moore. I was a student when Moore taught at Cambridge and can claim in some sense to have been a student under Moore. Therefore I shall do what I believe Moore would do if he were alive. First, I shall address myself directly to what the other contributors to this volume have said. And second, I shall do this, as G. E. Moore would, in the most practical and matter-of-fact way, so that the principles which divide me from the other authors shall be starkly plain.

I sense in some of the authors of the papers, and in the discussion, an odd duality. On the one hand, they want to formulate a system which they think of as a rigid science of values. On the other hand, they are out of sympathy with natural science as it is really practiced, and there runs under what they say the haunting conviction that the practice of science is destroying the values for which they care. The very people who ask for a science of values are filled with a deep distrust for modern science, which they fear and do not understand.

Plainly, these people use the word "science" in different senses in the two contexts. When they speak of a science of values, they mean an *a priori* set of absolute judgments, arranged to hang together in a formal system. But when they speak of science in the world around them, they mean, rightly, what Dr. Henry Margenau ably described: a complex of changing concepts whose only reality is that they give order to and are tested by the empirical facts of nature. There is nothing absolute about the concepts of natural science, and they link together to form a flexible framework which is always building and always being rebuilt; but the one thing that the framework must fit, obstinately, is the facts. It is this tyranny of the facts not as they ought to be but as they are that distresses people who fear that the spread of science is robbing them of some freedom of judgment. They feel that scientists have no spiritual urges and no human scruples, because the only success that science acknowledges is success in conforming to the material facts of the world.

THE PRACTICE OF SCIENCE

The signs of this latent opposition to science, which appears now whenever values are debated, have already been audible in the discussions of this Conference. In order to bring this opposition into the open and to come to grips with it, I have altered the original intention of this address. I had intended to analyze the nature of values and to demonstrate the rich and necessary tension which goes on always between opposing values. From this tension, this two-sidedness of values, I had intended to argue that whatever can be said about the relations between values, though it may be true and profound, cannot in any reasonable sense be called a science. But it seems to me now that these considerations are less important to this Conference—and this volume—than is the downright discussion of the issue which threatens to divide it. It is less important at this moment to speculate about a possible science of values than to discuss realistically what are the values of science. I shall therefore take as my subject the values of science.

The Committee which called this Conference expressed the hope, in its invitation, that the study of values had reached a point at which "we need no longer be content only with exhortation, with authoritarian statements, or with *a priori* thinking." The alternative to exhortation, to authority and to *a priori* thinking is the study of values as they actually appear in the behavior of people. Nothing that we say is practical, nothing is even reasonable, if it neglects this empirical study: this, as your Committee implied, is fundamental. I am therefore returning to the purpose of this Conference in making a short but strictly empirical examination of the way in which some of the values in our society are evolved.

I shall confine myself to some human and, in a sense, social values such as inform and govern the relations between people. And I shall confine myself particularly to values that arise in the civilization in which we now live. The characteristic mark of this civilization, the special activity to which it is committed, is the practice of science. Dr. Henry Margenau has given a clear exposition of the principles which underlie this practice. Science is the activity of arranging the known facts in groups under general concepts, and the concepts are judged by the factual outcome of the actions which we base on them. So, in all practical matters, ours is a society which judges belief by the outcome of the actions which it inspires. As Dr. Margenau explained, we believe in gravitation because we are thereby led to act in a way which works in our world. And as he also implied, if we are to believe in values, they must lead us to act in a way that works in the society that hopes to live and to survive by them.

The concept of gravitation is, at bottom, a compact and orderly means to describe how things fall. In this sense, the concepts of science are all means to describe how things fall out. Therefore critics of science usually call it a neutral activity, because its concepts, however subtle we make them, still tell us only what happens and not what they think ought to happen.

This is a sad jumble of language, which confuses the activity of science with its findings. The findings of science are indeed neutral, if by this word is meant that they describe and do not exhort. It is difficult to see what else the findings could be, unless the critics still believe, as the alchemists did, that science ought to command and to overpower nature. If the criticism is that science discovers facts and not spells, then I gladly accept it.

But, of course, the facts discovered must not be confused with the activity that discovers them. And the activity of science is not neutral: it is firmly directed and strictly judged. In practicing science, we accept from the outset an end which is laid down for us. The end of science is to discover what is true about the world. The activity of science is directed to seek the truth, and it is judged by the criterion of being true to the facts.

TRUTH AS VALUE

We can only practice science if we value the truth. This is the cardinal point that has never been seen clearly enough, either by critics or by scientists themselves. Because they have been preoccupied with the findings of science, they have overlooked that the activity of science is something different from its findings. When we practice science we look for new facts, we find an order among the facts by grouping them under concepts, and we judge the concepts by testing whether their implications turn out to be true to other new facts. This procedure is meaningless, and indeed cannot be carried out, if we do not care what is true and what is false.

When critics say that science is neutral, they mean that the findings of science are neither good nor bad in themselves; and they usually go on to say that therefore the use to which the findings are put must be determined by values which are not implied by the findings. So far, the argument is faultless; Dr. Margenau stated it himself in his exposition. The use to which the facts are put must be determined by values which are brought in from outside the facts. But now the critics turn the argument into a verbal trick. To use the findings of science, we must have values from outside the findings; but the critics blandly read this to mean that we must have values from outside science. Even if this were true, it is certainly not implied by the argument.

What the critics are anxious to say, of course, is that the scientific civilization in which we live is not taught any values by its science.

And it is true that we are not taught any values by the facts that science finds, by the machines that it builds, and even by the visions that it opens. The facts, the machines, the visions still require to be directed by what has been called a normative injunction, or what I prefer to call an agreed end. But, of course, although the facts do not supply such an injunction or end, the activity of science does. The activity of science is committed to truth as an end in itself.

Here critics can argue, with justice, that men believed that truth is a value long before they heard of science. I could argue in turn that this belief had often defined truth very oddly; that truth as I define it, truth to fact, was not valued in dogmatic societies; and that the acceptance by any society of the material fact as an arbiter of truth really makes it a scientific society. But these are all debating points, and they are beside the point. It is beside the point to argue about the history of truth as a value: who discovered it, who brought it into our civilization. The point, the only point, is that truth is central to science. A scientific civilization like ours cannot exist unless it accepts truth to fact as its cardinal value. If our civilization did not have this value, then it would have to evolve it, for it could not live without it.

I have established that the activity of science presupposes that truth is an end in itself. From this fundamental proposition, it is possible to go several ways. For example, it is possible to discuss what is implied by saying that a scientific description is true if it corresponds with the facts. For it is certain, as Dr. Margenau pointed out, that such a correspondence cannot be perfect. In the nature of things, the description can match the facts only with a certain coarseness, with what engineers call some tolerance. A scientist therefore has to decide what coarseness he accepts, if he is ever to come to conclusions. This decision is itself an act of judgment, and I suspect that it has subtle things to teach us about how we judge and how we value. Certainly it should teach us what I have missed in other speakers, the sense that science involves the scientist as a person; a discovery has to be made by a man, not by a machine, because every discovery hinges on a critical judgment.

TRUTH IN SOCIETY

However, I want to go another way from my fundamental proposition that science must value truth. I want to take the proposition beyond the individual scientist and ask what it implies in the society made up of men like him. This is a natural extension; we are all of us concerned not merely with our personal values but with the values of our whole society. But it is also an important extension for another reason. Many of the choices in which a man's values are expressed are precisely choices between what he would like to do as an individual and what he is asked to do as a member of a community. The social values are generated by this confrontation of individual wish and communal will. There are no problems of social values until the man has to find a posture to his society, and the society has to find its attitude to him: until each has to adjust itself to the other.

Therefore we have only begun the elucidation of modern values when we have found that science must necessarily value truth. For truth is an individual value, which dictates the conduct of a scientist alone with his work. It becomes a source of social values only when a whole society accepts the assumption that no belief will survive if it conflicts with factual truth. This is the unspoken assumption which our society makes. It is equivalent to setting up truth as the overriding value for our society, and to agree that the discovery of the truth is an end in itself, the supreme end, not only for individuals but for society as a whole. It follows that a whole nexus of social values should be deducible, by logical steps, from the single injunction that society has a duty to seek the truth.

I have said that our scientific society takes it for granted that it should seek the truth: and this description is characteristic of it. For the description implies that the truth is still being sought, and will go on being sought always; the truth has not already been found. A society that believes that the truth has been finally found, for example, in politics or in religion, simply imposes it; it is an authoritarian society. And what goes deeper, a society that believes that the truth has been found or revealed, that the truth is known, resists all change; for what is there to change for? When we say that our society seeks the truth, we imply that it acknowledges that it must itself change and evolve with the truth. The social values which I shall derive are, at bottom, a mechanism by which a society arranges that it shall evolve. They grow from the search for the truth in a scientific society, because the search demands that the society shall evolve.

VALUES DERIVED FROM TRUTH

A man who looks for the truth must be independent, and a society which values the truth must safeguard his independence. An age of reason may be anxious to persuade the unreasonable—and independent minds are always unreasonable—but it must be more anxious to ensure that they are not browbeaten. So Voltaire in his life was as belligerent for the independence of those who did not share his beliefs as for his own. A scientific society must set a high value on independence of mind, however angular and troublesome those who have it are to the rest of us.

The value which our society gives to independence is in direct contrast to the value which other societies have given to authority. This Conference would not think of accepting what I say, even in the rather traditional fields of values, if I were to give as my ground only the authority of some earlier thinker. The Conference may be interested by my recollections of G. E. Moore, and attracted by my claim that I am arguing here as he would. But this is not because the Conference accepts Moore as an authority, or me as his interpreter—and indeed, my philosophy is clearly quite different from Moore's. No, if Moore is respected here, it is because he has an independent mind; and what I recalled when I began to speak was the independence of his method. Our society as a whole is intellectually more interested in methods than in results, because the independent mind expresses itself most eloquently in the creation of an original method.

We value independence of mind because it safeguards originality, and originality is the tool with which new discoveries are made. But although originality is only a tool, it has become a value in our society, because it is necessary to its evolution. So high is the value which a scientific society places on originality that it has ousted the value which the arts used to place on tradition. The strange and, to me, admirable result has been that the arts have become more and more imaginative, more eccentric and personal in the last hundred years; and this has certainly been caused by the pressure for originality from what the critics call the impersonal field of science.

I do not claim that originality is always a virtue, any more than I claim that independence or even truth itself is always so. What I am showing is that originality has become a value in our society, as independence has, because both are means to foster its overriding value, the unending search for truth. There are occasions when originality, like the other values, becomes a bore. Whenever I go to an exhibition of children's paintings, I see several hundred examples of studied and uniform originality, and I sometimes suspect that originality is being taught as a school subject. I find this dull, but no more so than I should have found the studied and uniform conformity of children's paintings a hundred years ago, when tradition was taught as a school subject. The fact is that a child's painting is no more like art than a child's essay is like literature; what is dull in it today, what was dull a hundred years ago, is not the originality or the tradition, but the childishness. The child's painting has no more merit than an intelligence test; that is, it gives a hint of what the child's mind may do later; and as a scientist, I would rather be bored by the hint that it will dissent than by the conviction that it will conform.

Independence and originality are qualities of mind, and when a society elevates them to values, as ours has done, it must protect them by giving a special value to their expression. This is why we place a value on dissent. The high moments of dissent are monuments in our literature: the writings of Milton, the Declaration of Independence, the sermons of John Wesley and the poetry of Shelley. True, we find it more comfortable if dissent takes place somewhere else: in the past or in another country. In this country,

we like best to read about the dissent which Russian intellectuals
have been expressing since the death of Stalin; and no doubt Russians prefer to praise the dissenting voices in the West. But when
we have smiled at these human foibles, we recognize behind them
that dissent is accepted as a value in the intellectual structure of our
civilisation. And it is a value which derives from the practice of
science: from the experience that progress comes only when the
accepted concepts are openly challenged, whether by Copernicus,
by Charles Darwin or by Albert Einstein, and when the challenger
insists that the facts are looked at afresh because they have out-
grown the old concepts. Dissent is an instrument of intellectual
evolution.

A society which values dissent must provide safeguards for those
who express it. These safeguards are the most familiar values in the
repertory of the political orator: freedom of thought, freedom of
speech and writing, and freedom of movement and assembly. But
we must not take them for granted because lip-service to them has
become hackneyed, and we must not suppose that they are self-
evident and natural values in any society. Plato did not offer freedom of speech and writing in his republic. Freedom is valued in a
society only when the society wants to encourage dissent and to
stimulate originality and independence. Freedom is therefore essential to a scientific society, a society in evolution. It is merely a
nuisance, and is discouraged, in a static society. Yet freedom is the
basic acknowledgment that the individual is more important than
his society: and we see once again that science, in despite of its
critics, prizes the individual as other systems do not.

INERTIAL VALUES

So far, I have only deduced, from the conditions for the practice
of science, those values which make for change. But a society must
also have values which resist change; it must, in engineering terms,
have a certain inertia, by which it resists the overthrow of what it
holds to be true now, and makes the truth of tomorrow fight for life.
These inertial values are, of course, more common in other, static

societies; but they are also present and important in a scientific society. Respect, honor and dignity are necessary to the stability of science as of any other social activity, and their value can therefore be demonstrated from the conditions for the practice of science, in the same way that I have demonstrated the evolutionary values. But because the inertial values hold in other societies, because they are necessary to the existence of any society at all, I shall not discuss them further here. Instead, I shall make only one point about them, which is this: in a scientific society, the inertial values are reached by a different path from that which leads to them in other societies.

In a scientific society such values as respect, honor and dignity are approached across the value of tolerance, which forms as it were a bridge from the evolutionary values. Tolerance is a modern value, because it is a necessary condition for the coherence of a society in which different men have different opinions. Thus tolerance is essential to make a scientific society possible, and to link the work of the past with that of the future. Moreover, tolerance in this sense is not a negative value: it must grow out of an active respect for others. It is not enough in science to agree that other men are entitled to their opinions; we must believe that the opinions of others are interesting in themselves, and deserve our respect even when we think them wrong. And in science we think that other men are wrong, but not that they are wicked. By contrast, all absolute doctrines think that those who are wrong are deliberately and wickedly wrong, and may be subjected to any suffering to correct them. The tragedy of the political division of the world today is that it has this doctrinal intolerance: the statesmen of the West believe that those of the East are not merely wrong but wicked, and the statesmen of the East believe the same of us.

This is a good point at which to stop this impromptu exposition of some of the values of science. I have made no attempt to derive all the values which I believe a scientific society generates by the nature of its activity. And even if I had found logically all the values in science, I would not claim that they exhaust all the human values, and that the practice of science gives man and society all the values that they need. This has not been my purpose.

My purpose has been to meet head-on the current of mutiny against science that I have felt rising in this Conference, and that runs through so many discussions of values. This current always sets off with some harmless claim that science is neutral. But the harm is done by the confusion which is hidden in this innocent sentence. The findings of science are neutral, as every fact and every grouping of facts is neutral. But the activity of science which finds the facts and which orders them is not neutral. The activity of science is directed to one overriding end, which is to find the material truth. In our scientific society, this end is accepted as the supreme value.

From this cardinal value, some other values flow of necessity; and my purpose has been to show how this happens. It happens because a society which seeks the truth must provide means for its own evolution, and these means become values for it.

THE STUDY OF VALUES

In deriving some of these values, by way of examples, I have shown that there is indeed an empirical procedure for studying the values of a society. What I have been doing is to make, in outline, a short empirical study of a few values. All values are subtle, and the values of science are as subtle as any others. A value is not a mechanical rule of conduct, nor is it a blueprint of virtue. A value is a concept which groups together some modes of behavior in our society. In this sense, when I say that originality is a value for our society, I am just as empirical and as descriptive as when I say that gravitation is a phenomenon of our planetary system. And when I seek the reason for the value given to originality by tracing it back to the demand for truth, I am doing exactly what I should do if I were looking for the cause of gravitation in the more fundamental structure of matter.

This does not mean that values are mere descriptions of our behavior: and that for two reasons. First, the interplay of values is more complex than any mechanical compounding of forces: it creates a tension which is the stuff of our lives, and which would have been my theme in this paper if things had gone differently. But second, and more simply, values are concepts which describe our behaviour only when we understand what directs that behaviour overall. Science is directed by the search for truth, and all societies are directed by the search for stability. The values of our scientific society describe our behavior as it is directed to make an evolving society which shall also be stable.

It is almost three hundred years since scientists first banded together in the Royal Society of England and the *Académie Royale* of France. What scientists thought to be true then seems very primitive to us now; Isaac Newton was still a youth then, and even gravitation had not been thought of. Every scientific theory has changed profoundly, and several times, in these three hundred years. Yet the society of scientists has remained stable, and binds together Englishmen and Frenchmen, and Americans and Russians, in a unity of spirit, a community of principles, more profound than any other body of men. Does this impressive history really lend colour to the myth that science is inhuman and impersonal? Does it really suggest that the activity of science generates no values to unite those who practise it?

The point of my analysis today has not been to defend science from its critics. My point has been to attack what I believe to be a fundamental error of method in the critics, and which I have heard here: the error of looking for values outside our activity. If values are to be discussed in a useful way, then they must be discussed empirically, in the realistic setting of the world in which they operate. Values take their richness from the tension between each man and his society, and we should not be human if this tension disappeared: we should be a mechanical insect society. For this very reason, it is useless to discuss values as personal acts of faith and to disregard the society which must give them currency. If we do this, we shall always end by importing the values of some past tradition, and regretting that they do not fit us better. There are some traditional values alive in our scientific society today; but whether they are traditional or whether they are new, they are alive not by accident, but because they are appropriate: because they fit into, and grow from, the activity of science. It is time that those who discuss values learn the reach of that activity and the power of the values which spring from its modest search for the factual truth.

Human Values in a Changing World

—————————— LUDWIG VON BERTALANFFY

THE PRESENT conference differs radically from conventional scientific meetings as they are continually going on all over the globe. In such meetings we usually talk about new contributions to science, be it some field of mathematics, atomic physics, cancer, psychiatry, or whatever our professional specialty may be. Small or allegedly important, conservative or upsetting previous observations and doctrines—it is new data, new facts, new interpretations or theory one has to present at a meeting of the conventional sort. To use the terminology of this conference, a certain value, that of scientific knowledge, is implicitly taken for granted and not subject to discussion.

The present meeting is different. None of us, I believe, has discovered a new human value which he now wants to disclose, like a hitherto hidden jewel, to a world prepared or unprepared to accept it. Our task rather is taking stock of what has been commonly accepted as human values, and this very question is disquietingly symptomatic. Asking the question implies that values have become doubtful and are not taken for granted anymore. Hence I propose some sentences from Nietzsche's *Will to Power*[1] as a suitable starting point for this discussion: "What I relate," Nietzsche wrote in 1888, "is the history of the next two centuries. I describe what is coming, what can no longer come differently: the advent of nihilism.

[1] F. Nietzsche, *The Will to Power*, Preface.

. . . Our whole European culture is moving for some time now, with a tortured tension that is growing from decade to decade, as toward a catastrophe: restlessly, violently, headlong. . . . Why has the advent of nihilism become necessary? Because the values we had hitherto thus draw their final consequence; because we must experience nihilism before we can find out what value these 'values' really had."

PROGRESS IS QUESTIONABLE

Nietzsche regarded Christianity as the value system to be discarded and replaced by a new one. One possible answer to Nietzsche's demand for new values was the notion of progress, the belief that science and technology will carry mankind into a paradisiac future. It needs no elaborate discussion that, up to comparatively recent times, the belief in progress was the dominant ideology of our civilization, and that now we have become doubtful. As this question unavoidably leads to platitudes, let us quickly dispose of it. It is an obvious fact that yesterday I flew from Los Angeles to Boston in eight hours, while this trip took me four days by train twenty years ago; that the number of automobiles, washing machines, and television sets is multiplying; that the situation of the American worker today is incomparable to that of fifty years ago, or even to that of his European colleague; that the average life span has increased some twenty years in the past few decades, and so forth *ad infinitum*. Let us also pass the dangers inherent in this development: the hydrogen bomb, the possible social and psychological implications of automation, the Malthusian menace of further overcrowding our planet in consequence of the advances of modern medicine, and all the rest. Whether the sum total of human happiness and misery has increased, decreased, or remained approximately constant during the course of human history nobody can tell because there is no yardstick to measure it. Considering two total and a number of minor wars within the life span of one generation, the balance does not automatically jump in favor of our epoch as against the Thirty-Years' War, the Spanish Inquisition, or the French Revolution.

We must, therefore, dig deeper. It goes without saying that the notion of progress is intimately connected with the biological notion of evolution. As in geological times the living world has advanced from lowest to ever higher animal and plant species, so mankind progresses from primitive to ever more advanced states, the peak presently attained being Western civilization of the twentieth century. This implies a problem which, I presume, is the question posed to me in a discussion on human values: Can human values be derived from and reduced to biological values? It may be surprising or even shocking to some of you that the answer of at least one biologist is a well-considered "No."

BIOLOGICAL AND HUMAN VALUES

The basis of the parallel between organic evolution and human progress is what is known as the postulate of reductionism: that is, that biology should eventually be reduced to physics and chemistry and, correspondingly, the behavioral and social sciences to biology. Put in a somewhat different way: as a living organism is an intricate physicochemical system, so—it is assumed—human behavior is a particularly involved complex of the ways and factors of behavior present in subhuman species.

In my opinion, this is not so. I rather believe that the field of science, speaking in the way of gross oversimplification, consists of three major levels: physical nature; organisms; and human behavior, individual and social.

Let me make clear what I do not mean and what I do mean by this statement. I do not mean that there are absolute discontinuities between those levels. Being a biologist with strong leanings toward physical theory, I obviously do not mean that physics and chemisty are not the indispensable groundwork of biology. In a similar way, biology is the indispensable groundwork of the science of human behavior. What I do mean, however, is that the notion of emergence is essentially correct: each higher level presents new features that surpass those of the lower levels.

Let us apply this scheme to human affairs. What is unique and characteristic in human behavior? The answer, I believe, is simple and unequivocal. The monopoly of man is the creation of symbolic universes in language, thought, and all other forms of behavior.

Man's unique position in nature is based upon the predominance of symbols in his life.[2] Except for the immediate satisfaction of biological needs, man lives in a universe not of things but of symbolic stand-ins for things. A coin, for example, is a symbol for a certain amount of work done or utilities available; a document is a symbol of *res gestae;* a word or concept is a symbol of a thing or relationship; a book and a scientific theory are fantastic piles of accumulated symbols; and so forth ad infinitum.

This, then, indicates the difference between biological and specifically human values. Compared to the biological categories of "useful" or "harmful" for the survival of the individual and the species, what we call human values are essentially symbolic universes that have developed in history. You will find this definition applicable to any field of human activity, be it science, technology, art, morals, or religion. These symbolic universes may be adaptive and utilitarian in the biological sense, as when technology allows man to control nature. They may be indifferent, such as Greek sculpture or Renaissance painting which hardly can be claimed to have contributed toward better adaptation and survival. They may be outright deleterious if the breakdown of his little symbolic universe leads an individual to commit suicide, or the conflict of larger symbolic worlds leads to war and extermination on a large scale.

The viewpoint that I have brought forward appears to open many considerations of which I can follow only a few. Take, for example, the neurological and evolutionary aspect. The prerequisite for man's unique achievement obviously is the evolution of his brain. Speaking in terms of a crude oversimplification justly deserving the ire of the neurologist, we may distinguish the old brain or paleencephalon, the organ of primitive functions, instincts, and drives, and the new brain, the cortex or neencephalon which is the organ of the day per-

---

[2] L. von Bertalanffy, "A Biologist Looks at Human Nature," *Sci. Monthly,* 1956, 82:33 ff.

sonality, of conscious perception, feeling, voluntary action and, in particular, of the symbolic functions characteristic of man. Now if we survey the series of brains from lower vertebrates up to man, the characteristic is progressive cerebralization, that is, increase in the quantity and complexity of the forebrain. Consequently, what we call human progress is essentially an intellectual affair, made possible by the enormous increase of the forebrain. Owing to this, man was able to build up the symbolic worlds of speech and thought, and some progress was made in science and technology during the five thousand years of recorded history.

No development, however, is seen on the instinctual side, for the perfectly good reason that there is no anatomical substratum for it. This applies to both positive and negative aspects of behavior. Rousseau's idyllic image of the good natural man, spoiled only by civilization, and Freud's image of man as a born aggressor, patricide, and fornicator, precariously kept in bounds by the Censor, are equally romantic and unrealistic. Man is a tolerably monogamous species, he is a social animal, and he has inborn parental and filial instincts. This instinctual equipment, however, is not specifically human even though it may be the basis for conventional moral codes. Rather it is shared by any number of animal species which partly exhibit such instincts in far greater perfection. And there is, of course, the debit side of the ledger. We have progressed, in some five thousand years, from primitive mythology to quantum theory, and in some 150 years from the steam engine to the hydrogen bomb. But it would be a slightly optimistic view that general moral standards have progressed since Laotse, the Buddha, or Christ. This is a simple consequence of anatomy, namely, that the human cortex provides some 10 billions of neurons for intellectual achievements, but hardly a basis for a parallel development on the emotional and instinctual side.

The same problem can be envisaged from the viewpoint of cultural anthropology and history. The man-created symbolic universe partly depends on categories which are universally human, and partly on categories developed historically within a certain civilization.[3] The first fact accounts for the conformity of a Golden Rule of behavior common to all higher religions; the second, for the solecisms of moral codes. Moral values are indeed different for modern Europeans, Pueblo Indians, Kwakiutls, and Dobus as Ruth Benedict has so vividly depicted in her *Patterns of Culture;*[4] so much so that normal ways of behavior in one culture would be considered schizophrenic in another one. This all depends on the symbolic framework of cultures or even different frames of reference within one culture: what is penalized as murder in civilian life is labeled heroism in the frame of reference of war.

NIHILISM—THE BREAKDOWN OF A SYMBOLIC UNIVERSE

If we accept the viewpoint offered, Nietzsche's quest quoted in the beginning, and many disquieting phenomena, fall into place like pieces of a jigsaw puzzle. The phenomenon termed nihilism by Nietzsche is nothing else than the imminent breakdown of a symbolic universe. You will find this definition applicable to any field of human behavior and activity. The economic symbol of money has lost its connection with reality; a banknote does not represent any more a fixed quantity of gold or of commodities but is subject to continuous re-evaluation, to inflation, sometimes at an astronomical scale, and other machinations. Art used to be a symbol-system representative of a certain period in a certain culture. Today's "art" seems to extend from the finger-painting of a chimpanzee, recently reproduced in *Life* magazine and presenting a good example of modern nonrepresentative pictures, to the homey covers of the *Saturday Evening Post.* Even the symbolic universe of science, which is about the only solid thing we have, is shaky in certain aspects and places. The same symbol, democracy, means exactly the opposite when uttered in the West or in the Communist world. The symbolic system of religion which, abstracting from its intrinsic values, at any rate has developed organically in the long course of history, is supplanted by kaleidoscopically changing pseudo-

[3] L. von Bertalanffy, "An Essay on the Relativity of Categories," *Philosophy of Sci.,* 1955, 22:243ff.

[4] R. Benedict, *Patterns of Culture,* Houghton Mifflin, 1934.

religions, be they scientific progress, psychoanalysis, nationalism, soap opera, or tranquilizers.

All this does not mean that we necessarily behave worse than our predecessors, or that our predecessors were better than we are. It does mean, however, that there used to be established symbolic standards which were taken for granted even by the trespasser, sinner, and reformer, while now they seem to be disappearing.

I will illustrate this only by a few examples taken at random. Take, for instance, a problem in which we educators are immediately concerned, that "Johnny can't read" and, what is worse, that Johnnie doesn't much care to read. In spite of general and supposedly progressive education, we feel the advent of a new illiteracy, nourished by comics, television, and talkies. At the adult level, it is the same phenomenon when the so-called intelligentsia is labeled as a bunch of sissies or Communists, and Babbitt becomes the image of ideal humanity. What else is this than the breakdown of a symbolic universe, laboriously and under a thousand pains erected in the course of history?

Another facet is what I have called the return to the conditioned reflex. Permit me to quote my definition of this phenomenon:

The dignity of man rests on rational behavior—that is, behavior directed by symbolic anticipation of a goal. In modern man, however, this *vis a fronte*, to use Aristotle's term, consisting of goals the individual or the society sets itself, is largely replaced by the primitive *vis a tergo* of conditional reaction.

The modern methods of propaganda, from the advertisement of a tooth paste to that of political programs and systems, do not appeal to rationality in man but rather force upon him certain ways of behavior by means of a continuous repetition of stimuli coupled with emotional rewards or punishments. This method is essentially the same as that applied to Pavlovian dogs when they were drilled to respond to a meaningless stimulus with reactions prescribed by the experimenter. . . . If a slogan, however insipid, is repeated a sufficient number of times and is emotionally coupled with the promise of a reward or the menace of punishment, it is nearly unavoidable that the human animal establishes the condi-

72 NEW KNOWLEDGE IN HUMAN VALUES

tioned reaction as desired. Furthermore, to apply this method successfully, the conditioning process must be adjusted to the greatest common
denominator; that is, the appeal has to be made to the lowest intelligence
level. The result is mass man—that is, abolishment of individual discrimination and decision and its replacement by universal conditioned
reflexes.[5]

The recent book *The Hidden Persuaders*, by Vance Packard,[6] is
an excellent and amply documented elaboration of this theme.

Still another aspect is what might be called cultural regression,
using the term precisely in the psychoanalytic sense. Partly, even
the term "mental fetalization," in the sense Bolk used the word for
certain anatomic characteristics, would seem in place. The comic
strip, the peeping tom in the modern form of scandal magazines, the
touching infantility of television, the well-filled refrigerator as a sort
of nourishing womb, the penis symbolism of the Cadillac,[7] the
father image of Eisenhower—all these and many other things are
nothing but regression to infantile states. This does not mean that
automobiles, refrigerators, or Eisenhower may not in themselves be
excellent things; but it does mean that the attitude is not that of
what psychoanalysts call a mature ego.

No wonder, then, that the breakdown of the symbolic universe
leads to the experience of being lost in a meaningless world. This
experience, as formulated by individuals of a high intellectual
standard, is existentialist philosophy.

For the many who lack sophistication, there are two other outlets:
crime and mental disease. Juvenile delinquency reaching a peak
under optimum economic conditions—what else can it mean than
the practice of a philosophy of meaninglessness?

[5] L. von Bertalanffy, A Biologist Looks at Human Nature, p. 40.
[6] V. Packard, *The Hidden Persuaders*, McKay, 1957.
[7] "The fundamental fact about American male psychology is the fear of im-
potence. Let's give the men, therefore, the One Big Symbol that will make them
feel that they are *not* impotent. Let's give them great big cars, glittering all
over and pointed at the ends, with 275 h.p. under the hood, so that they can
feel like men!" S. T. Hayakawa, "Sexual Fantasy and the 1957 Car," *Etc.*, 1957,
14:163ff.

And there is that other outlet—mental ailment to the tune of some 10 million cases in the United States, or the 52 per cent mental cases of all hospitalized patients.[8] It is often maintained that the stress of modern life is at the basis of the increase of mental derangement. This stress is bad enough, but the theory is demonstrably false. It is a statistical fact that in times of extreme stress, as for example, the blitz in England, neurotic disorders decreased rather than increased.[9] Measured in terms of stress, all of Europe, after war and postwar experience, should be a gigantic madhouse, which patently it is not. It appears that the shoe is rather on the other foot: neurosis reaches its peak not when biological survival but rather when the symbolic superstructure is at stake. When life becomes intolerably dull, void, and meaningless—what can a person do but develop a neurosis? These neurosogenic or even psychosogenic conditions can even be reproduced in the laboratory as in the well-known Montreal experiments[10] where subjects, isolated from incoming stimuli, developed a model psychosis with intolerable anxiety, hallucinations, and the rest.

Is There a Remedy?

All these considerations, which could be continued for a Thousand and One Nights, are apt to show that culture, that is, a framework of symbolic values, is not a mere plaything for the human animal or luxury of the intelligentsia; it is the very backbone of society and, among many other things, an important psychohygienic factor.

What, then, can we offer for a reevaluation of human values? For a minority, there is what Maslow has so aptly labeled and described under the term "peak experience."[11] This, however, is reserved for an esoteric few. I am neither concerned with, nor competent on, matters theological. However, looking at things from a detached,

[8] W. Menninger, in *Los Angeles Times,* September 14, 1957.
[9] M. K. Opler, *Culture, Psychiatry, and Human Values,* Thomas, 1956, p. 67f.
[10] D. Bindra, Presentation in: *Discussions on Child Development,* ed. by J. M. Tanner and B. Inhelder, 1957, vol. 2, Tavistock Publications, Ltd.
[11] A. H. Maslow, "Cognition of Being in the Peak Experiences." To be published, *Journal of Genetic Psychology,* 1959.

scientific and historical viewpoint, it appears that the value system of Christianity has proved to be singularly persistent and adaptable to varying cultural frameworks. Of course, this means that I am in contradiction to Nietzsche with whom I started these considerations.

In summary, the diagnosis I have tried to make may appear pessimistic. There are, however, some hopeful aspects. Our present conference and other developments clearly show that these problems are no longer by-passed and neglected but are a matter of serious concern. Where there is insight and a will, there might be a way. Thus, I believe the purpose of our meeting will be fulfilled by making it understood that a new symbolic universe of values must be found or an old one reinstated if mankind is to be saved from the pit of meaninglessness, suicide, and atomic fire.

Human Nature as a Product of Evolution *

_____

A CENTURY ago, in 1858, Darwin and Wallace showed that the world of life did not suddenly spring into existence in the state in which we observe it today. Instead, life is the outcome of perhaps more than two billion years of evolutionary development. Darwin's work *The Descent of Man* appeared in 1871. It showed that man is a part of nature and one of the products of the evolutionary process.

Man is a zoological species. But this species has evolved properties so unique and unprecedented on the animal level that in man the biological evolution has transcended itself. Over and over again, some biologists made themselves ridiculous by urging solutions of human social and political problems based on the assumption that man is nothing but an animal. How dangerous may be such false keys to human riddles is shown by the fruits of one of these errors—the race theory. We have seen it being used under Hitler to justify murder on an unprecedented scale, and it contributes to the unhappiness of human beings from South Africa to Arkansas.

BIOLOGICAL AND HISTORICAL DEVELOPMENT

Human nature has been molded by evolutionary forces which were basically the same as those which operated in the living world

* The author wishes to acknowledge his obligations to his colleagues and friends for discussions which have helped to clarify some of the ideas presented in this article, particularly to Drs. J. A. Beardmore, L. C. Birch, L. C. Dunn, and G. L. Stebbins.

at large. Man has certainly not freed himself from all the shackles of his animal frame. Yet, in man the evolutionary forces have formed a pattern so singular that man has reached heavenward and acquired powers which no other organism even remotely approached. Man's powers now include the power to destroy himself if he so chooses. But they include also the knowledge which may permit man to direct the further evolution of his nature along the paths which he will select. We must avoid the vulgar error of mistaking the biological man for the whole man. Nevertheless, human nature cannot be adequately understood except as a product of its historical development, which is in part biological development.

It is not my purpose here to set forth in any detail the unique features of the human biological nature and of human evolution. I can only attempt to indicate in broad lines the evolutionary forces which impinge upon man, particularly in the formation of his conscience. Two general characteristics of the evolutionary process must be kept in mind in any discussion of the origins of human nature. First, evolution is utilitarian. Secondly, it is opportunistic. Evolution is utilitarian because the main directing force of evolutionary change is natural selection. The action of natural selection is usually to maintain or to enhance the adaptedness of life to its environments. Evolution is opportunistic because natural selection lacks a prescience of the future. The evolution of life and of man has not been planned in advance; it is a natural creative process which contains an element of freedom but also a risk of failure. The biological nature of man, like that of any other living species, has been shaped as it has because it enabled mankind to go on living and to spread to populate the earth. But, unless evolution is consciously managed, it is appallingly myopic. At any given time it tends to make the species successful in the environment which prevails at that particular time, quite regardless of the future needs. Hence the apparent paradox: living species change almost always in the direction of a greater adaptedness, and yet most of them end sooner or later by becoming extinct.

By any reasonable criteria of biological achievement, man is thus far the most successful product of organic evolution. Mankind has not only increased rapidly in numbers but spread to all parts of the world. Man has adapted himself to his environments not only by making his biological nature conform to the environments, but also by forcing the environments to conform to his nature. He has controlled, or will soon be able to control, all other organisms which could conceivably compete with him or to prey on him. The chances of extinction of man as a species are negligible, except through his own folly.

Man's biological success certainly does not mean that his biological nature is free from faults and flaws. Far from this; man is a paradoxical creature full of internal contradictions. On the one hand, he is a being endowed with reason and compassion. Although we no longer share the happy assurance of the Age of Enlightenment that men would naturally lead virtuous lives if only certain political and educational reforms will be made, most of us still believe that democracy may be the least imperfect method to achieve some degree of happiness for most people. On the other hand, we often witness the sorry spectacle of apparently enlightened and contented people behaving in most unlovely ways. And Freud and his followers persuade us that we are born with a confused host of desires which can only with greatest difficulty be brought in accord with the requirements of living in any human society, and then mostly by means of suppression or of sublimation. It would seem that the most vengeful believers in original sin and damnation held opinions about human nature which were hardly less favorable than those held by some of the Freudians.

Now, a mixture of excellence and taint in human nature is what could be expected on biological grounds. For one thing, a species living in a rapidly changing environment is necessarily adapted best to the conditions which have lapsed, and is only in the process of adaptation to the present conditions. Civilized as well as so-called primitive people carry genes which were implanted by natural selection acting when men lived under conditions very different from those in which they now live. Coon believes that the human biological equipment took essentially its present form during the paleolithic hunting stage, but only very few of the carriers of this equipment now live by hunting.

THE EVOLUTIONARY ADVANTAGE—INTELLIGENCE

Another consideration is still more pertinent. The opportunism inherent in biological evolution results in defects and imperfections being tolerated, provided that the handicaps imposed by them are compensated for by a superiority in other qualities. The biological success of the human species became a reality notwithstanding the fact that man is, for his bulk, neither particularly strong nor particularly agile nor resistant to inclement weather. Man became a winner in the evolutionary race because of the powers of his brain, not those of his body. Natural selection cannot improve the strength, or the resistance, or the intelligence separately from other qualities. It is the man as a whole who survives or dies, raises a family or remains childless. A supple intellect may offset the drawbacks of a relatively flabby body. Natural selection gives therefore even less assurance of an all-round perfection of the biological organization of a species than of its continued existence.

The unique human quality which has brought about the biological ascendancy of our species is the ability to think in terms of symbols and abstractions. This ability has permitted the development of the peculiarly human mode of communication, by means of symbolic languages. Such languages are only faintly foreshadowed on the animal level. Communication by speech, and later by writing, has enabled man to evolve a stock of learned traditions and skills which constitute culture. The transmission of biological heredity is a process vastly less efficient than that of culture. The former is transferred exclusively from parents to children and other direct descendants by the genes in the sex cells. The latter is passed by teaching and training, in principle to any normal human being willing to receive it, and, after the invention of writing and printing, potentially independently of distance in space and in time. Acquired bodily characteristics are not inherited; acquired cultural traits can be transmitted together with the traditional ones, and thus added to the cultural patrimony. The genetic equipment of mankind endows it with a capacity of cardinal importance, that to acquire and to transmit from generation to generation the knowledge and the skills to control the environment. Every succeeding generation can, if it so chooses, stand on the shoulders of the preceding ones and aspire to ever greater attainments. The emergence of this genetic equipment was the evolutionary masterstroke which placed our species at the summit of the living world.

Interesting attempts have been made to understand the origin of human values as a part of the genetic equipment of our species. In recent years, Julian Huxley has been the most active protagonist of this view. Indeed, it is reasonably safe to assume that certain urges related to the world of values are genetically conditioned. Man is a mammal, and one of the characteristic adaptations in mammals is parental care of the progeny. Parental love rises from the depths of human nature. Since man is a social animal, he usually profits more from amicable than from pugnacious disposition and behavior. Natural selection may have implanted in us dispositions suitable for living in organized groups. It is, however, difficult to account on this basis for the systems of values which we find in human societies. Many ways of behavior which are regarded as ethical or praise-worthy enhance neither the chances of survival nor of reproductive success of the persons so behaving. And yet, the selective value of a genetic equipment is measured precisely by the contribution which its carriers make to the succeeding generations. The "surviving fittest" is, according to this view, nothing more spectacular than the parent of the largest number of surviving children and grand-children. The origin of human values through natural selection is an over-simplification which can hardly be sustained. Human values are a part of our cultural heritage; they have been forged in the fires of cultural, not of biological, evolution. Their dependence on biological underpinnings of our nature is very real but indirect.

Reference has already been made to the cheerful creed of the Age of Enlightenment. The celebrated *tabula rasa* theory of John

Locke asserted that the human mind is formed entirely by experience and education. But this equality of identical blankness at birth would, according to Rousseau, make everybody good—"Man is naturally good and only by institutions is he made bad." The natural man is a noble savage, untouched by the evil influences of civilization. Nowadays the belief in noble savagery has fallen in disuse, but the confidence in natural goodness of man is ably defended by Ashley Montagu. "It is not evil babies who grow up into evil human beings, but an evil society which turns good babies into disordered adults, and it does so on a regimen of frustration. Babies are born good and desirous of continuing to be good."

The *tabula rasa* theory can just as easily be combined with the belief that man is naturally bad. The classical example is Hobbes' view that the natural state of man is *"bellum omnium contra omnes,"* perpetual war of all against all. This sounds very much like Darwin's inexorable struggle for existence. The so-called social Darwinism, which Darwin himself would probably have repudiated with disgust, is a cleverly contrived hodgepodge of Hobbes, Malthus, Darwin, and biological racism. Far from being a *tabula rasa* at birth, the personality is determined by our genes, and every one of us is born with genes different from everybody else. Moreover, the racists, from Gobineau to Darlington, claim that some people are born good or superior, while others are predestined by their heredities to be evil, or inferior, or both. Environment and education are powerless to change the qualities set by the genes. By a singular coincidence, the racist himself almost always belongs to the group of people who are genetically the best and most superior.

That human cultural evolution is conditioned by the genetic endowment of our species is evident enough. A person acquires his cultural traits by learning, beginning with the process of socialization in infancy. But the possession of normal human genes is necessary for receptivity to the socializing influences of the human social milieu. The genes of a microcephalic idiot make learning impossible. An ape, a monkey, a parrot, or a dog can learn many different things, but not many of these which a human child learns easily.

The evolution of culture became possible only when some basis for it had been blocked out in biological evolution. However, culture reacted back on biology, and the chief trend in the biological development of mankind has been to give full play to the cultural development.

The autonomy of cultural evolution does not mean that an impenetrable wall separates our culture from our genes. The autonomy of culture means that while the genes make it possible they do not determine its contents. Similarly, human genes determine the capacity of speech, but they do not determine what is said. The evidence of autonomy comes from the radical cultural changes which many human societies underwent without apparent genetic alterations. The ancestors of most of us were, a hundred or even less generations ago, rude barbarians eking out precarious existence from the niggardly nature of the forest zone of Europe. The industrial revolution has altered the occupations and the modes of life of many millions of people within very few generations. It is most probable that some genetic changes are taking place at all times in all human populations. But there is no reason to believe that the differences between our cultural state and those of our ancestors two, or twenty, or a hundred generations ago are to an appreciable degree due to differences between our genes.

Again and again, attempts have been made to postulate genetic changes that could be supposed to be responsible for the vicissitudes of human history. The decline of Rome has been ascribed to the alleged dysgenic practices of the latter-day Romans. Disintegration of our own civilization has been confidently predicted because of the high birth rates of the economically less fortunate classes. A detailed discussion of these matters is obviously impossible here, but it is not unfair to say that none of the above attempts have given fully convincing results. The state of the genetic equipment of human populations must be carefully watched, especially if many people try to insure their security by sowing more atomic bombs. Meanwhile, enormous improvements of the human lot may be expected from amelioration of the environment.

GENES OR CULTURE?

The ability of man to undergo acculturation, to change his occupations, his whole mode of life, and even his beliefs, hopes, and desires without corresponding genetic change is biologically most extraordinary. Organisms other than man are usually specialized for a single or for a few alternative modes of life; adaptation to new environments is possible only by way of evolutionary changes in the genetic equipment of the species. Man can adapt to new environments by changing his culture, or by changing the environments by means of his culture. This is one of the most fundamental properties of human biological nature. The *tabula rasa* theory seemed to follow from the everyday observation that people can, more or less easily, at least in comparison with animals, adjust themselves to new circumstances and new tasks.

The observation is correct but the conclusion drawn from it is false. The crucial fact is that human social and cultural environments are singularly inconstant, both in terms of an individual's life, and even more in terms of the destinies of families, tribes, and races. Biological heredity is simply too rigid, and biological evolution is too slow to serve as mechanisms of adaptation to the restlessly variable human environments. The cultural heritage is, as pointed out above, both more flexible and vastly more easily transmissible. This is in itself a sufficient reason why the genes which facilitated the transmission of the cultural heritage were established by natural selection in human evolution. They yielded an adaptive mechanism of an overwhelming potency, which worked especially well under the unique and biologically unprecedented conditions of the human estate. The ability of the organism to compensate for changes in its external environments in such ways that its normal functioning proceeds undisturbed is known as homeostasis. Human ability to profit by experience, learning and education is a singularly efficient homeostatic mechanism.

The doctrine of *tabula rasa* seemed useful to those who believed that all men have been created equal. Equality is, however, an ethical and not a biological concept. It is an outcome of the cultural, not of the biological, evolution. Equality is not predicated upon biological identity. As a matter of fact, no two persons in the world, identical twins excepted, carry the same genes. It does not follow from this that men are "free and unequal." Human personality development is remarkably responsive to variations in the cultural environments. The followers of the *tabula rasa* doctrine took this for evidence that people are really all alike. Precisely the reverse conclusion is warranted. The plasticity of the human developmental pattern is a method of making people different, depending upon the conditions in which they live. People are diverse but equal.

METHODS OF ADAPTATION

Man is proficient in controlling his physical surroundings. Thanks to advances of technology, the physical conditions under which people live in different climes are now less diverse than they would have been had all of us remained in primitive cultural states. Conversely, civilization increases enormously the range of vocations, functions, and roles which people are called upon to assume. In what ways could the evolutionary process make provisions for adaptation to this virtually infinite variety of functions? Biologically, two methods are possible. The first is genetic specialization. This may be illustrated by an analogy with breeds of dogs, horses, or other domesticated forms. There are hunting dogs, watch dogs, and dogs to captivate the heart of a superannuated spinster. The second method is homeostasis and developmental plasticity. To give a zoological example—a Drosophila fly coming from a well-fed larva may weigh three times as much as one from a starved larva. A fly larva faced with a food scarcity does not die, it merely gives an undersized adult.

Man's adjustment to his sociocultural environments makes use of both methods. Moreover, these methods are not alternative, as they are often imagined to be. They are complementary. Modification by experience and training is conjoined with genetic diversity. True, the developmental plasticity is, by and large, the more important of the two methods. Its progressive refinement has been, as pointed out above, adaptively the most significant feature of human evolution. The demands which human society makes on the individual are too diversified, and, most important, too rapidly changing with time to make genetic specialization alone competent to insure the perpetuation of our species, at least in its civilization stage. Genetic diversity yields, however, an additional increment of adaptive potentialities.

The genetic equipments of the human species do not make all men inherently good or irrevocably bad, virtuous or wicked, clever or stupid, cheerful or morose. They rather provide man with a range of potentialities, to be realized according to circumstances. Moreover, there is no such thing as a genetic equipment common to all, or even to all "normal" men. The variety of genetic equipment is very great, almost coextensive with the numbers of men who live, have lived, and will live. Every person is a carrier of an unprecedented and non-recurrent gene pattern. Human natures are diverse, and so are their outlooks on life.

To quote George Sarton:

Men understand the world in different ways. The main difference lies in this, that some men are more abstract-minded, and they naturally think first of unity and of God, of wholeness, of infinity and other such concepts, while the minds of other men are concrete and they cogitate about health and disease, profit and loss. They invent gadgets and remedies; they are less interested in knowing anything than in applying whatever knowledge they may already have to practical problems; they try to make things work and pay, to heal and teach. The first are called dreamers; the second kind are recognized as practical and useful. History has often proved the shortsightedness of the practical men and vindicated the "lazy" dreamers; it has also proved that the dreamers are often mistaken.

Unfortunately, we do not know to what extent the differences between the "dreamers" and the "practical men" are caused by variations in their genes and in their environments. Both are probably involved to some extent. In any case, a society which has some dreamers and some practical men is better off than a community of dreamers alone or exclusively of practical men. Human societies, and especially civilized societies, thrive on diversity, whether environmentally or genetically induced, because human societies have so many different functions to be served. The evolution of man has, indeed, provided the biological foundations for educability and occupational versatility on one hand, and for genetic diversity on the other. The great riddle is how best to make use of the diversity of men equal in rights to secure the greatest happiness of the greatest number. Who is bold enough to claim that he has fully solved this riddle?

BIBLIOGRAPHY

For more detailed discussions of the genetic determinants of human nature see:

Dobzhansky, T., *The Biological Basis of Human Freedom,* Columbia University, 1956.

——, *Evolution, Genetics, and Man,* John Wiley, 1955.

Simpson, G. G., *The Meaning of Evolution,* Yale University, 1949.

A somewhat different conception of the evolutionary basis of human nature has recently been developed in a series of books and articles of J. S. Huxley, particularly in:

Huxley, J. S., *Evolution in Action,* Harper, 1953.

A still different conception has been ably presented by:

Montagu, M. F. Ashley, *The Direction of Human Development,* Harper, 1955.

Comments on Art

THE PRESENT human situation resembles that of a lost child. The order, and thus the surety of existence, seem to be lost. Industrial civilization has torn us out of the relatedness that people knew in a smaller world. The forces of nature that were brought by gradual domestication into a human scale have again become alien forces: now they approach us menacingly along the avenues opened by science and technology. In this complex, changing world, we feel alone. We feel that we have lost parental guidance. Old mores, feelings and concepts which were both guides and shelter in a smaller and calmer world, have been swept away in the turmoil of new dynamic conditions. Like a lost child, we try to cope with the apparently hostile, new scale of things, without a measure to make them perceivable. We are even worse off than a lost child, for we have no hope of finding the parents, the old interpreters, because the world is on the move and this movement is not reversable. Our dominant reaction is fear—a fear which keeps us from accepting the challenge of our wider and potentially richer world. Insecure and afraid, we freeze our feelings and ideas, and we do not know how to take action to eliminate the basis of our fears.

No longer secure in our relationship to the world around us, we lose our ability to live a free and complete life. Our self-confidence is gone; we are unable to respond with courageous acceptance to the challenges that face us. Instead of using all that we have—eye, heart, brain—mobilizing all our faculties and capacities in a common focus, we react with frantic one-sided intensity. One aspect of ourself lives at the expense of the other. Our thoughts disregard and discredit our emotions, push them into the background, and thus lose contact with the energy and richness the emotions may provide. Our feelings are thereby frustrated and go underground or into dangerous blind alleys. Our sensibilities are also frozen. We are incapable of absorbing the new landscape, with its wealth of new sensations; therefore we cannot reinforce ourselves with the joys of light, color and forms, the rhythm of sound and movement essential to healthy growth. The inner wholeness, the essential key to a healthy act is gone. Nietzsche once commented on literature: "What is the characteristic of all literary decadence? It is that life no longer resides in the whole. The word gets the upper hand and jumps out of the sentence. The sentence stretches too far and obscures the meaning of the page. The page acquires life at the expense of the whole. The whole is no longer a whole." His comment is bitterly true for our contemporary life. Confused and cornered by the impact of the complex world, we have lost the ability to perceive the world as a connected whole and to react to it with healthy openness. The part has taken over the upper hand. With dazzling pace we shift focus from one aspect of our inner or outer horizon to another. Without an ability to live with undivided inner loyalties and without finding a sense of loyalty to the complete horizon of our contemporary scene, we gradually diminish our strength.

The Tasks We Face

We have then two interdependent tasks in front of us. We have to span the gap between man and his newly won possessions, knowledge and power; to build a foundation safe and broad enough to hold our common physical life securely on a twentieth-century standard, and we have to build bridges within ourselves and reach an inner oneness, a union of our sensory, emotional and rational aspects of life.

What inner guide do we have to meet these tasks? To realize

completeness, we have to have some inner models, some concrete vital experiences of order, harmony and self-realization. We have to have some inner seeds which contain patterns of "wholeness." As the perfectly patterned group of atoms, a small fraction of a cell, radiate orderly patterns and become the guide and guardian of the development of the organism, so we have to have in more complex dimensions guides and guardians.

Love is the closest to this inner model. Love in a personal or in a deep religious sense translates every experience to an embrace so that we project our basic sense of belonging to everything and everybody we may encounter. In love, or with a deep love, the world becomes a friendly world; the cloudy day becomes a sunny day and faces become the faces of friends. A strongly-felt loyalty to somebody or a deeply felt loyalty to men generates a growing chain of loyalties to everything we encounter.

There is another inner model which parallels the role of love. Artistic experience in making or reliving an artistic form can also serve as an inner guide and guardian.

THE ARTISTIC EXPERIENCE

What is the nature of an artistic experience? First of all it is an orderer. As common perception gathers a number of sense impressions into a *gestalt*, a pattern-vision, this heightened perception of artistic vision collates sense impressions into vision of the high patterning of works of art, with their harmony, balance, melodic sequence and rhythm. The uncomplicated symmetry of prehistoric tools; the intricate axial inversions of neolithic ornaments; the rhythmic variations of Peruvian fabrics; the orderly pulsation of the mosaic of San Vitale; and the convincing unity of shapes and colors in the paintings of Piero della Francesca, Sesshu, Bellini, Juan Gris or Mondrian; all these visual syntheses document convincingly man's supreme ability to focus and unify the diffused variety of the changing, seen world. Our sensibilities need to be sustained with the joy of felt order. As a basic aspect of the human organism, the artistic form is a significant organizer of life, enabling us to deal with the environment and directing and controlling our development. Artistic images order our thoughts and feelings as the genetic material orders the composition, growth and reproduction of our bodies. The artistic images we share encode our common culture; our private images encode our inner, unique world, impressing on us both the richness of the sensed and the order of the understood.

But there is another still deeper role of the artistic experience. We respond to the forms and images of artists because their harmonies, rhythms, colors, and shapes touch us not just on one level of our being or another, but, as Yeats has put it: they "could not move us at all, if our thought did not rush out to the edge of our flesh and it is so with all good art, whether the victory of Samothrace which reminds the soles of our feet of swiftness, or the Odyssey that would send us out under the salt wind, or the young horsemen on the Parthenon that seem happier than our boyhood ever was, and in boyhood's way."

And between the pulsating life of our sensation and the intense richness of our emotion up to their final symbolic focus there is a continuous analogue. In this aspect of many-layered, analogous experience, participation in a work of art often supplies us with deep ties with the world around us. The physical base outside us which stimulated us and our sensations within are bridged. Our sensations, feelings, and thoughts march in a unison of completeness. Whitehead described religion as "world loyalty," and in a certain sense artistic experience leads us to such world loyalty. It gives us what one may express with a paradox, our vertical horizon, our depth horizon. For no level of human response is neglected in an optimum form of an artistic statement. Sensations, the emotional and rational illumination are spanned in a living, unbroken, complete spectrum. Through experiencing it we are bound with deep loyalties to our total horizon.

THE DECAY OF THE ARTISTIC EXPERIENCE

In a climate of chaos and frustration these basic keys to a richer life in art have also come close to disappearing.

The industrial world sprang up without regarding our human need to find what Walt Whitman called the "primal sanities of nature." Our technical wonders have not provided us with the wide visions of harmony and order but, increasing without plan, have jumbled the basic wealth of the mechanical era into a dazzling kaleidoscopic pattern which shocks and numbs our sensibilities.

The modern metropolis, a giant focus of our unsettled world, spreads out upon the land in widening rings of visual disorder. At its core, bludgeoning us with their vulgar images, massive structures blot out open space; industrial areas beyond are dumped with factory buildings and dingy barracks where we house our poor; the residential fringes are dotted with characterless cottages repeated endlessly. Everywhere, smoke and dirt screen out the sun; and our containers, advertisements, commercial entertainment, films, our home furnishings and clothes, our gestures and facial expressions mount up to grotesque, formless aggregates lacking sincerity, scale, and cleanliness.

This is the world we continue to reproduce, and this is the world that shapes our vision. Our distorted surroundings, by distorting us, have robbed us of the power to make our experience rich and coherent. When visual responses are warped visual creativeness is impaired.

The starvation of the eye has paralleled the decline of the rhythmic joy in work. For the workers, unable to sense the total process of making, have been deprived of their power to organize their work rhythmically and have lost the "joy in labor" that is the elementary sap of every creative act, and that William Morris called their only birthright.

Because of these failings, the man of our time has come close to losing two of his important resources: the outer richness of the environment, and the inner richness of sensed unity derived from rhythmically articulated work.

But still more fatal, the creative vision has lost not only the basic nourishment of our sensations, but it has lost its broadest background—its relatedness to the complete natural world. The artist, like his fellow man, has gradually become closed in within a limited world. When scientific insights, with their magnificent constructs, encompassed and unified vistas of nature on a never dreamt of scale, the artist remained only an outsider hardly able to follow the outlines of the new wonderful spans of unity. While the scientists with uncompromising courage linked the old models of the planetary system with the new models of the smallest unit, the atom, and fused time and space and mass with energy in a consistent and legible construct, the artist timidly reduced his vistas to the narrow ranges of reacting to personal hurts.

ART AND THE NATURE OF MAN

Our great task is to bring man in scale again with the entire horizon of nature, so that he can sense it in all its wealth and promises, harmonies and mysteries. In ignorance and pride and by insecurity, we have severed ourselves from our broader background. We have to re-establish our bonds and recognize our loyalties on this all-inclusive level. Eastern philosophy and art had an age-old awareness that men lived most fully by opening themselves to the universal rhythm of nature. With deep insights, Eastern philosophers and artists responded to inner and outer correspondences and reached stages of wonderful tranquillity. The artists of our century, groping for self-realization, for an inner freedom, for the true ecstasy of spontaneity, jealously followed the expressive intensity and spontaneity of oriental art. But they did so without recognizing that the freedom of oriental art grew from its recognition of the continuity between man and nature. Our artists borrowed the exterior appearances and techniques of Eastern art, their calligraphic fluency with the uninhibited traceries of lines, their moods of nature feelings; our architects borrowed the attitudes of blending the man-created shelter into its broadest natural abode.

If one were to write a synoptic history of the last eighty years of artistic transformations, the dominant thread would, I am sure, be the assimilation of Eastern dreams and vision. Underlying this assimilation is an important truth: artistic sensibility, the seismograph of every creative act, has registered the main need of our time. It has sensed the urgent need to form a new sense of wholeness by accepting the deep continuities between man and nature.

"No one will fathom nature who possesses no sense of nature, no inward organ for creating and dividing nature, who does not, as though spontaneously, recognize and distinguish nature everywhere, who does not with inborn creative joy, a rich and fervent kinship with all things, mingle with all of nature's creatures through the medium of feeling, who does not feel his way into them," wrote the German poet Novalis at the beginning of the nineteenth century.

At the end of the century Charles S. Peirce expressed the same idea but with different emphasis: "That every scientific explanation of natural phenomenon is a hypothesis that there is something in nature to which the human reason is analogous; and that it really is so all the successes of science in its applications to human convenience are witnesses."

This has to be restated once more only with a yet still different emphasis: Novalis's "fervent kinship with all things" can only be reached by being able to face these things in the natural world as it is given to us. But the world of nature known to our fathers is changed beyond recognition. Science has opened up new resources for new sights and sounds, new tastes and textures. To accept the essential continuity between man and nature, we have to accept nature in its new dimensions. And our artists will live up to their great historical challenge if they can embrace these new dimensions and make them their own.

BIBLIOGRAPHY

Kahnweiler, D. H., *Juan Gris, His Life and Work*, Lund Humphries, 1947.
Kepes, Gyorgy, *Language of Vision*, Paul Theobald, 1944.
———, *The New Landscape*, Paul Theobald, 1956.
Klee, Paul, *Über die moderne Kunst*, Verlag Bentelli, Bern-Bumpliz, 1945.
Mondrian, Piet, *Plastic Art and Pure Plastic Art*, Wittenborn, 1945.

Morris, William, *Hope and Fears for Art,* 1882.

Morris, William, *Signs of Change,* 1888.

Needham, Joseph, *Science & Civilisation in China,* vol. II, Cambridge University, 1956.

Nietzsche, F., *The Case of Wagner,* vol. XI of *The Works of F. Nietzsche,* Allen and Unwin.

Novalis, F., *The Novices of Sais,* Curt Valentin, 1949.

Peirce, C. S., *Collected Papers,* C. Hartshorne and Paul Weiss (eds.), Harvard University, 1931.

Read, Herbert, *The Grass Roots of Art,* Wittenborn, 1947.

Sakanishi, Shio, *The Spirit of the Brush,* John Murray, 1939.

Sze, Mai-Mai, *The Tao of Painting,* Bollingen Series, Pantheon Books, 1956.

Human Values in Zen

_____ DAISETZ TEITARO SUZUKI

NOT A SCHOLAR

WE ARE requested to say something objective, something scientific, in regard to human values. But I am afraid I have nothing to say which is so characterized. The fact is that I am not a scholar, I am just a plain, ordinary layman deeply interested in the advance and enhancement of human culture in general. It is for this reason that I may be permitted to express my humble view concerning the promotion of "unselfish behavior." As to its "causes and conditions," I am sure there are many able speakers who have been carrying on their investigations and may have something objective and scientific and highly contributive to human welfare. It is not mine to follow their examples.

VALUES OLD, HOW TO REVIVIFY

The point I wish to make is that there is something "new," though not scientific or objective perhaps, in the way of evaluating human behavior. The fact is that this something "new" is really not at all new, it is very ancient, and its being ancient makes it new because there is nothing new under the sun and what is old is new when it is viewed from an angle hitherto neglected.

All the values in the broad field of human activity may be stamped as old and dilapidated and even worn out in the sense that ever since the dawn of civilization we have been talking about them con-

94

stantly. And because of this constant talk the values inestimably valuable are weatherbeaten and have lost their freshness and consequently their viability.

One way to resuscitate them is to re-evaluate them and see what is that which ultimately constitutes their value. When we do this we discover that all values come from unselfish motives. Any act with its base in an egoistic source is bad, hateful, and ugly, and goes against the general welfare of humanity. Egoism is thus always found at the basis of such an act. The ego is the mischief-maker. Even when we do something, objectively speaking, good and benefiting all of us, the act may not be judged as genuinely good if we find the shadow of ego lurking behind it.

VALUES, SUBJECTIVE AND OBJECTIVE

Roughly speaking, values have two aspects: subjective and objective, and I like to emphasize the subjective, and state that a value is valueless when it is not subjectively free from an egoistic impulse. In terms of Taoism or Mahayana Buddhism, the value is a value when it is a no-value. Psychologically, when all the values are shut up in the depths of the unconscious or in the limbo of oblivion, we have the values in their genuine form. Lao-tze says that what can be designated as this or that is not Tao. Tao is nameless. The very moment you say, "It is good," the good loses its goodness. The really good is just so, and no more, no less. The good is just-so-ness. So with the rest of human values.

When God saw the world created in response to his fiat, "Let there be light," he said, "It is good." This "good" has nothing to do with any human way of evaluating things. The "good" is the isness of things, it is not something added to them from an external source. If it is, it is valueless. Anything of value is something inherent in it. When a thing is genuinely in its isness, it is valuable. A painted beauty is no beauty. The beautiful need not claim itself to be beautiful, it stands before us and we all know it is beautiful.

Some may say that this kind of beauty or goodness or truth is not human but divine and that we are asked to talk about human values. But I should like to ask if there is anything that is divine which is not at the same time human. The human and the divine are one, for what is humanly valuable is so only because it is divine. This is the reason why I say that the old is new and the new is old.

THE DIVINE AND THE BEAUTIFUL

Bashō (1644–1694), the founder of the modern Japanese poetical form known today as haiku, had this to utter when he saw Mount Yoshino covered with cherry blossoms:

> What a sight!
> What a sight!
> Nothing more!
> Mount Yoshino, flower-bedecked!*

A feeling when at its highest and deepest refuses to be wordy. It utters—and not coherently. To be wordy and coherent and logical is the function of the intellect. The feeling—especially what I like to call primary, that is, what we feel even before any designation or differentiation could have taken place, the sheer feeling of being just-so, even before our intellectual discrimination made its start in our consciousness—this is what I like to be understood as the primary feeling.

Some again may protest, "How presumptuous and arrogant you are, to confuse what is divine and what is human!"

But I protest on my part: "How self-degrading you are not to identify what is human with what is divine!" How can we exist even for a moment without being divine? That we are at all is of God, we owe everything to God. Even not to be of God is of God. How can we escape from being of God? Things are humanly valuable just because they are of God.

When we pursue this line of thought, everything we judge to be

---

* Another translation:
> Wonderful!
> Wonderful!
> Only this!
> Mount Yoshino flowering!

Shakespeare also has something to this effect: "O wonderful, wonderful, and most wonderful wonderful!"

of value, to be meaningful, to be worth preserving or conserving as humanly desirable, is all of God. Human values so called then acquire a new, fresh, and inspiring significance.

BUDDHIST ANATMAN AND LOVE (MAHAKARUNA)

Love is regarded by every one of us as a great force remolding and ameliorating the structure of human community. There are no thinkers or religious leaders who do not emphasize the importance of Love in our communal life. Love corresponds to the Buddhist idea of *mahākarunā*, and according to Buddhists the Buddha-heart is no other than *mahākarunā* itself. *Mahākarunā* is equivalent to *agape* as distinguished from *eros*.

Christians would say *eros* is mixed up with egoistic interests. To purge it of all such impurities the ego must be sacrificed, that is, crucified, and then regenerated. Crucifixion and resurrection symbolize it.

In this respect Buddhism differs from the Christian doctrine. For Buddhists tell us that there is from the beginning no ego and therefore that there is no need of crucifying it. This is known as the doctrine of non-ego or *nirātman* or *anatta*. When we realize that the *ātman is nonexistent, mahākarunā* asserts itself, as *mahākarunā* constitutes the Buddha-heart, and the Buddha-heart is no other than the human heart.

Apparently, there is much misunderstanding about the doctrine of *anatta* which is construed as negativistic. The misunderstanding in fact rises from grammar. The prefix *a* or *an* is deprivative. But the *anatta* is not to be interpreted from the purely linguistic point of view, for the doctrine is based on an existential experience. The denial of the ego does not stop just with the denial. Experience goes much more deeply and is more informative of reality than linguistics. Even when the ego is found nonexistent as an entity, life goes on as ever, regardless of our conceptual turmoil. Even when Buddha is reported to have found "the house-builder" who is no more to build him a house, and further, even when it is said that his "mind has gone to an utter dissolution and all his desires are destroyed," he never ceased to keep up his activities as the great teacher of the Dharma (truth), which is still alive together with his personality even after his entrance into *parinirvāna* more than twenty-four centuries ago. I like to ask, "What is that which thus continues to be living among us?"

This cannot be anything else but Life, that is, Love, or *mahākaruṇā*. As long as the conceptual delusion of an ego-entity subsists, *mahākaruṇā* remains dormant, it invariably finds itself beclouded by the delusive ego, and its activity is refracted, warped. In spite of this, it occasionally breaks through the clouds of egotism, and deeds of pure altruism are performed to the wonderment of the agent himself. This is why Mencius upholds human nature to be inherently good, free from ego-centered impulses. "Creative altruism" is not something foreign to human beings. The creativity is obstructed only when intellection grows too rampantly and unwarrantedly.

A modern Japanese Zen master tells us:

> While alive
> Be a dead man—
> Thoroughly dead,
> And then act as you will,
> And all is good.

This is a most significant saying and directly points to the creative altruistic way of living. Probably, there is nothing new in this Zen master's advice. I do not think there is, and yet how refreshingly new it is! We all love to live, to be alive, and yet are we really living? We may be living in a way, but not as we ought to, as human beings honorable and dignified. We can readily understand what a miserable life each one of us is leading when we reflect within ourselves, or when we read our daily papers.

We must die once while living and live a new life. Paradise must be lost and regained. It's a good thing that God once chased us out of the Garden of Eden because of our eating the fruit of knowledge. We must eat another fruit of knowledge which nullifies, or rather revivifies in its own way, the effect of the first fruit. The first fruit killed us. Being killed, we must not stay killed, we must revive. This is possible when we eat a second fruit of knowledge, which is a new knowledge tapping the source of creativity.

ZEN ON "CREATIVE ALTRUISM"

There are two Zen stories which I wish to quote in connection with "human values" or with "creative altruism," for, according to my view, the stories illuminatingly point out where lies the new way of living.

There was a great Zen master in China during the T'ang dynasty. He is said to have lived 120 years, and his name was Jūshin of Jōshū. In the monastery compounds where he resided, there was a stone-bridge reputed all over the empire. Once a visiting monk asked the master, "We hear so much of your stone-bridge, but as I see it it is no more than a rickety old log-bridge." Jōshū answered, "You just see the log-bridge and do not see the stone one." The monk asked, "What then is the stone-bridge?" "Horses pass over it, donkeys pass over it," was the reply.

Not only horses and donkeys, but in these days automobiles of any description pass over it. The bridge is solidly built, as solidly as the earth itself. The wise and the stupid, the rich and the poor, the noble and the humble, the young and the old—they all walk it in full confidence, with the feeling of utmost security as if they were the earth itself.

Two monks were engaged in a heated discussion about the ultimate truth that does not permit equivocation. The discussion took the form of the Tathāgata's ever indulging in ambiguities. One said that his words can never be ambiguous. The other then asked, "What are the Tathāgata's words?" The first monk answered, "How could the deaf hear them?" The second one remarked, "Sure enough, you have fallen into a secondary stage." "What then are the Tathāgata's words?" The question was immediately followed by this: "Have a cup of tea, O my brother-monk."

"Have a cup of tea" is one of the favorite phrases of the Zen monks in Japan as well as in China, when a visitor comes it is customary to treat him to a cup of tea, it is an act of courtesy in our daily life. Once a Chinese Zen master of the tenth century was asked, "What is the temple (*sanghārāma*)?" "Just this." "What is the person in the temple?" "What?! What!?" "What will you do when a visitor calls on you?" "Have a cup of tea." Such an epigrammatic dialogue known as *mondo*, "question and answer," illustrates a typical *weltanschauung* and *lebensanschauung* of the Zen master. Take "the temple" for the objective world, and "the person" for the subject, and "the visitor's calling" for human situation, and the whole *mondo* will begin to assume a much greater significance than a monkish life in the mountain retreat.

LIFE, SOCIAL AND INDIVIDUAL

Some may object after reading the two Zen stories here cited, saying: "You may be all right as far as individuals are concerned, but how about our social, or communal, or international life? We as individuals on the whole seem to be decent, well-behaving, orderly, law-abiding, trustworthy, but as soon as we live as a group in whatever form it may take, we lose all the fine qualities we have shown as individuals, and the devil, or whatever devilishness is still alive in every one of us perhaps, lifts his head and most violently asserts himself. This we all know. How should we deal with this ugly fact?"

This is indeed the crux of our modern world situation. I have been long wrestling with the problem, but so far I have not been able to solve it. All that I can say at present is: whatever form our group life may take, its constituents are individuals after all. Let, therefore, the constituent individuals be thoroughly purged of all their defiled ingredients and have their individual *mahākarunā* regain its original purity and work out its way without being hindered by our human overintellectualization. For this purpose, my two Zen stories are to be thoroughly, experientially studied and assimilated into our daily life.

THE PRODIGAL SON

We all know the story of the prodigal son. There is a similar story in a Buddhist *sūtra* known as the *Lotus Gospel*. Probably, they come from the same original source. What interests me here is that whatever wanderings a man may have to go through he invariably longs for his home and wants to return. The lost paradise is to be regained. Otherwise, we have no security. It is strange that we have to lose in order to gain. Time loses itself in the infinity and returns to itself again. We are historical beings and as such we go through all the vicissitudes of an historical being. But we are so made as to transcend history in order to secure the Pure Land of eternal happiness. History cannot be denied but to be really an historical being man is to go beyond history. History is time. As long as he is in time, he is enslaved by his future as well as his present. He cannot help being the plaything of all kinds of affective disturbances, among which we may specify such things as recollection and anticipation. He then can never be master of himself. Without being master of himself he can never be free and creative.

The prodigal son is a miserable creature during his wanderings. But the time comes upon him when he suddenly realizes that his home is nowhere else but in his wanderings. In fact, he has been carrying his home all the time on his shoulders throughout his long, long wanderings and wayfarings. With this realization his past and his future crystallize themselves, as it were, in his absolute present, he is the eternal now, he stands in the "here-now," he is master of himself. He is no more a creature. Yes, he is a creature and yet not a creature, for while his creatureliness does not go beyond the superficial realm of objectivity, he is yet no more in it, he has gone beyond it. That is to say, he is back to himself and is in himself, he stands in his "here-now," he is not a slave to anybody or anything, but a master and lord of the universe, the storehouse of infinite possibilities.

As limited beings we have to talk in terms of time and history, and this is where logicians and linguists have their special field of study. But we are more than that, we also belong to the realm of eternals. And as such we are entitled to resort to experiences attainable in it. The thing, however, which we ought not to forget is that the infinity is not something distinguishable from the finite and thus in possession of an independent entity—which makes it one of the finite. While it may not be quite exact to say that the infinite is the finite, the infinite is not to be regarded as a kind of quiddity existing as such in the finite. After all, finite and infinite are words conceptually distinguishable, and therefore subject to ambiguities. In our actual life no such things take place, and those who have an experience in this field know at once what the monk meant when he told his monk-friend to have a cup of tea. From the ordinary conceptual point of view, we may expostulate, "What has the absolute truth to do with sipping a cup of tea?" The Zen master will answer: "It is from this sipping that creative altruism makes its start and that if anything new can come out of human values it is from the cup of tea taken by the two monks."

SCIENCE AND VALUE

After writing so far, I come to think of another possible objection coming from the audience, which is: "So far so good, perhaps, Mr. Speaker, but your talk lacks precision. The stone-bridge which is trodden by the lame as well as by the athlete, and a cup of tea which is sipped not only by two friendly monks but by each one of us in his daily life—in what logical connection does the bridge or the tea stand to the issue which is the chief concern of today's Conference? Can't you give us a precise position you take in the discussion?"

To answer this, I am afraid, will take more time than we can afford here. But this much I can say: the word "precise," along with other cognate terms, belongs to the field of sciences, dealing with things subject to quantitative measurements, and those terms themselves, strictly speaking, are only approximately definite. The sciences limit themselves, and within these limits they can talk about definability and verifiability. Once beyond them, all the scientific or logical terminology will lose its value, and we have to resort to expressions paradoxical or contradictory or nonsensical or full of absurdities. And the strange fact is that it is those extraordinary expressions that will more "precisely," or more definitively, tell the experiences belonging to the realm of ultimate reality.

It is not exact to call those experiences intuitional in its usual sense. Lacking a more appropriate English term "intuition" is used with the following reservation: for instance, in the case of Zen the experience is not between subject and object, but it is of a something which is neither subject nor object, becoming conscious of itself.

Probably to make the matter more intelligible to our Christian audience, I may be allowed to resort to Christian terminology. The experience referred to is God becoming conscious of himself, or the Godhead objectifying himself as creator God. To explain further: when God was in himself, something happened, humanly speaking, and he willed to create the world. It is in fact better to say that God could not help willing to create the world; in God, necessity and free-will are one; and when this willing took place in him, he became conscious of himself. This is the Zen experience.

I am going into theology, I'm afraid. I have many more things to say in this connection to avoid possible misunderstandings. But I must stop with this remark:

There is after all nothing new under the sun. The oldest is the newest and the newest is the oldest.

KNOWLEDGE AND BEHAVIOR

While preparing this paper, I received a kind of memorandum released, I believe, for the press with the date of September 29 (Sunday), 1957, in which I note the following (in abstract): "The old ways of handling the great problems of modern time are insufficient and altogether inadequate. We are here to attack them 'scientifically' and find the new ways of applying the new additional knowledge thus gained to the solution of the multitude of personal and social complexities which confront us now as the outcome of the advancing technology and industrialization."

In view of these statements, my presentation so far may seem to have nothing to do with the scientific treatment of the problems required of us to solve in a new way. It may further appear to be a kind of "exhortation" or a bit of "*a priori* thinking" as is condemned by the Program Committee. I am fully conscious of my paper not

containing anything toward constructing a science of human values.
I have no time however to justify my position; I only wish to say a
few words more about "knowledge" or sciences generally.

There is no doubt this is the age of reason and technology, but at
the same time we all know that it is not science and technology that
will solve the problems confronting or rather threatening us these
days so ominously. Before this fact, science and technology are
utterly helpless. They are, on the contrary, fiercely fanning up the
flames of war between nations, between races, between cultures. We
talk about peace, disarmament, mutual confidence, reconciliation,
and many other things, and yet we are not even to stop the testing
of nuclear weapons, when we are fully aware of the fact that any
substantial increase in nuclear explosions is surely a great danger
not only to the human race but to all living beings. We claim that
the defense measures are needed for prevention of war, but did they
ever stop war? Are we not all the more bending our scientific and
technological ingenuities toward the possible event of a war of
mutual extermination? In many ways we seem to be rational and
far-sighted enough, but reason never keeps us within limits of
rationality. When we want to break through reason, we do it quite
readily regardless of science and technology. We make use of them
to promote irrationality.

What moves human beings is decidedly not science and the rationality of human nature; nor does the scientific treatment of anything and whatever knowledge accruing therefrom help us in any
practical way to solve the problems such as we are facing at present.
To believe in them is a modern supersitition.

If science or knowledge per se can *do* anything, let the scientist
or the learned man take the reins of government and see if he accomplishes anything. It is the man and not his knowledge that does
things. I do not know exactly how old the world history is. But, for
the sake of argument, let it be ten thousand years. During this time
we have accumulated a large amount of knowledge, and our ways
of living have made wonderful advance. But are we better men and
women than those brothers and sisters of, say, two thousand years

ago, in Europe or in China or India? Essentially, human nature has not changed. One instance will suffice to prove this. How did we behave before and during World War II? And how are we behaving after it?

If science and knowledge and technology and industrial civilization can accomplish anything in the way of alleviating any kind of tension we are feeling at present on all sides, let us find some means whereby all the leading statesmen of all nations, beginning with Eisenhower and Krushchev, come to this school of science and technology and after three or four years of study go back to their respective positions and resume their business as before. What can we expect of them then? Do we not know that we'll be facing the same state of affairs as before? As long as the man himself does not go through a transformation no amount of science and knowledge will improve the human situation in which we all are at this moment. The politicians, individually, may be good, respectable men, but when they are at the head of a group, small or large, the leaders are no more leaders, they are democrats. They follow the masses whose mentality requires ages to be lifted up above the level of mediocrity.

Let us, therefore, be patient and wait another one thousand, or two thousand, or even a million, years, for that matter, but in the meantime work steadily, continuously, and with all our moral and spiritual resources toward improving human nature basically. For this purpose, the best method is to follow, individually and collectively, the old ways of discipline. This is also, I am sure, the new method of enhancing the sense of creative altruism.

BIBLIOGRAPHY

Suzuki, D. T., *Essays in Zen Buddhism*, 1st Series, Luzac, 1927. Republished, Rider, 1950.

——, *Essays in Zen Buddhism*, 2nd Series, Luzac, 1933. Republished, Rider, 1950.

——, *Essays in Zen Buddhism*, 3rd Series, Luzac, 1934. Republished, Rider, 1953.

——, *An Introduction to Zen Buddhism*, Eastern Buddhist Society, 1934. Republished, Rider, 1948.

——, *The Lankāvatāra Sūtra*, George Routledge, 1932. Republished, 1957.

——, *Manual of Zen Buddhism*, Eastern Buddhist Society, 1935. Republished, Rider, 1950.

——, *Mysticism: Christian and Buddhist*, Harper, 1957.

——, *Outlines of Mahāyāna Buddhism*, Luzac, 1907.

——, *Studies in the Lankāvatāra Sūtra*, George Routledge, 1930.

——, *Studies in Zen*, Rider, 1955.

——, *Zen Buddhism and Its Influence on Japanese Culture*, Eastern Buddhist Society, 1938.

Existence and Values

——————————— WALTER A. WEISSKOPF

THE PROBLEM

IT MAY require some explanation why an economist, asked to contribute some ideas on the problem of values, chooses to leave his own field and delves instead into ontology and psychology. The lack of a common world view drives the specialist beyond his field. A basic reorientation is needed today, and thus the specialist has to become a philosopher.

The problem of value was formulated for our time by Kant when he split the world apart into a realm of pure and of practical reason. With this step the cognitive and the normative spheres were separated; this prevented any conclusion from "what is" to "what ought to be." A science of values became a contradiction *in adjecto*. Science, as it developed in the modern world, applies logic to observed facts. Neither logic nor factual observation were able to say anything about ends and values, especially about ultimate ends. This type of science could only deal with values as facts. It analyzed value-attitudes in various cultures and came to the conclusion that values are relative and culture-bound. This situation created great difficulties in our civilization, in which science is supposed to be the ultimate arbiter. It was felt that only values supported by science would be valid goals of human endeavor; but science left us without a guide for our aspirations. This opened the locks to irrational forces and contributed an important cause to the destructivity of mass movements that have shocked mankind during our lifetime. The fault lies as much with scientism as with the advocates of irrationalism. By excluding important elements of being and existence from its world view and by de-rationalizing the dimension of values, scientism created a power vacuum and the forces of irrationality moved in. Scientism misunderstood the basic structure of human existence. Values have their place in the existential scheme. If this scheme is ignored, values are eliminated from the picture of the universe.

THE EXISTENTIAL STRUCTURE

The existential structure is found in human experience. Man experiences everything in terms of a dialectical trinity, consisting of a basic antinomy, a polarity of the two antinomic poles, and an ultimate unity of the two. The basic split or antinomy is derived from the dichotomy of subject and object, of "myself" and the world.[1] Whatever we experience is split into two: a subject which experiences, and an object which is experienced. This applies not only to thought but to all human remembering, imagining, feeling, willing, and acting. The polarity of the two branches of the antinomy implies that they are interdependent; one cannot be without the other. Self and world determine each other; subject and object cannot exist, do not exist, in isolation from each other. This polarity is the intermediate link between the antinomy and the ultimate unity of the two poles. They are only different aspects of something which is ontologically one. This trinity is most lucidly symbolized by the sign of the Tao in Chinese philosophy, by the two intertwined halves in black and white, included in the union of the circle.

The basic source of the split in human existence is *consciousness*. Man can *transcend* any given situation because he is aware of it. Man "is" and, at the same time, he is conscious of his being. This establishes a cleavage between himself as conscious subject and the objective situation of which he is conscious. Transcendence

[1] P. Tillich, *Systematic Theology*, University of Chicago Press, 1951, vol. I, pp. 94, 168, and R. Kroner, *Culture and Faith*, University of Chicago Press, 1951, 31ff.

through consciousness is the basis of human freedom. By transcending the given situation through his consciousness man frees himself within certain limits from the necessities of this situation. This opens up alternatives; the dimension of actuality is left behind and the realm of potentiality is entered, creating the possibility of choice and the necessity of decision based on guiding values. The entire sequence of transcendence through consciousness, grasping of potential alternatives and the exercise of choice based on values, constitutes man's freedom.

Values, then, are a concomitant of freedom. What is the ground of values and what determines their content? On the level of concrete actuality, historical conditions, society and culture determine the content of values. The ultimate ground of values, however, is rooted in the ultimate ground of being. Values have an ontological source. Even those who reject metaphysical arguments can learn from history that all cultures derived their ultimate values from a basic concept or symbol which stood for the ground of being, such as God, nature, the universe, etc. Wherever the awareness of this relation between the ground of being and values was lost, values began to disintegrate.

The universal content of ultimate values stems from the basic existential trinity of antinomy, polarity and the union of opposites. *This union is the essence of ultimate values.* Ontologically, the ground of being is that dimension in which all antinomies are united and harmonized. It is the all-inclusive essence in which conflicts are dissolved in unity. It is the rational structure of the universe together with its depth dimension, the "creative ground, the infinite and unconditional power of being."[2] It cannot be described, defined and named but merely symbolized, perhaps grasped in rare peak experiences, "in a flash of understanding so that the mind is flooded with light."[3] It is, for those who do not shy away from the name, God.

[2] P. Tillich, *Systematic Theology,* University of Chicago Press, 1957, vol. II, pp. 7, 23ff.

[3] Plato, Epistle VII, 344b, *Thirteen Epistles of Plato,* L. A. Post (ed.), Oxford University Press, 1925, p. 99.

One can, however, arrive at the same conclusion purely through existential analysis, leaving entirely open the question as to the "reality" of the "ground" of this union. One can easily detect in all of man's deepest strivings the attempt to negate, to cancel, to overcome the basic split in his existential situation. This split, caused by consciousness, estranges man from himself and from nature and imposes the burden of freedom. It is the ultimate source of human anxiety and suffering. Whether one explains this suffering and the longing for unity by the memory of a previous unity, or by man's dim awareness of a higher unified dimension of reality, the fact of the split and of suffering and of the longing to overcome it, remains.

UNION DOWNWARDS AND UPWARDS

Thus, the union of opposites and the harmonization of the basic existential split are the goals of human striving and form the essential content of ultimate human values. There are, however, two avenues towards this union which I shall call *union downwards* and *union upwards*. These two avenues stem from two basic tendencies of all living matter: a *regressive* tendency towards the dissolution of the existing state and the restoration of a previous, less complicated state on the one hand, and a tendency towards *individuation* on the other hand.

The split in human existence is of an ontological nature; it is part of the ontological structure which "is" on a supra-temporal level. The ontological structure has no beginning, no end, no growth and no history. However, man's *awareness* of the existential split is subject to a development which takes place on a phylogenetic and on an ontogenetic level. Both are interrelated because the individual repeats the development of mankind.

This evolution towards the awareness of the existential split starts with a state of primeval unity between self and world, individual and group, conscious and unconscious.[4] Everything is experienced as one. In phylogenetic development this stage is represented by the pre-literate cultures with their magical and mythical "thinking"

[4] E. Neumann, *The Origins and History of Consciousness*, Pantheon Books, 1954.

with their attitude of *participation mystique* in nature and within the group, and with the predominance of the collective unconscious. In ontogenetic development this stage is represented by the existence in utero and by early childhood where the individual has not become aware of his separation from the world and from others, and where all psychic events are dominated by the unconscious. In that stage the self-conscious human ego "exists" only as a potentiality.

This state is experienced and thought of as a state of complete bliss. There is a tendency to revert to this state which Freud has called the "death drive."[5] This term is unfortunate insofar as this drive does not aim at death. It is a manifestation of the inertia of living matter which leads to the restoration of a previous, less complicated, less tension-filled state of life.

This universal tendency may also be at work in the human striving to restore the original bliss and unity of the beginning and to revert to a situation without dichotomy and without the burden of consciousness and freedom. Resistance against consciousness and individuation develops because they cause anxiety. This leads to regression and to union downwards. Giving in to the "death-drive," to union downwards is a powerful force in human behavior because it represents one possible avenue towards the elimination of the dichotomies of existence. It manifests itself in the many avenues of escape such as ecstatic behavior, sex, intoxication, etc. An element of this "diving into an abyss" is a necessary ingredient even in the most positive, highest human striving. This will become clearer if we turn now to a discussion of "union upwards."

Union upwards is connected with the drive toward *individuation*. The question as to the origin of individuation is the age-old problem of the relation of being and becoming. Whatever the metaphysical answer may be: the fact remains that there is a tendency towards separation, differentiation and individuation in the cosmos and in human development. The process of individuation has been represented as a struggle between two principles. In the writings of Nietzsche, Bachofen, Jung and others they have been described as

[5] S. Freud, *Beyond the Pleasure Principle*, Hogarth Press, 1950.

the Dionysian, the female, the moon, the collective unconscious as against the Apollonian, the male, the sun, and the conscious ego. These two worlds, interlocked in struggle with each other, are related to the two drives. The motherly, female, telluric, Dionysian world is the object of the "death-drive," the Apollonian, male world of the head, of light, of the sun, the object of the drive towards individuation. Individuation thus consists in the gradual emancipation from original, preconscious unity. It is accompanied by growing differentiation and by a sharpening of distinctions in reasoning. In the sphere of the will it implies growing self-assertion and emphasis on free decision. Individuation is accompanied by an abandonment of collectively imposed values and their replacement by individually chosen ones. In Freudian parlance: the superego is replaced by the ego-ideal.

Union upwards is the striving for the harmonization of the existential antinomies without resistance to individuation. Union downwards negates individuation; union upwards affirms it. This may seem contradictory because union means to overcome separation, and individuation is separation. But, this situation is a dialectical one: union upwards is synthesis which takes place *after* the individual has emerged as a separate entity from the original state of unconscious unity. It is the same scheme that we find in utopias: a unitary paradisiac state at the beginning; an antithetic state of Fall and sin; and, as harmonious resolution, a synthesis which is on a higher plane than the original unity. Union upwards, then, is union which *affirms* individuation.

Union in general, and union upwards in particular are the goals of human striving. Therefore, they determine the content of ultimate values. In the Occidental tradition the ultimate values have been called truth, beauty, and love. Their realization consists of a union between a subject and an object. Knowledge of truth is brought about by a union between the knower and the known.[6] It implies a detached knowing center, separated from the object of knowledge, and, at the same time, the ability to unite itself with this object

---

[6] P. Tillich, *Systematic Theology*, vol. I, pp. 94, 168.

without destroying the detachment. This is union upwards which does not negate individuality but requires *amor intellectualis* and *eros* which drives the mind towards the true (Plato).

Likewise, creative and recreative experience of beauty in nature and art involves a union between the beauty in the viewer and beauty in the object; they merge and become one. Both the grasping of truth and of beauty imply a similar structure of reality in the subject and the object, the separation of the two, and, ultimately, their union.

The same is obviously the case in all love relations. Man's estrangement includes separation from others. Love, in the broadest meaning of the term, is the negation of this estrangement. All loving, warm, affectionate, intimate human relations are attempts to overcome isolation and to heal the split between the "I" and the others. Through love the other becomes a "Thou." [7]

Again, this is possible only because there is a common element in both. The "I" and the "Thou" are both persons. The "Thou" is the "I" of another human being; through love it is accepted as an "I" instead of as an object. I can identify with the Thou through empathic understanding. The process is the same as the grasping of truth and beauty; a separation of subject and object, a common element in both, and a union of the two. This is most obvious in the case of sexual love; but it is present in all forms of loving relations. Sexual love without the affirmation of the individuality of the loved one and without striving towards a higher fulfillment, is union downwards and not upwards. Love, in the highest sense, is union upwards which preserves and accepts the individuality of the "Thou."

REPRESSIVE AND INTEGRATIVE VALUE SYSTEMS

Value systems can also be classified under the headings of *repressive* and *integrative* systems. A repressive value system represents a failure of the attempt to establish union although a semblance of union is accomplished through the suppression of one branch of the

[7] M. Buber, *I and Thou*, T. and T. Clark, 1937.

antinomy. In such a system certain aspects of human existence are denied, condemned, repressed. A sharp dogmatic black and white distinction between good and bad is made. Guides for human action are formulated in terms of unequivocal, universal, abstract rejection and suppression of one generalized kind of action and approval its opposite.

Under the impact of Calvinism, Puritanism, and their secular descendants, this attitude has become prevalent in Western civilization. It shows all the features of what depth psychologists call repression. The repressed is not eliminated but only relegated into the unconscious. There it remains active and strives for realization. The censorship of the ego tries to prevent the repressed from coming to the surface but in vain. The attempts of repression lead sooner or later to the outbreak of the repressed in the form of neurotic symptoms and demonic possession. All this is applicable to the development of thought and values in modern times. The repression of irrational, demonic elements has led in the twentieth century to totalitarian mass movements and wars. This represents a dismal failure of repressive value attitudes.

This attitude of repression of one aspect of existence and reality is also reflected in positivistic, naturalistic, progressivistic modern thought which does not recognize the antinomic character of human existence. These schools of thought are repressive insofar as they deny the conflict between the tragic imperfections of man's actual existence and his potential ideal essence. This resulted in a glorification of the so-called forces of history and in a shallow belief in progress.[8] Human actuality in culture, history and society becomes the realization of essence. The obvious imperfections are only temporary maladjustments which will be eliminated by progress. More scientific knowledge, reforms of the economy, more money for research, etc. will supposedly take care of these maladjustments and eliminate for good the split between an ideal and a real world.

This kind of world view leads to a repressive value system because

[8] P. Tillich, *Systematic Theology*, vol. II, pp. 7, 23ff., and E. Voegelin, *The New Science of Politics*, University of Chicago Press, 1952, 107ff.

the ineluctable human predicament with its estrangement, its ambiguities and its demonic character is not acknowledged. These elements are repressed in cognition and, therefore, also in the system of values. The "enemy" is not faced, and, therefore, not defeated. It should be understood, however, that, like all value systems, a repressive one owes its origin also to the basic human goal of union of opposites. Through the repression of one branch of the antinomy the split is eliminated although in an imperfect and inefficient way.

Integrative value systems are based on the recognition of the ontological trinity with its antinomy, polarity and ultimate unity. They embrace both aspects of the antinomy and strive to unite them in synthesis. Both union downwards and union upwards have integrative elements. However, union downwards belongs, to some extent, to the category of repressive value systems because it negates individuation. Nevertheless, even union downwards is a union of opposites; it implies the existence of an antinomy which has to be harmonized.

The four types of value systems—repressive, integrative, union upwards, and union downwards—are not mutually exclusive classifications but rather elements which may be found in any concrete system of values. These systems can be evaluated according to the degree and the intensity of union which they accomplish. Lowest in this scale will be a repressive value system. Union downwards comes next; it removes the antinomy but negates individuation. Highest in this scale will be an integrative value system which leads to union upwards.

EXISTENTIAL ANALYSIS AND SOCIAL PROBLEMS

Can any conclusion be drawn from this existential analysis of values for our present situation? I believe that this is possible. Most of our spiritual, psychological and social problems can be traced back to the lack of integration and union. Erich Fromm has criticized man in our economy as totally alienated.[9] Alienation can be defined

[9] E. Fromm, *The Sane Society*, Rinehart, 1955, p. 124.

as the surrender of the total human being to an outside power or to a partial striving, a part of himself; alienation involves the absence of integration and union. Under the impact of technology and business we have become concerned exclusively with activity directed towards change and control of the external world, with things to be produced and consumed, with money, possessions and their power. The inner life has been neglected. In business, technology and science, we have come to accept the principles of expedient, utilitarian rationality, characterized by the strict separation of ends and means, by the assumption that ends are unequivocally given, and by the attitude that the economic principle (maximum effect with minimum effort) should be the supreme guide for action. This one-sided attitude deprives morality and nonutilitarian striving of their rational basis. The same one-sidedness and lack of integrative union can be found in our interpersonal relations. It is the root of our inability to love. Competitive acquisitiveness is not confined to the market place. It has generated a hostile attitude towards others which permeates all kinds of social and human relations. Again, it is the inability to even aspire towards integrative union which prevents us from practicing altruism and real love. Because we cannot even see the possibility of a union with the ground of being, we cannot unite with the other.

This situation is tied up with our economy and reflected in the image of man presented by economics. The "economic man" is the prototype of alienated man. He is confined to conscious, deliberate action. All spontaneous, emotional, nonutilitarian behavior is suppressed. Economic theory has, in spite of its lip-service to economic freedom, eliminated real freedom from its image of man by maintaining that perfect consciousness and knowledge permits only one, unequivocally determined kind of action, that is, action which leads to the maximization of material gain measured in terms of money. Man has been reduced by economics to a maximizing computer. He is supposed to be concerned only with choices between alternatives which can be reduced to the common denominator of money calculation. This led to a disintegration of those aspects of life where this measurement is inapplicable. Friendship, love, charity, creative activity, aesthetic, and religious experiences cannot be calculated according to the economic principle. The goals are not unequivocally given and no calculable relationship exists between means and ends which could serve as a guide for action. The expenditure of time, labor, material, and money cannot be used to evaluate the contemplation of the divine nor the greatness of a work of art. Through the enormous impact of economics on the modern world, its rules have obliterated other ways of life. This resulted in the reduction of human behavior to a small segment of its total potentialities and dimensions, that is, in alienation.

This is true in spite of the fact that man cannot avoid living in a state of predicament. The *ontological* aspects of estrangement have to be separated from the alienation created by socioeconomic and cultural conditions. The antinomies of existence are ineluctable; but they can be relieved or aggravated by society, economy, and culture. Our time has reached such a state of aggravation that a radical spiritual, intellectual, and ethical reversal has become imperative.

In a way, union, integration and balance is also the answer to some of our economic problems. In an economy of abundance with a high productive capacity, the problem is not increased efficiency and productivity. The sway of the economic principle which drives us toward an ever higher national product, towards more and bigger things and gadgets has to be broken. Our economy tends to grow into a tower of Babel which in the end must break down because of the limitlessness of our striving for more material goods. In order to balance the economy we have to integrate work with leisure, material need satisfaction with spiritual and intellectual pursuits. Growing technical efficiency and automation will require a basis for the distribution of income other than labor and work. This, in turn, will require a value reorientation; intellectual, artistic and spiritual creation will have to receive higher rewards than production of material goods and gadgets. A person will have to be rewarded rather on the basis of what he is than of what he does in the market place. This is not only an ethical postulate but will become an economic necessity when jobs will be scarce because of automation, but income will have to be widely distributed for the creation of purchasing power. All this implies union and integration: our economic activism will have to be tempered with a "passive," contemplative way of life.

To accomplish this we will have to abandon our almost exclusive reliance on reasoning with its analytical emphasis on differentiation and dissection, which has perpetuated all existential antinomies, accentuated the split in human existence, and prevented us from even perceiving the goal of ultimate union. We have come to a stop on the first level of the existential trinity, the level of the antinomies. Because of our fascination with pure logic and its sharp distinctions, we have been unable to perceive polar interrelations and ultimate unity. According to logic alone, a thing is either A or not A; if it is the one, it cannot be the other. To utilitarian reasoning, this seems to be the acme of truth. Only what Tillich calls ontological reason can grasp the polarity and ultimate unity of logically different entities. Because of our overemphasis on the intellect, we have divorced reason from emotion. We have ignored the depth-dimension, the abyss of reason. This prevented us from transcending the given, concrete differentiation of things and individuals and striving for ultimate unity. This puts an intolerable burden on our shoulders because it perpetuates inner and outer conflicts. It is as if we have condemned ourselves to an irremediable state of schizophrenia and destroyed all bridges between man and world, man and man, man and himself. Only by reopening the door to the depth, to the ground, can we strive toward a new union within ourselves, with the other, and with the eternal one.

Psychological Data and Value Theory

_____ ABRAHAM H. MASLOW

HUMANISTS for thousands of years have attempted to construct a naturalistic, psychological value system that could be derived from man's own nature, without the necessity of recourse to authority outside the human being himself. Many such theories have been offered throughout history. They have all failed for mass purposes exactly as all other value theories have failed. We have about as many scoundrels in the world today as we have ever had, and _many more_ neurotic, probably, than we have ever had.

These inadequate theories, most of them, rested on psychological assumptions of one sort or another. Today practically all of these can be shown, in the light of recently acquired knowledge, to be false, inadequate, incomplete, or in some other way lacking. But it is my belief that developments in the science and art of psychology, in the last few decades, make it possible for us for the first time to feel confident that this age-old hope may be fulfilled if only we work hard enough. We know how to criticize the old theories, we know, even though dimly, the shape of the theories to come, and, most of all, we know where to look and what to do in order to fill in the gaps in knowledge, that will permit us to answer the age-old questions, "What is the good life? What is the good man? How can people be taught to desire and prefer the good life? How ought children to be brought up to be sound adults?, etc." That is, we think that a scientific ethic may be possible, and we think we know how to go about constructing it.

The following section will discuss briefly a few of the promising lines of evidence and of research, their relevance to past and future value theories, along with a discussion of the theoretical and factual advances we must make in the near future. Since my space is too short to assay the level of confidence of these various data, I think it safer to judge them all as more or less probable rather than as certain.

FREE CHOICE EXPERIMENTS: HOMEOSTASIS

Hundreds of experiments have been made that demonstrate a universal inborn ability in all sorts of animals to select a beneficial diet if enough alternatives are presented from among which they are permitted free choice. This wisdom of the body is often retained under less usual conditions, *e.g.*, adrenalectomized animals can keep themselves alive by readjusting their self-chosen diet, pregnant animals will nicely adjust their diets to the needs of the growing embryo, etc.

We now know this is by no means a perfect wisdom. These appetites are less efficient, for instance, in reflecting body need for vitamins. Lower animals protect themselves against poisons more efficiently than higher animals and humans. Previously formed habits of preference may quite overshadow present metabolic needs.[1] And most of all, in the human being, and especially in the neurotic human being, all sorts of forces can contaminate this wisdom of the body, although it never seems to be lost altogether.

The general principle is true not only for selection of food but also for all sorts of other body needs, as the famous homeostasis experiments have shown.[2]

It seems quite clear that all organisms are more self-governing, self-regulating, and autonomous than we thought twenty-five years ago. The organism deserves a good deal of trust and we are learning

[1] P. T. Young, "The Experimental Analysis of Appetite," *Psychol. Bull.*, 1941, 38:129–164.

[2] W. B. Cannon, *Wisdom of the Body*, Norton, 1932.

steadily to rely on this internal wisdom of our babies with reference to choice of diet, time of weaning, amount of sleep, time of toilet training, need for activity, and a lot else.

But more recently we have been learning, especially from physically and mentally sick people, that there are good choosers and bad choosers. We have learned, especially from the psychoanalysts, much about the hidden causes of such behavior and have learned to respect these causes.

In this connection we have available a startling experiment,[3] which we have been trying to repeat at Brandeis, that is pregnant with implications for value theory. It turns out that chickens allowed to choose their own diet vary widely in their ability to choose what is good for them. The good choosers become stronger, larger, more dominant than the poor choosers, which means that they get the best of everything. If then the diet chosen by the good choosers is forced upon the poor choosers, it is found that *they* now get stronger, bigger, healthier, and more dominant, although never reaching the level of the good choosers. That is, good choosers can choose better than bad choosers what is better for the bad choosers themselves. If similar findings are made in human beings, as I think they will be, we are in for a good deal of reconstruction of all sorts of theories. So far as human value theory is concerned, no theory will be adequate that rests simply on the statistical description of the choices of unselected human beings. To average the choices of good and bad choosers, of healthy and sick people is useless. Only the choices and tastes and judgments of healthy human beings will tell us much about what is good for the human species in the long run. The choices of neurotic people can tell us mostly what is good for keeping a neurosis stabilized, just as the choices of a brain-injured man are good for preventing a catastrophic breakdown, or as the choices of an adrenalectomized animal may keep *him* from dying but would kill a healthy animal.

[3] W. F. Dove, "A Study of Individuality in the Nutritive Instincts; of the Causes and Effects of Variation in the Selection of Food," *Amer. Nat.*, 1935, 69:469–544.

I think that this is the main reef on which most hedonistic value theories and ethical theories have foundered. Pathologically motivated pleasures cannot be averaged with healthily motivated pleasures.

Furthermore, any ethical code will have to deal with the fact of constitutional differences not only in chickens and rats but also in men, as Sheldon[4] and Morris[5] have shown. Some values are common to all (healthy) mankind, but also some other values will *not* be common to all mankind, but only to some types of people, or to specific individuals. What I have called the basic needs are probably common to all mankind and are therefore shared values. But idiosyncratic needs generate idiosyncratic values.

Constitutional differences in individuals generate preferences among ways of relating to self, and to culture and to the world, *i.e.*, generate values. These researches support and are supported by the universal experience of clinicians with individual differences. This is also true of the ethnological data that make sense of cultural diversity by postulating that each culture selects for exploitation, suppression, approval or disapproval, a small segment of the range of human constitutional possibilities. This is all in line with the biological data and theories and self-actualization theories which show that an organ system presses to express itself, in a word, to function. The muscular person likes to use his muscles, indeed, *has* to use them in order to self-actualize and to achieve the subjective feeling of harmonious, uninhibited, satisfying functioning which is so important an aspect of psychological health. People with intelligence must use their intelligence, people with eyes must use their eyes, people with the capacity to love have the *impulse* to love and the *need* to love in order to feel healthy. Capacities clamor to be used, and cease their clamor only when they *are* used sufficiently. That is to say, capacities are needs, and therefore are intrinsic values as well. To the extent that capacities differ, so will values also differ.

[4] W. Sheldon, *The Varieties of Temperament*, Harper, 1942.
[5] C. Morris, *Varieties of Human Value*, University of Chicago Press, 1956.

BASIC NEEDS AND THEIR HIERARCHICAL ARRANGEMENT

It has by now been sufficiently demonstrated that the human being has, as part of his intrinsic construction, not only physiological needs, but also truly psychological ones. They may be considered as deficiencies which must be optimally fulfilled by the environment to avoid sickness and to avoid subjective ill-being. They can be called basic, or biological, and likened to the need for salt, or calcium or vitamin D because:

1. The person yearns for their gratification persistently.
2. Their deprivation makes the person sicken and wither, or stunts his growth.
3. Gratifying them is therapeutic, curing the deficiency-illness.
4. Steady supplies forestall these illnesses.
5. Healthy people do not demonstrate these deficiencies.

But these needs or values are related to each other in a hierarchical and developmental way, in an order of strength and of priority. Safety is a more prepotent, or stronger, more pressing, earlier appearing, more vital need than love, for instance, and the need for food is usually stronger than either. Furthermore *all* these basic needs may be considered to be simply steps along the time path to general self-actualization, under which all basic needs can be subsumed.

By taking these data into account, we can solve many value problems that philosophers have struggled with ineffectually for centuries. For one thing, it looks as if *there were* a single ultimate value for mankind, a far goal toward which all men strive. This is called variously by different authors self-actualization, self-realization, integration, psychological health, individuation, autonomy, creativity, productivity, but they all agree that this amounts to realizing the potentialities of the person, that is to say, becoming fully human, everything that the person *can* become.

But it is also true that the person himself does not know this. We, the psychologists observing and studying, have constructed this concept in order to integrate and explain lots of diverse data. So far as the person himself is concerned, all *he* knows is that he is desperate for love, and thinks he will be forever happy and content if he gets it. He does not know in advance that he will strive on *after* this gratification has come, and that gratification of one basic need opens consciousness to domination by another, "higher" need. So far as he is concerned, *the* absolute, ultimate value, synonymous with life itself, is whichever need in the hierarchy he is dominated by during a particular period. These basic needs or basic values therefore may be treated *both* as ends and as steps toward a single end-goal. It is true that there is a single, ultimate value or end of life, and *also* it is just as true that we have a hierarchical and developmental system of values, complexly interrelated.

This also helps to solve the apparent paradox of contrast between Being and Becoming. It is true that human beings strive perpetually toward ultimate humanness, which itself is anyway a different kind of Becoming and growing. It's as if we were doomed forever to try to arrive at a state to which we could never attain. Fortunately we now know this not to be true, or at least it is not the only truth. There is another truth which integrates with it. We are again and again rewarded for good Becoming by transient states of absolute Being, which I have summarized as peak-experiences. Achieving basic-need gratifications gives us many peak-experiences, each of which are absolute delights, perfect in themselves, and needing no more than themselves to validate life. This is like rejecting the notion that a Heaven lies someplace beyond the end of the path of life. Heaven, so to speak, lies waiting for us throughout life, ready to step into for a time and to enjoy before we have to come back to our ordinary life of striving. And once we have been in it, we can remember it forever, and feed ourselves on this memory and be sustained in time of stress.[6]

Not only this, but the process of moment to moment growth is itself intrinsically rewarding and delightful in an absolute sense. If they are not mountain peak-experiences, at least they are foothill-experiences, little glimpses of absolute, self-validative delights, little

[6] A. H. Maslow, "Cognition of Being in the Peak Experiences," *Journal of Genetic Psychology*, 1959. In press.

moments of Being. Being and Becoming are *not* contradictory or mutually exclusive. Approaching and arriving are both in themselves rewarding.[7]

I should make it clear here that I want to differentiate the Heaven ahead (of growth and transcendence) from the "Heaven" behind (of regression). The "high Nirvana" is very different in important ways from the "low Nirvana" even though most clinicians confuse them because they are also similar in some ways.

SELF-ACTUALIZATION: GROWTH

I have published in another place a survey of all the evidence that forces us in the direction of a concept of healthy growth or of self-actualizing tendencies.[8] This is partly deductive evidence in the sense of pointing out that, unless we postulate such a concept, much of human behavior makes no sense. This is on the same scientific principle that led to the discovery of a hitherto unseen planet that *had* to be there in order to make sense of a lot of other observed data.

There is also some direct evidence, or rather the beginnings of direct evidence which needs much more research, to get to the point of certainty. The only direct study of self-actualizing people I know is the one I made,[9] and it is a very shaky business to rest on just one study made by just one person when we take into account the known pitfalls of sampling error, of wish-fulfillment, of projection, etc. However, the conclusions of this study have been so strongly paralleled in the clinical and philosophical conclusions of Rogers, of Fromm, of Goldstein, of Angyal, of Murray, of C. Bühler, of Horney, Jung, Nuttin, and many others that I shall proceed under the assumption that more careful research will not contradict my findings radically. We can certainly now assert that at least a reasonable, theoretical, and empirical case has been made for the presence within the human being of a tendency toward, or need for, growing in a

[7] A. H. Maslow, "Defense and Growth," *Merrill-Palmer Quarterly*, 1956, 36–47.

[8] A. H. Maslow, *Motivation and Personality*, Harper, 1954.

[9] *Ibid.*

direction that can be summarized in general as self-actualization, or psychological health or maturation, and specifically as growth toward each and all of the sub-aspects of self-actualization. That is to say, the human being has within him a pressure (among other pressures) toward unity of personality, toward spontaneous expressiveness, toward full individuality and identity, toward seeing the truth rather than being blind, toward being creative, toward being good, and a lot else. That is, the human being is so constructed that he presses toward fuller and fuller being and this means pressing toward what most people would call good values, toward serenity, kindness, courage, knowledge, honesty, love, unselfishness, and goodness.

Few in number though they be, we can learn a great deal from the direct study of these highly evolved, most mature, psychologically healthiest individuals, and from the study of the peak moments of average individuals, moments in which they become transiently self-actualized. This is because they are in very real empirical and theoretical ways, *most fully human.* For instance, they are people who have retained and developed all their human capacities, especially those capacities which define the human being and differentiate him from let us say the monkey. (This accords with Hartman's[10] axiological approach to the same problem of defining the good human being as the one who has more of the characteristics which define the concept "human being.") From a developmental point of view, they are more fully evolved because not fixated at immature or incomplete levels of growth. This is no more mysterious, or a *priori*, or question-begging than the selection of a type specimen of butterfly by a taxonomist or the most physically healthy young man by the physician. They both look for the "perfect or mature or magnificent specimen" for the exemplar, and so have I. One procedure is as repeatable in principle as the other.

Full humanness can be defined not only in terms of the degree to which the definition of the concept "human" is fulfilled, *i.e.* the species norm. It also has a descriptive, cataloguing, measurable,

[10] R. S. Hartman, *The Structure of Value*, forthcoming.

psychological definition. We now have from a few research beginnings and from countless clinical experiences some notion of the characteristics both of the fully evolved human being and of the well-growing human being. These characteristics are not only neutrally describable; they are also subjectively rewarding, and pleasurable and reinforcing.

Among the objectively describable and measurable characteristics of the healthy human specimen are:

1. Clearer, more efficient perception of reality.
2. More openness to experience.
3. Increased integration, wholeness, and unity of the person.
4. Increased spontaneity, expressiveness; full functioning; aliveness.
5. A real self; a firm identity; autonomy; uniqueness.
6. Increased objectivity, detachment, transcendence of self.
7. Recovery of creativeness.
8. Ability to fuse concreteness and abstractness, primary and secondary process cognition, etc.
9. Democratic character structure.
10. Ability to love, etc.

These all need research confirmation and exploration but it is clear that such researches are feasible.

In addition, there are subjective confirmations or reinforcements of self-actualization or of good growth toward it. These are the feelings of zest in living, of happiness or euphoria, of serenity, of joy, of calmness, of responsibility, of confidence in one's ability to handle stresses, anxieties, and problems. The subjective signs of self-betrayal, of fixation, of regression, and of living by fear rather than by growth are such feelings as anxiety, despair, boredom, inability to enjoy, intrinsic guilt, intrinsic shame, aimlessness, feelings of emptiness, of lack of identity, etc.

These subjective reactions are also susceptible of research exploration. We have clinical techniques available for studying them.

It is the free choices of such self-actualizing people (in those situations where real choice is possible from among a variety of possibilities) that I claim can be descriptively studied as a naturalistic value system with which the hopes of the observer absolutely have nothing to do, *i.e.*, it is "scientific." I do not say "He *ought* to choose this or that" but only "Healthy people, permitted to choose, are *observed* to choose this or that." This is like asking "What *are* the values of the best human beings" rather than "What *should* be their values?" or "What *ought* they do?" (Compare this with Aristotle's belief that "it is the things which are valuable and pleasant to a good man that are really valuable and pleasant.")

Furthermore I think these findings can be generalized to most of the human species because it looks to me (and to others) as if *all* or most people tend toward self-actualization (this is seen most clearly in the experiences in psychotherapy, especially of the uncovering sort), and as if, in principle at least, all people are capable of self-actualization.

If the various extant religions may be taken as expressions of human aspiration, *i.e.*, what people would *like* to become if only they could, then we can see here too a validation of the affirmation that all people yearn toward self-actualization or tend toward it. This is so because our description of the actual characteristics of self-actualizing people parallels at many points the ideals urged by the religions, *e.g.*, the transcendence of self, the fusion of the true, the good and the beautiful, contribution to others, wisdom, honesty and naturalness, the transcendence of selfish and personal motivations, the giving up of "lower" desires in favor of "higher" ones, the easy differentiation between ends (tranquility, serenity, peace) and means (money, power, status), the decrease of hostility, cruelty and destructiveness and the increase of friendliness, gentleness and kindness, etc.

1. One conclusion from all these free choice experiments, from developments in dynamic motivation theory and from examination of psychotherapy is a very revolutionary one that no other large culture has ever arrived at, namely, that our deepest needs are *not*, in themselves, dangerous or evil or bad. This opens up the prospect of resolving the dichotomy between Apollonian and Dionysian,

classical and romantic, scientific and poetic, between reason and impulse, work and play, verbal and preverbal, maturity and child-likeness, masculine and feminine, growth and regression.

2. The main social parallel to this change in our philosophy of human nature is the rapidly growing tendency to perceive the culture as an instrument of need-gratification as well as of frustration and control. We can now reject, as a localism, the almost universal mistake that the interests of the individual and of society are *of necessity* mutually exclusive and antagonistic, or that civilization is primarily a mechanism for controlling and policing human instinctoid impulses.[11] All these age-old axioms are swept away by the new possibility of defining the main function of a healthy culture and each of its institutions as the fostering of universal self-actualization.

3. In healthy people only is there a good correlation between subjective delight in the experience, impulse to the experience, or wish for it, and "basic need" for the experience (it's good for him in the long run). Only such people uniformly yearn for what is good for them and for others, and then are able wholeheartedly to enjoy it, and approve of it. For such people virtue is its own reward in the sense of being enjoyed in itself. They spontaneously tend to do right because that is what they *want* to do, what they *need* to do, what they enjoy, what they approve of doing, and what they will continue to enjoy.

It is this unity, this network of positive intercorrelation that falls apart into separateness and conflict as the person gets psychologically sick. Then what he wants to do may be bad for him; even if he does it he may not enjoy it; even if he enjoys it he may simultaneously disapprove of it so that the enjoyment is itself poisoned or may disappear quickly. What he enjoys at first he may not enjoy later. His impulses, desires, and enjoyments then become a poor guide to living. He must accordingly mistrust and fear the impulses and the enjoyments which lead him astray, and so he is caught in conflict, dissociation, indecision; in a word, he is caught in civil war.

So far as philosophical theory is concerned, many historical dilem-

[11] H. Marcuse, *Eros and Civilization*, Beacon Press, 1955.

mas and contradictions are resolved by this finding. Hedonistic theory *does* work for healthy people; it does *not* work for sick people. The true, the good and the beautiful *do* correlate some, but only in healthy people do they correlate strongly.

4. Self-actualization is a relatively achieved "state of affairs" in a few people. In most people, however, it is rather a hope, a yearning, a drive, a "something" wished for but not yet achieved, showing itself clinically as drive toward health, integration, growth, etc. The projective tests are also able to detect these trends as potentialities rather than as overt behavior, just as an X-ray can detect incipient pathology before it has appeared on the surface.

This means for us that that which the person *is* and that which the person *could be* exist simultaneously for the psychologist, thereby resolving the dichotomy between Being and Becoming. Potentialities not only *will* be or could be; they also *are*. Self-actualization values as goals exist and are real even though not yet actualized. The human being is simultaneously that which he is and that which he yearns to be.

GROWTH AND ENVIRONMENT

Man demonstrates *in his own nature* a pressure toward fuller and fuller Being, more and more perfect actualization of his humanness in exactly the same naturalistic, scientific sense than an acorn may be said to be "pressing toward" being an oak tree, or that a tiger can be observed to "push toward" being tigerish, or a horse toward being equine. Man is ultimately *not* molded or shaped into humanness or taught to be human. The role of the environment is ultimately to permit him or help him to actualize *his own* potentialities, not *its* potentialities. The environment does not give him potentialities and capacities; he *has* them in inchoate or embryonic form, just exactly as he has embryonic arms and legs. And creativeness, spontaneity, selfhood, authenticity, caring for others, being able to love, yearning for truth are embryonic potentialities belonging to his species-membership just as much as are his arms and legs and brain and eyes.

This is not in contradiction to the data already amassed which show clearly that living in a family and in a culture are absolutely necessary to *actualize* these psychological potentials that define humanness. Let us avoid this confusion. A mother or a culture does not create a human being. It does not implant within him the ability to love, or to be curious, or to philosophize, or to symbolize, or to be creative. Rather, it permits or fosters or encourages or helps what exists in embryo to become real and actual. The same mother or the same culture, treating a kitten or a puppy in exactly the same way, cannot make it into a human being. The culture is sun and food and water: it is not the seed.

"INSTINCT" THEORY

The group of thinkers who have been working with self-actualization, with self, with authentic humanness, etc., have pretty firmly established their case that man has a tendency to realize himself. By implication he is exhorted to be true to his own nature, to trust, himself, to be authentic, spontaneous, honestly expressive, to look for the sources of his actions in his own deep inner nature.

But, of course, this is an ideal counsel. They do not sufficiently warn that most adults don't know *how* to be authentic and that if they "express" themselves, they may bring catastrophe not only upon themselves but upon others as well. What answer must be given to the rapist or the sadist who asks "Why should I too not trust and express myself?"

These thinkers as a group have been remiss in several respects. They have *implied* without making explicit that if you can behave authentically, you *will* behave well, that if you emit action from within, it will be good and right behavior. What is very clearly implied is that this inner core, this real self, is good, trustworthy, ethical. This is an affirmation that is clearly separable from the affirmation that man actualizes himself, and needs to be separately proven (as I think it will be). Furthermore, these writers as a group very definitely have ducked the crucial statement about this inner core, *i.e.*, that it *must* in some degree be inherited or else everything else they say is so much hash.

In other words, we must grapple with "instinct" theory, or, as I prefer to call it, basic need theory, that is to say, with the study of the original, intrinsic, heredity-determined needs, urges, wishes, and, I may say, values of mankind. We can't play both the biology game and the sociology game simultaneously. We can't affirm *both* that culture does everything and anything and that man has an inherent nature. The one is incompatible with the other.

And of all the problems in this area of instinct, the one of which we know least and should know most is that of aggression, hostility, hatred, and destructiveness. The Freudians claim this to be instinctive: most other dynamic psychologists claim it to be not directly instinctive but rather an ever-present reaction to frustration of instinctoid or basic needs. The truth is that we don't really know. Clinical experience hasn't settled the problem because equally good clinicians come to these divergent conclusions. What we need is hard, firm research.

THE PROBLEM OF CONTROLS AND LIMITS

Another problem confronting the morals-from-within theorists is to account for the easy self-discipline which is customarily found in self-actualizing, authentic, genuine people and which is *not* found in average people.

In these healthy people we find duty and pleasure to be the same thing, as are also work and play, self-interest and altruism, individualism and selflessness. We know they *are* that way, but not how they *get* that way. I have the clear impression that such authentic, fully human persons are the actualization of what *any* human being could be. And yet we are confronted with the sad fact that so few people achieve this goal, perhaps only one in a hundred, or two hundred. We can be hopeful for mankind because in principle anyone *could* become a good and healthy man. But we must also feel sad because so few actually *do* become good men. If we wish to find out why some do and some don't, then the research problem presents itself of studying the life history of self-actualizing men to find out how they get that way.

We know already that the main prerequisite of healthy growth is gratification of the basic needs, especially in early life. (Neurosis is very often a deficiency disease, like avitaminosis.) But we have *also* learned that unbridled indulgence and gratification has its own dangerous consequences, *e.g.*, psychopathic personality, irresponsibility, inability to bear stress, spoiling, immaturity, certain character disorders. Research findings are rare, but there is now available a large store of clinical and educational experience which allows us to make a reasonable guess that the young child needs not only gratification; he needs also to learn the limitations that the physical world puts upon his gratifications, and he has to learn that other human beings seek for gratifications, too, even his mother and father, *i.e.*, they are not only means to his ends. This means control, delay, limits, renunciation, frustration-tolerance, and discipline. Only to the self-disciplined and responsible person can we say, "Do as you will, and it will probably be all right."

REGRESSIVE FORCES: PSYCHOPATHOLOGY

And now we must face the problem of what stands in the way of growth; that is to say, the problems of cessation of growth and evasion of growth, of fixation, regression, and defensiveness, in a word, the attractiveness of psychopathology, or, as other people would prefer to say, the problem of evil.

Why do so many people have no real identity, so little power to make their own decisions and choices?

1. These impulses and directional tendencies toward self-fulfillment, though instinctive, are very weak, so that, in contrast with all other animals who have strong instincts, these impulses are very easily drowned out by habit, by wrong cultural attitudes toward them, by traumatic episodes, by erroneous education. Therefore, the problem of choice and of responsibility is far, far more acute in humans than in any other species.

2. There has been a special tendency in Western culture, historically determined, to assume that these instinctoid needs of the human being, his so-called animal nature, are bad or evil. As a con-

sequence, many cultural institutions are set up for the express purpose of controlling, inhibiting, suppressing and repressing this original nature of man.[12]

3. There are two sets of forces pulling at the individual, not just one.[13] In addition to the pressures forward toward health, there are also regressive pressures backward, toward sickness and weakness. We can either move forward toward a "high Nirvana," or backward to a "low Nirvana."

I think the main factual defect in the value theories and ethical theories of the past and the present has been insufficient knowledge of psychopathology and psychotherapy. Throughout history, learned men have set out before mankind the rewards of virtue, the beauties of goodness, the intrinsic desirability of psychological health and self-fulfillment. It's all as plain as ABC, and yet most people perversely refuse to step into the happiness and self-respect that is offered them. Nothing is left to the teachers but irritation, impatience, disillusionment, alternations between scolding, exhortation, and hopelessness. A good many have thrown up their hands altogether and talked about original sin or intrinsic evil and concluded that man could be saved only by extrahuman forces.

Meanwhile there lies available the huge, rich, and illuminating literature of dynamic psychology and psychopathology, a great store of information on man's weaknesses, and fears.[14] We know much about *why* men do wrong things, *why* they bring about their own unhappiness and their self-destruction, *why* they are perverted and sick. And out of this has come the insight that human evil is largely human weakness, forgivable, understandable and also, in principle, curable.

I find it sometimes amusing, sometimes saddening that so many scholars and scientists, so many philosophers and theologians, who talk about human values, of good and evil, proceed in complete dis-

---

[12] A. H. Maslow, *Motivation and Personality;* A. M. Montagu, *The Direction of Human Development,* Harper, 1955.

[13] A. H. Maslow, "Defense and Growth," 36–47.

[14] O. Fenichel, *The Psychoanalytic Theory of Neuroses,* Norton, 1945.

regard of the plain fact that professional psychotherapists every day, as a matter of course, change and improve human nature, help people to become more strong, virtuous, creative, kind, loving altruistic, serene. These are only some of the consequences of improved self-knowledge and self-acceptance. There are many others as well that can come in greater or lesser degree.[15]

The subject is far too complex even to touch here. All I can do is draw a few conclusions for value theory.

1. Self-knowledge seems to be the major path of self-improvement, though not the only one.

2. Self-knowledge and self-improvement are very difficult for most people. They usually need great courage and long struggle.

3. Though the help of a skilled professional therapist makes this process much easier, it is by no means the only way. Much that has been learned from therapy can be applied to education, to family life, and to the guidance of one's own life.

4. Only by such study of psychopathology and therapy can one learn a proper respect for and appreciation of the forces of fear, of regression, of defense, of safety. Respecting and understanding these forces makes it much more possible to help oneself and others to grow toward health. False optimism sooner or later means disillusionment, anger and hopelessness.

5. To sum up, we can never really understand human weakness without also understanding human health. Otherwise we make the mistake of pathologizing everything. But also we can never fully understand or help human strength without also understanding human weakness. Otherwise we fall into the errors of overoptimistic reliance on rationality alone.

If we wish to help humans to become more fully human, we must realize not only that they try to realize themselves but that they are also reluctant or afraid or unable to do so. Only by fully appreciating this dialectic between sickness and health can we help to tip the balance in favor of health.

[15] C. Rogers, *Client-Centered Therapy*, Houghton Mifflin, 1951.

BIBLIOGRAPHY

Allport, G., *Becoming,* Yale University, 1955.

Bowlby, Jr., *Maternal Care and Mental Health,* World Health Organization, Geneva, 1952.

Bucke, R., *Cosmic Consciousness,* Dutton, 1923.

Goldstein, K., *The Organism,* American Book, 1939.

Harlow, H., "Motivation as a Factor in the Acquisition of New Responses," in *Current Theory and Research in Motivation,* University of Nebraska, 1953.

Maslow, A. H., "Deficiency Motivation and Growth Motivation," in Jones, R. M. (ed.), *Nebraska Motivation Symposium 1955,* University of Nebraska, 1955.

———, "A Philosophy of Psychology," in Fairchild, J. (ed.), *Personal Problems and Psychological Frontiers,* Sheridan House, 1957.

———, Power relationships and patterns of personal development, in Kornhauser, A. (ed.), *Problems of Power in American Democracy,* Wayne University, 1957.

———, Two kinds of cognition and their integration, *General Semantics Bulletin,* 1957, Nos. 20–21.

Moustakas, C. (ed.), *The Self,* Harper, 1956.

Normative Compatibility in the Light of Social Science

_____ GORDON W. ALLPORT

SEVERAL of the contributors to this symposium have made the point that although moral values cannot be derived from natural data nor from science, they can in some sense be validated (confirmed or disconfirmed) by the activity of science. This point has been made by both natural scientists and social scientists on our program. I find myself in full agreement.

Likewise I agree with Professor Maslow when he says that the validating capacity of social science is still somewhat feeble. Its data and methods are coarse and imprecise. One critic complained that "social science is nothing but journalism without a dateline." However that may be, I offer my paper in support of the proposition that modern social science, for all its imperfections, can now aid us in selecting from among the moral imperatives prescribed by various philosophers as guides to social policy. It can do so by helping us test broad types of ethical theory in the light of our modern knowledge of human nature and human collectivities.

TESTING ETHICAL THEORY BY SOCIAL SCIENCE

By way of illustration, and without offering detailed evidence at this time, let me mention some of the broad types of ethical theory that seem to fare badly when they are exposed to social-scientific analysis.

Theories of *renunciation or asceticism*, to give one example, make the error of assuming that men seek a life that is one-sided rather than one that is full and abundant. According to this view morality is largely a matter of repression or negation—a denial of much or most of man's endowment for growth. We cannot, of course, deny that this path of life, with its implied beatific vision, may be well suited for a few; but it is doomed to failure if it is prescribed for the masses of mankind.

Authoritarian morality, of which we have seen much in our day, defines goodness merely in terms of obedience. The adult, with all his potentialities for growth, is kept at the childhood level. While it is easy for many people to adopt the authoritarian code in order to "escape from freedom," the result, we know, is stultification, tyranny, and war and therefore the destruction of virtually all values.

Legalistic theories prescribe morality in terms of "thou shalts" or "thou shalt nots." The psychological error here is that the letter of the law, being inflexible, does not guide men in the novel and changing encounters of daily life.

Utopian theories are inept, not because they counsel perfection—because all morality does that—but because they plot no pathway from today's quandaries to the ultimate beatitude they depict.

Utilitarian ethics—in fact every version of *hedonism*—fixes men's minds on a will o' the wisp. Happiness can never be a tangible goal; it can only be a by-product of otherwise motivated activity. We may add that in the mid-nineteenth century ethical hedonism (*laissez-faire*) was given an explicit trial in the social policies of Britain and America and succeeded in creating moral dilemmas not in solving them. In short, its failure was experimentally demonstrated much as the failure of authoritarian morality has been demonstrated in our own day.

With these negative examples before us, we now ask what type of ethical theory does social science find most congruent with recent researches on human nature and on human aggregates.

Before answering this question let us remind ourselves that all theories of moral conduct have one primary purpose: they set before us some appropriate formula for handling conflict—whether the conflict be between warring interests in one individual or among individuals. In testing rival ethical theories, therefore, it is necessary to know a good deal about the interests of men—about the motives that are likely to come into conflict within the person or between persons or groups of persons.

DESIRES VERSUS DEMANDS

Although our present interest is in validatable moral theory, and not in motivation, let me refer to one relevant finding concerning motivation that comes from industrial research. Summarizing a number of studies of motivation and morale in industry, Likert concludes that workers have, in effect, two primary sets of interests. They want ego-recognition, a broad motivational category that includes credit for work done, economic security, praise, and many other forms of self-esteem. But they also want, no less urgently, affiliation with the group, a dimension that includes pleasant relations with the foreman, a sense of participation in team work, and above all the satisfaction of conducting themselves in terms of the values and normative expectations prevailing within the group of co-workers.[1]

The point is important. In industry, and probably in any form of human association, men wish to preserve their self-esteem—their self-love—and simultaneously wish to have warm, affiliative relations with their fellows. No one seems initially to want to hate. Hatred grows up as a consequence of blocked self-esteem and blocked affection.

Now it has been further discovered that high production, high morale, and successful relations can be achieved only when formulae are discovered that permit the adequate expression of these two sets of interests on the part of all participants. The movement called "human relations in industry" teaches this lesson over and over again, whether it be in terms of labor-management councils, group decision, the retraining of foremen, or basic changes in managerial philos-

[1] Rensis Likert, *Motivational Dimensions in Administration,* University of Michigan, 1951.

ophy.[2] In former days industry ran almost entirely on the basis of punishment, or, we may say, subtraction. Workers were asked to give up their identity, their pride, their social impulses during the hours they were earning a living. Today the saying is, "The whole man goes to work." Realizing this fact, certain industries now have counsellors on personal and family problems. Through improved communication the individual is given a means of participating in his own destiny. His private life and his work life are integrated; the interests of management and employees come together to a greater degree than formerly. I am not saying that Utopia is achieved in industry, but only that experimentation has already gone far enough to demonstrate the validity of ethical theory that advocates the resolution of conflict through the harmonious *integration of interests*.

This approach to morality does not aim at the reconciling of conflicting *demands*. Demands are usually nothing more than ways and means prematurely conceived to be the only channels for the realization of desires. All theories of the enlargement of interests stress the distinction between demands and desires, that is to say, between instrumental and intrinsic values, and insist that the moral individual himself must at every step distinguish between his demands and his desires. E. B. Holt calls the process *discrimination*, Ralph Barton Perry calls it *reflection*.[3]

I can illustrate the distinction by borrowing a classic incident from Mary Follett. It seems that, in a certain part of Vermont, dairy farmers who lived up the hill from the railway station and those who lived down the hill from the station both claimed the right to unload their milk supply first at the platform. Their demands were irreconcilable, and for a long time a feud prevailed. Finally they perceived their error. Their root desire was not, as they thought, to "unload first." This was a demand. The underlying desire of both factions was

[2] The story is told in F. Roethlisberger and W. J. Dickson, *Management and the Worker*, Harvard University Press, 1939; and in S. D. Hoslett, *Human Factors in Management*, Harper & Brothers, 1946.

[3] E. B. Holt, *The Freudian Wish and Its Place in Ethics*, Henry Holt, 1915; R. B. Perry, *Realms of Value: a Critique of Human Civilization*, Harvard University Press, 1954, Chap. 6.

not to be kept waiting. Profiting from this discriminative insight they joined forces on a Saturday afternoon, lengthened the railway platform and thereafter were both able to unload "first."

Although the illustration may seem a bit pat, it does contain the paradigm for moral action: two or more conflicting sets of apparent purposes collide; they are analyzed reflectively and so purged of preconceived ways and means; the root desires themselves are then brought to fulfillment through the invention of a larger framework that renders them compatible rather than incompatible as they at first seemed to be. In Professor Weisskopf's terms, a "union upward" is achieved.

The Principle of Enlargement of Interests

Wartime research is filled with examples of our principle. I shall cite one study, drawn from Stouffer's investigation of the American soldier.[4] Men in combat, we should expect, would show the maximum of destructive, self-preserving motivation. They were asked the question, "When the going was tough, how much did it help you to think that you couldn't let the other men down?" Approximately *two-thirds* said that it "helped a lot." Thus the affiliative motive even under extreme stress seems to hold twice as many men to their task as does the motive of hate. The point to note is that an enlargement of interest systems to include one's comrades is, even in the time of physical combat, a natural bent of man.

Successful psychotherapy offers a basic illustration of the principle. The most elementary formula for encouraging a patient is to assure him that "lots of people suffer from your difficulty." Most patients brighten when they know that they are not alone in their misery. Such assurance does not, of course, solve the patient's problem but he finds that even this imaginative integration of interests proves helpful. True neuroses, we know, are best defined as stubborn self-centeredness. No therapist can cure a phobia, obsession, prejudice, or hostility by the method of subtraction. He can only assist the patient

---

[4] S. A. Stouffer *et al., The American Soldier,* Princeton University Press, 1949, vol. 2, p. 178.

to achieve a value-system and outlook that will blanket or absorb the troublesome factor.

The successful resolution of *social* conflict proceeds always along the same lines. Take the issue of desegregation, a problem of the first magnitude not only in this country but in the world at large. On the social level it is a matter of bringing resistant provincial interests in line with more inclusive national and world values. On the personal level, it is a problem of enlarging the outlook of individuals who live now according to an exclusionist formula that secures for them self-esteem at the expense of dark-skinned people. At present they are willing to form no inclusive unit with the federal majority in this country nor with the world majority; nor will they form inclusive units with the Negro minority in their midst. They are not able even to resolve the moral dilemma in their own breasts. In all directions the principle of inclusion fails.

At the moment this particular problem is most acute in the United States and in South Africa. Although I have not the space to diagnose the situation in detail, let me say briefly that so far as South Africa is concerned the chief blunder of the Nationalist Party government, morally and politically, lies in its failure to consult with the Bantu peoples concerning their own destiny. The master group *tells* the servant group, who outnumber the masters three to one, that they have nothing to contribute to the life of the multiracial society excepting manual labor. Thus the cultural pride, love of homeland, and all other normal human aspirations and abilities of the Bantus are excluded from the existing matrix of values. The policy of apartheid extends to housing, transportation, schools, public assemblies, recreation, and politics, so that there is no legal opportunity to become acquainted. And needless to say the precondition of all normative compatibility *is* communication.

Both South Africa and the United States are exciting test cases for social science at the present time, the one following officially a policy of *excluding* interests, the other an official policy of *inclusion*. The world is watching the outcome.

We could pile up evidence from areas of conflict I have not yet touched upon—from family, classroom, neighborhood, municipality, and deliberative assemblies, but I shall limit myself to the question of how far it is possible for people, especially for children, to learn the moral principle of discrimination and inclusion.

THE PROCESS OF ENLARGEMENT IN CHILDHOOD

A study by Piaget and his associates is enlightening.[5] These investigators find that the children around six and seven years of age, living in the city of Geneva, are unable to think of themselves as both Genevese and as Swiss. Given a crayon and asked to draw a circle for Geneva and for Switzerland, they ordinarily draw two circles side by side. And they insist that if they are Genevese they cannot simultaneously be Swiss. As for foreign lands, the children suffer from even greater cognitive impoverishment. Concerning Italy they know only that their father visited Italy, or an aunt comes from there. Even loyalty to the homeland does not yet exist. The child's affective reactions are wholly egocentric. "I like Lausanne because I ate chocolate there." "I like Bern because my uncle lives there." In Piaget's language, these children have not yet commenced the process of "decentering," that is, from the unit of self to any larger social unit.

Ages eight and nine are transitional. Although the child draws a circle for Geneva properly inside the circle for Switzerland, he still has difficulty translating spatial enclosure into terms of social enclosure. He may say, for example, "I'm Swiss now so I can't be Genevese any longer." True, the concept of the homeland is gradually growing, but in a self-centered way. The child says, "I like Switzerland because I was born there." As for foreign lands, he knows of their existence but commonly views them with scorn. The French are dirty; the Americans want war; and people living in other lands all wish they were Swiss, of course. The child at this age has taken bits of conversation from his home and school and fitted them to this own affective self-centeredness.

Only at the age of ten and eleven do we find that decentering has

[5] J. Piaget and Anne-Marie Weil, "The Development in Children of the Idea of the Homeland of Relations with Other Countries," *International Soc. Sci. Bull.*, 1951, 3:561–578.

made appreciable progress. Egocentricity begins to give way to the principles of reciprocity and inclusion. The child of ten or eleven understands his dual membership in a smaller and larger political unit. He also gives fewer personal reasons for his affective attachment to his homeland. Switzerland now becomes the land of the Red Cross; it is the country without war. Further, the child understands that members of other countries are as attached to their own lands as he is to his—this is the principle of "reciprocity." But cognitive reciprocity does not necessarily mean that the child is capable of seeing good in all the peoples he knows about. He may still despise them. Whether the child outgrows his affective provincialism along with his cognitive provincialism seems to depend largely on the attitudes he learns from his parents.

Now this study teaches us certain lessons. For one thing, it shows that maturation and time are needed to achieve a decentering from the unit of self to a progressively larger social unit. Further, this process may be arrested at any stage along the way, especially in its affective aspects. It is significant Piaget gives no evidence that his children (at least up to fourteen years of age) discern the possibility of membership in any supranational grouping. Decentering has not reached the point where the child feels himself as belonging to the European region, to be a supporter of the United Nations; certainly none mentions his membership in the inclusive collective of mankind. Even if in later years such a cognitive enlargement takes place, the chances are that the corresponding affective enlargement will be lacking. Using Piaget's terms, we may then say that adults in all nations are still incompletely decentered. Cognitively they may stumble at the threshold of supranational chambers, but affectively they fail to enter.

RESOLVING INTERNATIONAL CONFLICTS

A study conducted in Belgium by de Bie shows how few adults are concerned with identification across national boundaries. Even those of a higher level of education have little sense of international relationships. Membership in any unit larger than the nation simply is not a psychological reality. Let international problems be handled by our leaders, they say.[6] And most, though not all, leaders, we know, lack affective, or even cognitive, decentering beyond the sphere of purely national interests.

In its *Tensions and Technology* Series, UNESCO has recently published a volume entitled *The Nature of Conflict*, surveying much relevant research. In summing up the results, R. C. Angell concludes that interacting nations will enjoy peace only when they become parts of a social system that embraces them.[7] It is not necessary to destroy national loyalties, but only to include them. In Angell's words, "The social system which is painfully coming to birth will grow out of national states, but their structures will not be annihilated in the process." J. C. Flugel has made the same point: "We must probably agree that intra-group behavior is on the whole far more moral than inter-group behavior; and in so far as the latter is moral it is often because the groups in question are for certain purposes themselves members of a larger group, so that it can at bottom be reduced to behavior of the intra-group variety."[8]

Such conclusions are based on a considerable amount of historical and contemporary research. This research, broadly speaking, indicates the relative futility of the moral creeds and strategies that are hortatory, authoritarian, hedonistic, legalistic, or Utopian. To abolish war some of these theories have said: let us give up our prejudices, our malice and our fear; let us remove barriers to trade, to communications and travel; let nations surrender land, money, aspirations, armaments, pride, and sovereignty. Though it is necessary that some of these subtractions take place, they will not do so if the approach is negative. Each and every local interest, deplored by us as making for international discord, serves a legitimate purpose so long as no

[6] P. de Bie, "Certain Psychological Aspects of Benelux," *International Soc. Sci. Bull.*, 1951, 3:540–552.

[7] R. C. Angell, "Discovering Paths to Peace," Chap. 4 in *The Nature of Conflict*, UNESCO, 1957.

[8] J. C. Flugel, "Some Neglected Aspects of World Integration," Chap. 6 in T. H. Pear (ed.), *Psychological Factors of Peace and War*, Hutchinson & Co., 1950.

social system exists to transcend nationhood. To state the case psychologically, individuals who favor the conditions making for war do so because they have no embracing circle of loyalties or expectations that would render these present conditions maladaptive to their purposes. Conflicts of value are never solved by the process of direct collision or defeat, nor by the double-edged subtraction that comes through compromise, but only through a process of inclusion and recentering.

Although the subtractive, authoritarian, legalistic, and utopian moralities still prevail, we view with hope certain signs of progress. The United Nations, of course, is organized for the express purpose of resolving conflict through the enlargement of interest systems. True, its major activities seem for the present to be hopelessly blocked by a centering on national interests. There are even signs of regress in the present violent upsurge of national, religious, and linguistic provincialism. So we must count our gains humbly: evidences of regional grouping, increased student and personnel exchanges (though evaluative studies of this policy seem to show somewhat less gain than we might hope).[9] We note progress against illiteracy which eventually may establish a firmer ground for communication. International bodies of scientists and other scholars are all to the good. So too the Olympic games. But perhaps our firmest gain is the widening circle of enlightenment and discussion that our common problems have evoked, as exemplified in the present symposium.

Returning to Piaget's research for a moment, we can surely say of the average adult that cognitively and affectively he is potentially capable of considerable decentering. The average man has no difficulty at all thinking of himself at one and the same time as a member of his family, neighborhood, town, state, and nation. Along the way he manages to include his church, lodge, and friendship circles. The principle is thus established that larger loyalties do not clash so long as they allow for the maximum possible inclusion of smaller loyalties. Trouble, to be sure, arises when values conflict at the same level. A

[9] *Journal of Social Issues*, 1956, 12, No. 1; *Annals of the American Academy of Political and Social Science*, 1954, Vol. 295.

bigamist cannot comfortably apportion his loyalty between two wives, nor a traitor serve two countries. But still it is clearly within the capacity of men to continue the decentering process illustrated by Piaget's children, and to go well beyond them. Empirically we can point, as Professor Sorokin and Professor Maslow have done, to individuals who have already realized this capacity.[10] Unfortunately, they are still relatively few in numbers.

Nothing that I have said is intended to detract from the positive values of rivalry, or of pride in one's kin and kind. Rival scientists struggle vigorously to prove their respective theories against their opponents but they do so within the frame of loyalty to science as a whole. What is good in free enterprise comes from competition regulated by common loyalty to the rules of the game. One's pride in one's way of life is not incompatible with an attitude of "let both grow together until the harvest." To critics who reply that conflict is the essence of existence, that "to live is to struggle; to survive is to conquer," we reply that we do not aim to eliminate struggle but to establish it within a framework that will actually lead to survival in a fully human sense and not to extermination in a strictly literal sense.

Preparing the Individual

The root of the matter, of course, lies in the posture of the individual's mentality. Psychologists today like to speak of "cognitive style." Now the style of mind that welcomes rivalry within the constraints of potential inclusion is marked by a kind of *tentativeness*. It does not insist upon the absolute validity of its equations; it prefers a way of life without prescribing it for all; it possesses humor; it maintains its loyalties within an expanding and yet discriminating frame. Its judgments are tentative, its religion heuristic, its ultimate sentiment compassion. There are, as we have said, people with this outlook. It is they who in this period of rapid social change give the

[10] P. A. Sorokin, *Altruistic Love: A Study of American Good Neighbors and Christian Saints,* Beacon Press, 1950; A. H. Maslow, *Motivation and Personality* Harper, 1954.

world such stability as it possesses. Our problem is to increase their numbers.

On this particular problem I will say only one thing at this time. The cognitive style I have defined is the precise opposite of the prejudiced style of life. The past decade or so has produced hundreds of studies of the sources and correlates of prejudice.[11] If the prejudiced style of life can be learned—and certainly it is not innate— then surely the tentative style, or, in Gandhi's terms, the "equi-minded" outlook can also be acquired. There is no simple formula for teaching it, but the books lie open for those who can adapt current research to educational policy for the home, school, and church. In the home there is much to be said for the method of the family conference wherein all the members from the oldest to the articulate youngest can seek a rational inclusive plan for the fulfillment of their interests. In schools, I suggest, we discard if necessary up to 10 per cent of the present content and replace it with suitably chosen instruction and experience in the principle of integration of interests. The lesson should include classroom and playground activities as well as studies in neighborhood, national, and international experiments in inclusion. In my opinion our knowledge to date warrants this deliberate change in educational policies.

FINAL WORD

But, of course, our knowledge, solid as some of it is, has many deficiencies. And since the emphasis of this Society is upon research, let me conclude by stating explicitly four implications of my remarks for a possible research program.

First, at the level of the individual person we need to know much more about the frame of mind that I have called tentative or equi-minded, for to me it seems to be the very essence of altruism. Research by Sorokin and by Maslow has given us valuable insights, but much more of the same order is needed.

Second, a problem of joint concern to psychology, anthropology, and philosophy confronts us. The moral guideline we have laid

---

[11] G. W. Allport, *The Nature of Prejudice,* Addison-Wesley, 1954.

down requires discrimination between root desires and demands, between intrinsic values and instrumentals. Now it seems probable that the root desires (not the demands) of men in all countries are very similar and therefore not incompatible. Hence I advocate cross-cultural investigations that will compare men's motives in many lands but always with a view to distinguishing their root desires from their demands.

Third, how can we develop symbols of inclusion that will assist children, and citizens, and statesmen to look beyond the confines of egocentricity? Without images it is impossible to form attitudes. Our symbols today are overwhelmingly local and nationalistic. We continue to view our membership circles, as did Piaget's children, as lying side by side, not as concentric. We have few symbols of inclusion, but even if effective supranational symbols existed, they would, of course, have no magic property. Men's choices can be only among sequences they have known, and so our problem of training involves also the giving of experience, especially in childhood, that will enlarge the cognitive style and turn the mind automatically toward the integrative mode of handling conflict.

Finally, continued philosophical research is needed concerning the principle I have outlined. The harmonious realization of abilities, interests, and purposes is, of course, a familiar theme in philosophies as diverse as those of Plato, Spinoza, Kant, Dewey, and Perry—to name but a few. What philosophy needs now to do, with the aid of social science, is to specify which inclusive sets of interest can best be achieved by which available techniques—in industry, in education, and in statescraft. Philosophy has the further critical task of refining the principle and examining instances where it may not fully apply. I am aware that not all conflicts are easily brought under our formula. Yet the philosophical task, I am convinced, is one of refinement and not of refutation, for the principle of maximal inclusion has the overwhelming testimony of social science in its support.

BIBLIOGRAPHY

Allport, G. W., *The Nature of Prejudice*, Addison-Wesley, 1954.

Chase, S., *The Proper Study of Mankind*, rev. ed., Harper, 1956.

Everett, W. G., *Moral Values*, Henry Holt, 1918, Chap. 7.

Follett, Mary P., *Creative Experience*, Longmans, Green, 1924.

———, *The New State*, Longmans, Green, 1920.

Holt, E. B., *The Freudian Wish and Its Place in Ethics*, Henry Holt, 1915.

Maslow, A. H., *Motivation and Personality*, Harper, 1954.

Perry, R. B., *Realms of Value*, Harvard University, 1954, Chaps. 1–7.

Sorokin, P. A. (ed.), *Forms and Techniques of Altruistic and Spiritual Growth*, Beacon Press, 1954.

Urban, W. M., *Fundamentals of Ethics*, Henry Holt, 1930, Chaps. 6–10.

Values, Psychology, and Human Existence

IN THIS paper, I want to present some substantiation and evidence for a thesis that is shared by a number of us.

The thesis is that *values are rooted in the very conditions of human existence; hence that our knowledge of these conditions, that is, of the "human situation," leads us to establishing values which have objective validity;* this validity exists, only with regard to the existence of man; outside of him there are no values.

MAN AND THE CONDITIONS OF HUMAN EXISTENCE

What is the nature of man, what are the special conditions of human existence, and what are the needs which are rooted in these conditions?

Man is torn away from the primary union with nature, which characterizes animal existence. Having at the same time reason and imagination, he is aware of his aloneness and separateness, of his powerlessness and ignorance, of the accidentalness of his birth and of his death. He could not face this state of being for a second if he could not find new ties with his fellow man which replace the old ones, regulated by instincts. Even if all his physiological needs were satisfied, he would experience his state of aloneness and individuation as a prison from which he had to break out in order to retain his sanity. In fact, the insane person is the one who has completely failed to establish any kind of union and is imprisoned, even if he is

151

not behind barred windows. The necessity to unite with other living beings, to be related to them, is an imperative need on the fulfillment of which man's sanity depends. This need is behind all phenomena which constitute the whole gamut of intimate human relations, of all passions which are called love in the broadest sense of the word.

There are several ways in which this union can be sought and achieved. Man can attempt to become one with the world by *submission* to a person, to a group, to an institution, to a God. In this way he transcends the separateness of his individual existence by becoming part of somebody or something bigger than himself and experiences his identity in connection with the power to which he has submitted. Another possibility of overcoming separateness lies in the opposite direction: man can try to unite himself with the world by having *power* over it, by making others a part of himself, and thus transcending his individual existence by domination.

The common element in both submission and domination is the symbiotic nature of relatedness. Both persons involved have lost their integrity and freedom; they live on each other and from each other, satisfying their craving for closeness, yet suffering from the lack of inner strength and self-reliance which would require freedom and independence, and furthermore constantly threatened by the conscious or unconscious hostility which is bound to arise from the symbiotic relationship. The realization of the submissive (masochistic) or the domineering (sadistic) passion never leads to satisfaction. They have a self-propelling dynamism, and because no amount of submission or domination (or possession or fame) is enough to give a sense of identity and union, more and more of it is sought. The ultimate result of these passions is defeat. It cannot be otherwise; although these passions aim at the establishment of a sense of union, they destroy the sense of integrity. The person driven by any one of these passions actually becomes dependent on others; instead of developing his own individual being, he is dependent on those to whom he submits, or whom he dominates.

There is only one passion which satisfies man's need to unite himself with the world and to acquire at the same time a sense of integrity and individuality, and this is *love*. *Love is union* with some-body, or something, outside oneself, *under the condition of retaining the separateness and integrity of one's own self.* It is an experience of sharing, of communion, which permits the full unfolding of one's own inner activity. The experience of love does away with the necessity of illusions. There is no need to inflate the image of the other person, or of myself, since the reality of active sharing and loving permits me to transcend my individualized existence and at the same time to experience myself as the bearer or the active powers which constitute the act of loving. What matters is the particular *quality* of loving, not the object. Love is in the experience of human solidarity with our fellow creatures, it is in the erotic love of man and woman, in the love of the mother for her child, and also in the love for oneself as a human being; it is in the mystical experi-ence of union. In the act of loving, I am one with All, and yet I am myself, a unique, separate, limited, mortal human being. Indeed, out of the very polarity between separateness and union, love is born and reborn.

Another aspect of the human situation, closely connected with the need for relatedness, is man's situation as a *creature* and his need to *transcend* this very state of the passive creature. Man is thrown into this world without his consent or will. In this respect he is not differ-ent from the animal, from the plants, or from inorganic matter. But being endowed with reason and imagination, he cannot be content with the passive role of the creature, with the role of dice cast out of a cup. He is driven by the urge to transcend the role of the creature, the accidentalness and passivity of his existence, by becoming a "creator."

Man can create life. This is the miraculous quality which he in-deed shares with all living beings, but with the difference that he alone is aware of being created and of being a creator. Man can create life, or rather, woman can create life, by giving birth to a child and by caring for the child until it is sufficiently grown to take care of his own needs. Man—man and woman—can create by plant-ing seeds, by producing material objects, by creating art, by creating ideas, by loving one another. In the act of creation man transcends himself as a creature, raises himself beyond the passivity and accidentalness of his existence into the realm of purposefulness and freedom. In man's need for transcendence lies one of the roots for love, as well as for art, religion, and material production.

To create presupposes activity and care. It presupposes love for that which one creates. How then does man solve the problem of transcending himself if he is not capable of creating, if he cannot love? *There is another answer to this need for transcendence; if I cannot create life, I can destroy it. To destroy life makes me also transcend it.* Indeed, that man can destroy life is just as miraculous a feat as that he can create it, for life is *the* miracle, the inexplicable. In the act of destruction, man sets himself above life; he transcends himself as a creature. Thus, the ultimate choice for man, inasmuch as he is driven to transcend himself, is to create or to destroy, to love or to hate. The enormous power of the will for destruction which we see in the history of man, and which we have witnessed so frightfully in our own time, is rooted in the nature of man, just as the drive to create is rooted in it. To say that man is capable of developing his primary potentiality for love and reason does not imply the naive belief in man's goodness. Destructiveness is a secondary potentiality, rooted in the very existence of man, and having the same intensity and power as any passion can have. But—and this is the essential point of my argument—it is the *alternative* to creativeness. Creation and destruction, love and hate, are not two instincts which exist independently. They are both answers to the same need for transcendence, and the will to destroy must rise when the will to create cannot be satisfied. However, the satisfaction of the need to create leads to happiness, destructiveness to suffering—most of all, for the destroyer himself.

A third need, again following the conditions of human existence, is that for *rootedness*. Man's birth as man means the beginning of his emergence from his natural home, the beginning of the severance of his natural ties. Yet this very severance is frightening; if man loses his natural roots, where is he and who is he? He would stand alone, without a home, without roots; he could not bear the isolation and helplessness of this position. He would become insane. He can dispense with the natural roots only insofar as he finds new *human* roots and only after he has found them can he feel at home again in this world. Is it surprising, then, to find a deep craving in man not to sever the natural ties, to fight against being torn away from nature, from mother, blood and soil?

The most elementary of the natural ties is the tie of the child to the mother. The child begins life in the mother's womb and exists there for a much longer time than is the case with most animals; even after birth, the child remains physically helpless and completely dependent on the mother; this period of helplessness and dependence again is much more protracted than with any animal. In the first years of life no full separation between child and mother has occurred. The satisfaction of all his physiological needs, of his vital need for warmth and affection depend on her; she has not only given birth to him, but she continues to give life to him. Her care is not dependent on anything the child does for her, on any obligation which the child has to fulfill; it is unconditional. She cares because the new creature is her child. The child, in these decisive first years of his life, has the experience of his mother as the fountain of life, as an all-enveloping, protective, nourishing power. Mother is food; she is love; she is warmth; she is earth. To be loved by her means to be alive, to be rooted, to be at home.

Just as birth means to leave the enveloping protection of the womb, growing up means to leave the protective orbit of the mother. Yet, even in the mature adult, the longing for this situation as it once existed never ceases completely, in spite of the fact that there is, indeed, a great difference between the adult and the child. The adult has the means to stand on his own feet, to take care of himself, to be responsible for himself and even for others, whereas the child is not yet capable of doing all this. But, considering the increased perplexities of life, the fragmentary nature of our knowledge, the accidentalness of adult existence, the unavoidable errors we make, the situation of the adult is by no means as different from that of the child as it is generally assumed. Every adult is in need of help, of warmth, of protection, in many ways differing and yet in many ways similar to the needs of the child. Is it surprising to find in the average adult a deep longing for the security and rootedness which the relationship to his mother once gave him? Is it not to be expected that he cannot give up this intense longing unless he finds other ways of being rooted?

In psychopathology we find ample evidence for this phenomenon of the refusal to leave the all-enveloping orbit of the mother. In the most extreme form we find the craving to return to the womb. A person obsessed by this desire may offer the picture of schizophrenia. He feels and acts like the foetus in the mother's womb, incapable of assuming even the most elementary functions of a small child. In many of the more severe neuroses we find the same craving, but as a repressed desire, manifested only in dreams, symptoms, and neurotic behavior, which results from the conflict between the deep desire to stay in the mother's womb and the adult part of the personality which tends to live a normal life. In dreams this craving appears in such symbols as being in a dark cave, in a one-man submarine, diving into deep water, etc. In the behavior of such a person, we find a fear of life and a deep fascination for death (death, in fantasy, being the return to the womb, to mother earth).

The less severe form of the fixation to mother is to be found in those cases where a person has permitted himself to be born, as it were, but where he is afraid to take the next step of birth, to be weaned from mother's breasts. People who have become arrested at this stage of birth have a deep craving to be mothered, nursed, protected by a motherly figure; they are the eternally dependent ones, who are frightened and insecure when motherly protection is withdrawn but optimistic and active when a loving mother or mother substitute is provided, either realistically or in fantasy.

Living is a process of continuous birth. The tragedy in the life of most of us is that we die before we are fully born. Being born, however, does not only mean to be free *from* the womb, the lap, the hand, etc., but also to be free *to* be active and creative. Just as the infant must breathe once the umbilical cord is cut, so man must be active and creative at every moment of birth. To the extent that man is fully born, he finds a new kind of rootedness; that lies in his creative relatedness to the world, and in the ensuing experience of solidarity with all men and with all nature. From being *passively* rooted in nature and in the womb, man becomes one again—but this time actively and creatively with all life.

Fourth, man needs to have a *sense of identity*. Man can be defined as the animal that can say "I," that can be aware of himself as a separate entity. The animal, being within nature and not transcending it, has no awareness of himself, has no need for a sense of identity. Man, being torn away from nature, being endowed with reason and imagination, needs to form a concept of himself, needs to say and to feel: "I am I." Because he is not *lived*, but *lives*, because he has lost the original unity with nature, has to make decisions, is aware of himself and of his neighbor as different persons, he must be able to sense himself as the subject of his actions. As with the need for relatedness, rootedness, and transcendence, this need for a sense of identity is so vital and imperative that man could not remain sane if he did not find some way of satisfying it. Man's sense of identity develops in the process of emerging from the "primary bonds" which tie him to mother and nature. The infant, still feeling one with mother, cannot yet say "I," nor has he any need for it. Only after he has conceived of the outer world as being separate and different from himself does he come to the awareness of himself as a distinct being, and one of the last words he learns to use is "I," in reference to himself.

In the development of *the human race* the degree to which man is aware of himself as a separate self depends on the extent to which he has emerged from the clan and the extent to which the process of individuation has developed. The member of a primitive clan might express his sense of identity in the formula "I am we"; he cannot yet conceive of himself as an "individual," existing apart from his group. In the medieval world, the individual was identified with his social role in the feudal hierarchy. The peasant was not a man who happened to be a peasant, the feudal lord not a man who happened to be a feudal lord. *He was* a peasant or a lord, and this sense of his unalterable station was an essential part of his sense of identity. When the feudal system broke down, this sense of identity was shaken and the acute question "Who am I?" arose—or, more precisely, "How do I know that I am I?" This is the question that was raised, in a philosophical form, by Descartes. He answered the quest for identity by saying, "I doubt—hence I think; I think—hence I am." This answer put all the emphasis on the experience of "I" as the subject of my *thinking* activity, and failed to see that the "I" is experienced also in the process of feeling and creative action.

The development of Western culture went in the direction of creating the basis for the full experience of individuality. By making the individual free politically and economically, by teaching him to think for himself and freeing him from an authoritarian pressure, one hoped to enable him to feel "I" in the sense that he was the center and active subject of his powers and experienced himself as such. But only a minority achieved the new experience of "I." For the majority, individualism was not much more than a façade behind which was hidden the failure to acquire an individual sense of identity.

Many substitutes for a truly individual sense of identity were sought for and found. Nation, religion, class, and occupation serve to furnish a sense of identity. "I am an American," "I am a Protestant," "I am a businessman," are the formulae that help a man experience a sense of identity after the original clan identity has disappeared and before a truly individual sense of identity has been acquired. These different identifications are, in contemporary society, usually employed together. They are in a broad sense status identifications, and they are more efficient if blended with older feudal remnants, as in European countries. In the United States, in which so little is left of feudal relics and in which there is so much social mobility, these status identifications are naturally less efficient, and the sense of identity is shifted more and more to the experience of conformity.

Inasmuch as I am not different, inasmuch as I am like the others and recognized by them as "a regular fellow," I can sense myself as "I." I am—"as you desire me"—as Pirandello put it in the title of one of his plays. Instead of the pre-individualistic clan identity, a new herd identity develops in which the sense of identity rests on the sense of an unquestionable belonging to the crowd. That this uniformity and conformity are often not recognized as such, and are covered by the illusion of individuality, does not alter the facts.

The problem of the sense of identity is not, as it is usually understood, merely a philosophical problem, or a problem concerning only our mind and thought. The need to feel a sense of identity stems from the very condition of human existence, and it is the source of the most intense strivings. Since I cannot remain sane without the sense of "I," I am driven to do almost anything to acquire this sense. Behind the intense passion for status and conformity is this very need, and it is sometimes even stronger than the need for physical survival. What could be more obvious than the fact that people are willing to risk their lives, to give up their love, to surrender their freedom, to sacrifice their own thoughts for the sake of being one of the herd, of conforming, and thus of acquiring a sense of identity, even though it is an illusory one.

REASON AND ORIENTATION IN THE WORLD

The fact that man has reason and imagination leads to the necessity not only for having a sense of his own identity but also for *orienting himself in the world intellectually*. This need can be compared with the process of physical orientation that develops in the first years of life and that is completed when the child can walk by himself, touch and handle things, knowing what they are. But when the ability to walk and to speak has been acquired, only the first step in the direction of orientation has been taken. Man finds himself surrounded by many puzzling phenomena and, having reason, he has to make sense of them, has to put them in some context which he can understand and which permits him to deal with them in his thoughts. The further his reason develops, the more adequate becomes his system of orientation, that is, the more it approximates reality. But even if man's frame of orientation is utterly illusory, it satisfies his need for some picture which is meaningful to him. Whether he believes in the power of a totem animal, in a rain god, or in the superiority and destiny of his race, his need for some frame of orientation is satisfied. Quite obviously, the picture of the world that he has depends on the development of his reason and of his knowledge. Although biologically the brain capacity of the human race has remained the same for thousands of generations, it takes a long evolutionary process to arrive at *objectivity*, that is, to acquire the faculty to see the world, nature, other persons, and oneself as they are and not distorted by desires and fears. The more man develops this objectivity, the more he is in touch with reality, the more he matures, the better can he create a human world in which he is at home. Reason is man's faculty for *grasping* the world by thought, in contradiction to intelligence, which is man's ability to *manipulate* the world with the help of thought. Reason is man's instrument for arriving at the truth, intelligence is man's instrument for manipulating the world more successfully; the former is essentially human, the latter belongs also to the animal part of man.

Reason is a faculty which must be practiced in order to develop, and it is indivisible. By this I mean that the faculty for objectivity refers to the knowledge of nature as well as to the knowledge of man, of society, and of oneself. If one lives in illusions about one sector of life, one's capacity for reason is restricted or damaged, and thus the use of reason is inhibited with regard to all other sectors. Reason in this respect is like love. Just as love is an orientation which refers to all objects and is incompatible with the restriction to one object, so is reason a human faculty which must embrace the whole of the world with which man is confronted.

The need for a frame of orientation exists on two levels; the first and the more fundamental need is to have *some* frame of orientation, regardless of whether it is true or false. Unless man has such a subjectively satisfactory frame of orientation, he cannot live sanely. On the second level, the need is to be in touch with reality by reason, to grasp the world objectively. But the necessity to develop his reason is not as immediate as that to develop some frame of orientation, since what is at stake for man in the latter case is his happiness and serenity, and not his sanity. This becomes clear if we study the function of *rationalization*. However unreasonable or immoral an action may be, man has an insuperable urge to rationalize it, that is, to prove to himself and to others that his action is determined by intelligence, common sense, or at least conventional morality. He has little difficulty in acting irrationally, but it is almost impossible for him not to give his action the appearance of reasonable motivation.

FEELING AND ORIENTATION TO THE WORLD

If man were only a disembodied intellect, his aim would be achieved by a comprehensive thought system. But since he is an entity endowed with a body as well as a mind, he has to react to the dichotomy of his existence not only in thinking but in the total process of living, in his feelings and actions. Hence any satisfying system of orientation contains not only intellectual elements but elements of feeling and sensing which are expressed in the relationship to an object of devotion.

The answers given to man's need for a system of orientation and an object of devotion differ widely both in content and in form. There are primitive systems such as animism and totemism in which natural objects or ancestors represent answers to man's quest for meaning. There are nontheistic systems, such as Buddhism, which are usually called religions although in their original form there is no concept of God. There are purely philosophical systems, such as Stoicism, and there are the monotheistic religious systems that give an answer to man's quest for meaning in reference to the concept of God.

But whatever their contents, they all respond to man's need to have not only some thought system but also an object of devotion that gives meaning to his existence and to his position in the world. Only the analysis of the various forms of religion can show which answers are better and which are worse solutions to man's quest for meaning and devotion, "better" or "worse" always considered from the standpoint of man's nature and his development.

Choices and Fulfillment

In discussing the various needs of man as they result from the conditions of his existence, I have tried to indicate that they have to be satisfied in some way or other lest man should become insane. But there are several ways in which each of these needs can be satisfied; the difference between these ways is the difference in their appropriateness for the development of man. The need to be related can be satisfied by submission, or by domination; but only in love is another human need fulfilled—that of independence and integrity of the self. The need for transcendence can be satisfied either by creativeness or by destructiveness; but only creativeness permits of joy—whereas destructiveness causes suffering for oneself and others. The need for rootedness can be satisfied regressively by fixation in nature and mother, or progressively by full birth in which new solidarity and oneness is achieved. Here again only in the latter case are individuality and integrity preserved. A frame of orientation may be irrational or rational; yet only the rational one can serve as a basis for the growth and development of the total personality. Eventually, the sense of identity can be based on primary ties with nature and clan, on adjustment to a group, or, on the other hand, on the full, creative development of the person. Again, only in the latter case can man achieve a sense of joy and strength.

The difference between the various answers is the difference between mental health and mental sickness, between suffering and joy, between stagnation and growth, between life and death, between good and evil. All answers that can be qualified as good have in common that they are consistent with the very nature of life, which is continuous birth and growth. All answers that can be qualified as bad have in common that they conflict with the nature of life, that they are conducive to stagnation and eventually to death. Indeed, at the moment man is born, life asks him a question, the question of human existence. He must answer this question at every moment of his life. *He* must answer it, not his mind, or his body, but *he*, the real person, his feet, his hands, his eyes, his stomach, his mind, his feeling—his real—and not an imagined or abstracted person. There are only a limited number of answers to the question of existence. We find these answers in the history of religion, from the most primitive to the highest. We find them also in the variety of characters, from the fullest sanity to the deepest psychosis.

In the foregoing remarks I have tried to outline these various answers, implying that each individual represents in himself the whole of humanity and its evolution. We find individuals who represent man on the most primitive level of history, and others who represent mankind as it will be thousands of years from now.

I said that the answer to life that corresponds to the reality of human existence is conducive to mental health. What is generally understood by mental health, however, is negative, rather than positive; the *absence of sickness, rather than the presence of well-being*. Actually there is even very little discussion in the psychiatric and psychological literature of what constitutes well-being.

Well-being I would describe as the *ability to be creative, to be aware, and to respond;* to be independent and fully active, and by this very fact to be one with the world. To be concerned with *being*, not with *having;* to experience joy in the very act of living—and to consider living creatively as the only meaning of life. Well-being is not an assumption in the *mind* of a person. It is expressed in his whole body, in the way he walks, talks, in the tonus of his muscles.

Certainly, anyone who wants to achieve this aim must struggle against many basic trends of modern culture. I want to mention very briefly only two. One, the idea of a *split between intellect and affect,* an idea which has been prevalent from Descartes to Freud. In this whole development (to which there are, of course, exceptions) the assumption is made that only the intellect is rational and that affect, by its very nature, is irrational. Freud has made this assumption very explicitly by saying that love by its very nature is neurotic, infantile, irrational. His aim was actually to help man succeed in dominating irrational affect by intellect; or, to put it into his own words, "Where there was Id—there shall be Ego." Yet this dogma of the split between affect and thought does not correspond to the reality of human existence, and is destructive of human growth. We cannot understand man fully nor achieve the aim of well-being unless we overcome the idea of this split, restore to man his original unity, and recognize that the split between affect and thought, body and mind, is nothing but a product of our own thought and does not correspond to the reality of man.

The other obstacle to the achievement of well-being, deeply rooted in the spirit of modern society, is the fact of man's dethronement from his supreme place. The nineteenth century said: God is dead; the twentieth century could say: man is dead. Means have been transformed into ends, the production and consumption of things has become the aim of life, to which living is subordinated. We produce things that act like men and men that act like things. Man has transformed himself into a thing and worships the products of his own hands; he is alienated from himself and has regressed to idolatry, even though he uses God's name. Emerson already saw that "things are in the saddle and ride mankind." Today many of us see it. The achievement of well-being is possible only under one condition: *if we put man back into the saddle.*

Culture and the Experience of Value

_____ DOROTHY LEE

MY PAPER will deal with culture as a factor in the experience of values; that is, it will discuss some ways in which culture mediates value for the experiencing individual. It will deal mainly not with human values but with value itself. By human values, by *a* value or a system of values, I mean the basis upon which an individual will choose one course rather than another, judged as better or worse, right or wrong. We can speak about human values, but we cannot know them directly. We infer them through their expression in behavior.

HUMAN VALUES AND VALUE

What I refer to as value—not *a* value—resides in the situation, in the field in which an individual participates. What I have called *a* value is a part of the cultural system; what I call *value* resides in the reality that is mediated by culture. According to this view, we experience value when our activity is permeated with satisfaction, when we find meaning in our life, when we feel good, when we act not out of calculating choice and not for extraneous purpose but rather because this is the only way that we, as ourselves, deeply want to act. I believe that value can be experienced only when relatedness with the surround is immediate and, in a sense, active; when the self is not only open to the experience of the other but also, to use Dewey's term, in transaction with the other. To experience the other on the basis of a prior category would be to introduce an interruption into the relationship. According to this view of value, prelabeling, analysis, assessment, calculation, measurement, evaluation, all erect barriers that may diminish or even destroy the value content of a situation.

The value experience I speak of here has reference to all reality. When the self is in transaction within a social situation, we speak of social value; though the experience itself is personal, it is bound to have value for the transacting other, also.

UNIVERSALITY OF SOCIAL VALUE

My thesis here is that the good is held to be social in all or nearly all societies and that cultures are structured in such a way as to maintain and enhance social value and, each in its own way, to furnish for the individual situations rich in social value. Cultures differ widely in the forms of the behavior patterns furnished, through which social value enters the life of the members of the society, and in the multiplicity and effectiveness of these patterns. They also differ in the kind of self they enable the growing individual to develop, the degree of sensitivity they foster, the definitions of self and of other they offer as basic to relatedness.

It is not difficult to discover the negative ways in which social value is given recognition. As Kluckhohn points out, there is in all societies an interdiction against "killing, indiscriminate lying and stealing within the in-group," and in fact, against whatever might bring about dissension, disruption, destruction within the recognized social unit, thus ensuring the persistence of good relations. However, the procedures through which the social bonds are strengthened and the avenues afforded for the experience and enhancement of social good are so varied that the universality of the positive aspect is not as easy to recognize.

In addition, there is a great difference in the conception of the social situation. In our own view, a social relationship exists when the ends of the relationship are human. But among many societies man can have social relations with nonhumans, such as the Oglala Dakota, for example, who extended kinship terms to Buffalo,

Thunder, Earth, and other natural phenomena. Many Australian groups appear to experience social value when they visit, during their walkabouts, a rock or a tree to which they are related, enduring hardships and short rations to do so. They perform rites of increase for animals, plants, and other natural objects to which they consider themselves related, apparently mainly by way of helping nature maintain itself, since many of the objects are inedible and may even be dangerous to man.

To show how culture mediates value, I shall speak first of two societies where, in different ways, there is an emphasis on infusing the life of the members with social value; and next I shall speak of the openness of the self, which makes immediate experience of value possible.

RELATEDNESS—ARAPESH

We take first the Arapesh of New Guinea, as they were when Margaret Mead visited them in 1931. For these people, the stress on the enhancement of social value was so strong as to overshadow all else. All their food-getting activities—their agriculture, their gathering, their hunting, and even the processing of the food—were hampered by constant interruptions, suffered continual interferences and distractions; there was appalling inefficiency and waste of time and energy. As a result, they never had enough to eat their fill, they always seemed hungry, even during their feasts, which themselves would have appeared to us pitifully meager even as everyday fare. Yet the Arapesh maintained the pattern of their situations in the face of near hunger; they persisted in arranging their working time uneconomically and in being prodigal with their presumably little energy. Their structuring of food-getting may have been inefficient from the point of view of food production, but it was eminently efficient from the point of view of infusing value into their lives.

The Arapesh depended mainly on agriculture for their food; but agriculture was difficult and not very profitable. The terrain is mountainous, so rugged that there is almost no level land. The garden plots might be separated from the hamlet by miles of difficult territory. The most economical way to cultivate them would have been to have one gardener plant a garden and work in it alone or with the help of his wife; yet up to six men would work on a small plot, often with their wives and children, traveling over forbidding territory from plot to distant plot, enjoying each other's society and the sharing of work. This means that a man planted several gardens, often widely separated; in one of them he was host and others came to help him; in the others, he was a guest. From the point of view of growing enough food, this was wasteful procedure. Yet, the Arapesh went beyond this. Margaret Mead writes: "The ideal distribution of food is for each person to eat food grown by another, eat game killed by another, eat pork from pigs that have been fed by people at . . . a distance." A man walked miles with his coconut saplings to plant them on the house sites of others, he gave his pigs to relatives in distant hamlets to feed and tend for him, he hunted only to give his kill away, since the lowest form of humanity was the man who ate his own kill, even one tiny bird. The system actually forbade a man to eat of his own kill; but it did not forbid him to give his pigs to his own wife to tend or to plant all his trees by his own house. Taboo and preference, however, went hand in hand toward creating a wide gap between ownership and possession: what a man possessed he did not own, what he owned he gave to another. This gap then provided continuing opportunities for experience in social value. Thus it was ensured that the Arapesh had little to eat; but it also meant that every mouthful they consumed had been the medium of social participation and contained social value.

Social value was channeled into experience through a variety of ways, regulations, attitudes, behavior patterns. Any surplus of food, for instance, however small, was always temporary, as it was always the occasion for inviting others to a feast. The kinship system again was seen as something to be manipulated as a medium for discovering avenues of relatedness. And, quite often, the relationship with a given individual would be traced through a rambling route which brought in a large number of intermediate relatives. For example, Margaret Mead speaks of a woman who, when offering food to a visiting brother, phrased this as giving food to her husband's brother-in-law.

Even incest regulations were phrased as having the function of enhancing relatedness. When Margaret Mead asked whether a man ever married his sister, she was met with incredulous amazement. Her informants inquired, in effect, "If we did so, where would we get brothers-in-law?" And, of course, to marry one's own sister instead of the sister of another man would deprive one of two sets of brothers-in-law, two wide-branching channels for relatedness and shared experience.

In fact, social value so permeated the lives of the Arapesh that it would have required deliberate effort to cut it out of experience. Mead describes how, even when a man was walking alone through the jungle, he was in a sense carrying his society with him, so that what he saw along the way was not a vine, a piece of wood, but rather a vine to be picked for Y's roof, a plank for R's house. And the walk he was taking most probably had reference to a social framework.

The enjoyment of the value in the social situation depended, I believe, on the presence of a capacity to apprehend with immediacy. There were no barriers between self and other, no gaps to be bridged. The Arapesh self could participate in the other, and in fact the relations between a man and his wife, a man and his child, were codified in this way. A man "grew" his wife, from the time when she came as a child to join the household of his parents. He "grew" her the food he grew or killed for her; that is, he gave her of his self. In the same way, a good father grew his children. Together, throughout the period of pregnancy, husband and wife grew the child. Before and after the birth of the child, the food the father provided, what he did, and what he refrained from doing all went into growing the child. His time, his energy, his physical exertion, his good will and concern, his skill, his very self became incorporated in his wife and children.

And this conception of the self, I believe, was basic to the experience of all social value. In all of these food is involved. "Good" food, valued food, is food grown by one person and given to another; so that the "ideal distribution of food" which Margaret Mead describes, is actually an extension of the principle of "growing" of the wife and child; it was putting one's self into the other. For the Arapesh this "growing" is identical with value. The word for *good* and *the good* (*jap*) is the same as the word for *grow*.

RELATEDNESS—OGLALA

In the culture of the Oglala Indians of this country, value was interpreted and infused into experience in an entirely different way, through an entirely different set of human values. Here relatedness was overtly recognized and sought as the ultimate value. It was indispensable for the growth and strengthening of a man to achieve relatedness with the manifestations of the Great Spirit—earth, plants, animals, stars, thunder, etc.—broadening in scope and intensifying through life. But relatedness was good in itself, relatedness ultimately to all; and man must be a worthy relative. So the emphasis was on rigorous development of the self, both through and for relatedness. In addition, a man was responsible for his social unit, or rather *as* his social unit, since he was an interpenetrating part of his camp circle, representing it in his person; and a holy man was eventually responsible for the actualization of the universe. Therefore, to enhance oneself, to strengthen oneself, meant to enhance the unit of relatedness.

Development of the individual in relatedness was initiated by the mother and eventually taken on by the growing boy. The mother initiated her unborn baby into relatedness with nature and continued to do so in various ways through his infancy. She took the very young baby out and merely pointed to natural manifestations, without labeling. Only after the baby experienced directly, only later, did she offer him concepts. She sang songs to him referring to the animals as his brothers, his cousins, his grandparents. Early in life he was also helped to develop sensitivity toward nature so that he might be enabled to relate openly. Standing Bear writes: "Children were taught to sit still—and look when apparently there was nothing to see, and to listen intently when all seemingly was quiet" . . . and to "become conscious of life about us in its multitude of forms." Categorizing and logic were not absent from the culture but they came afterward, after the immediate apprehension of *this*. After the child had been initiated into acquaintance with nature, he was guided into using this as observed data on the basis of which he could draw conclusions. Logic did not mediate experience but was founded upon experience. At the same time the growing individual was acquiring tremendous self-discipline and training himself in hardihood, in skills, in endurance of incredible physical pain and danger. On the face of it, all this is self-centered; yet it was actually social because only through the strength and development of the individual could the social unit prosper, and only through personal enhancement could the individual be worthy of relationship with the multitude of manifestations of the Great Spirit.

On the surface, Arapesh and Oglala mediated value in diametrically different ways, and their values were widely different. The Oglala valued what we call the manly, both in man and woman. The Arapesh valued that which Mead has called maternal. The Oglala food-getting was impressively efficient; if they hunted in groups, it was for more effective results, not for the sake of being together. The Oglala individual often spent time alone; and he sought his religious experience ultimately in solitude, alone in the midst of the manifestations of the Great Spirit with whom he sought communion. Yet, in his person, he represented his camp circle; his prayer to Wakan Tanka, The Great Spirit, was: Help me that my people may live. And into the pipe he smoked to The Great Spirit at this time had been introduced with painstaking symbolism all the four groups of animals, the cardinal directions, the seasons, the times of the day, the earth, the sky, the region below. At this time, while alone, with the pipe in his hand, the Oglala seeker represented the entire social unit, reaching out for communion with the entire universe. And this was the prime situation of social value.

RELATEDNESS AND THE OPEN SELF

It is obvious that at the base of both Arapesh and Oglala concepts of social value lies a conception of the self as open; otherwise, the value situations which I presented could not have been experienced. There was an assumption of a degree of continuity between self and other: the self was not an element, complete in itself, capable of being completely removed from the surround. When an Arapesh man left his territory, for example, a part of his very self stayed behind, in his wife, his children, and, to a lesser extent, his many relatives who had eaten of the food he had grown and of the game he had killed. Conversely, it had been possible for the Arapesh man to relate himself in this way to his wife and children and other relatives, and to find value in this relationship, because he had an open self.

In both the cultures that I presented, the conception of the open self lies at the base of the enculturation of the individual as well as of the structure of behavioral situations. But here the similarity stops. The two societies differ as to the way in which they present the open self to their members.

I believe that the fully open self was presupposed in the Arapesh culture, and the emphasis was on furnishing, finding, creating a multiplicity of occasions for the exercise of the open self in transaction. The Oglala concentrated on enhancing the openness of the self, on developing in the growing individual an immediacy of apprehension; on enabling the individual to transact within an increasingly broadening field, on refining and intensifying the experience of the open self. When the concept of the open self is present, we find it at the base of probably all patterned behavior.

Among the Wintu Indians of California, I found the concept of the self expressed in the morphology of the language. For example, in a Wintu tale that I recorded, a man, speaking of his sick son, added a suffix to the verb: *I am ill*, (*koyu*), and now said, "I am ill (*koyuma*) my son": and later, added the same suffix to *get well* (*modu*), and said, "I want to get well my son." With the aid of this suffix, a chief haranguing his people about the coming of the Whites was quoted as saying: "You shall hunger your children, you shall hunger your horses." When this suffix occurred with a verb such as *I ate*, I found it easy to translate the phrase as "I fed my child." But here I was probably violating the meaning of the Wintu speaker. *I fed* presupposes a separate, bounded self acting upon another separate bounded self; I did something, whether desired or not, *to* someone else. If there is consistency in the meaning of the suffix, I believe it must always be translated in such a way that it expresses some kind of immediate participation in the experience of the other; so that, I do not *feed my child,* but rather: "I eat in respect to my child," "I hunger in respect to my child," "I am ill in respect to my child"; that is, I am open to the experience of my child. This is only one of the many cases where the linguistic forms as well as the cultural structure of the Wintu expressed their peculiar formulation of the openness of the self.

To say that the self is open is not to say that the self is fused with, or submerged in, the other. In all the cultures that I have studied reference is made to a differentiated self. In the Wintu language, for example, in addition to the personal pronouns we have at least two suffixes whose function is to differentiate and emphasize the self; and, in the case that I cited above, the father who participated in the son's illness was named in distinction from the son. The Wintu did not use an *and* when they spoke of two or more individuals; in our terms, they would say not: John *and* Mary have arrived but: John Mary they have arrived. This may imply that the coming of John and the coming of Mary are not separate to be joined by an *and;* yet John and Mary were clearly differentiated.

When I was in my teens, I was tortured by a question that I think would never have disturbed the Wintu or the Arapesh or the Oglala. If I dashed out to save a child from death or maiming at the risk of my own life, would I be doing it for *the child's* sake or for *my* sake? Would my act be altruistic or selfish? Upon which of these values would my chosen action be based? Would I be saving his life so that he could enjoy it, or would I act only because I could not bear to live with myself if I did not try to save him? This question of course presupposed a conception of the self as closed, in limited, purposive interaction.

In a society where relatedness stems from the premise of the open self, such a question would be nonsense. In such societies, though the self and the other are differentiated, they are not mutually exclusive. The self contains some of the other, participates in the other, and is in part contained within the other. By this I do not mean what usually goes under the name of empathy. I mean rather that where such a concept of the self is operative, self-interest and other-interest are not clearly distinguished; so that what I do for my own good is necessarily also good for my unit, the surround, whether this is my family, my village, my tribe, my land, or even nature in general, the entire universe. So the Oglala Indian could concentrate his entire life in developing his self, through rigorous self-discipline and privation, through intense physical suffering, through the systematic sharpening of his senses and the refining of his sensitivity, thus making himself worthy of communion with nature, the manifestation of the Great Spirit, doing all this ultimately for the welfare of the camp circle. What he asked of Wakan Tanka, The Great Spirit, was: "Help me that my people may live," and he could say at this time: "I am the people." Was this egoism or altruism?

I can say, "Help *me* that *my people* may live," only when the self is continuous with the other; and when this is so, whether I enhance myself, whether I expose myself to illness or pollution, whether I allow myself to deteriorate, in every case this is not a matter involving only myself; it is not even a matter purely affecting others; it is rather a situation shared by the other because I am to some extent the other.

A corollary to this view of the self is that, in respecting the other, the self is simultaneously respected. If the other is enjoyed in its totality, it means that the self must also be enjoyed. I cannot trust the other, value the other, unless I also love and value myself. In societies where the individual is ideally at one with, in harmony with, society, nature, the universe, we find that the self has tremendous value. So the Navaho, for example, valuing harmony and relatedness with the universe, believed that to assume the attitude of supplication or of gratitude toward the divine was to devalue or humiliate the divine with whom he was to some degree identified. The Oglala man seeking power through communion with nature had "to prove to some bird or animal that he was a worthy friend," to quote from the autobiography of Standing Bear: "The animal would thereafter observe and learn from the dreamer," and the dreamer also "should do likewise." The Oglala man who sought a vision was, in Standing Bear's words: "Humble without cringing, without loss of spirit. He always *faced* the Powers in prayer; he never groveled on the earth, but with face lifted to the sky he spoke straight to his Mystery." He was in immediate relation to "his Mystery"; yet he was himself, differentiated and full of personal worth.

BIBLIOGRAPHY

Fortune, Reo, *Monographs of the American Ethnological Society*, J. J. Augustin, 1942.

The following of my papers deal to a greater or less extent with value and with the conception of the self:

Lee, Dorothy, Are basic needs ultimate? *J. Abn. and Soc. Psych.*, 1948, 43, 391–395.

———, Being and value in a primitive culture, *J. Philosophy*, 1949, 46, 401–415.

———, "Discrepancies in the Teaching of American Culture," in George D. Spindler (ed.), *Education and Anthropology*, Stanford University, 1955.

———, "Greek View of the Self," in Margaret Mead (ed.), *Cultural Patterns and Technical Change*, UNESCO, 1953, 80–88.

———, "The Joy of Work as Participation," in *The Hour of Insight: A Sequel to Moments of Personal Discovery*, Harper, 1953, 15–28.

———, Lineal and non-lineal codifications of reality, *Psychosomatic Medicine*, 1950, 12, 89–98.

——, Linguistic reflection of Wintu thought, *Intern. J. Amer. Linguistics*, 1944, *10*, 181–187.

——, Notes on the conception of the self among the Wintu Indians, *J. Abn. and Soc. Psych.*, 1950, *45*, No. 3.

——, Religious Perspectives in College Teaching," in *Anthropology*, Edward Hazen Foundation, 1951.

——, Stylistic use of the negative in Wintu, *Intern. J. Amer. Linguistics*, 1946, *12*, 79–81.

——, "Symbolization and Value," in *Symbols and Values, an Initial Study*, Thirteenth Symposium of the Conference on Science, Philosophy and Religion, 1954.

Mead, M., "The Arapesh of New Guinea," in *Cooperation and Competition Among Primitive Peoples*, McGraw-Hill, 1937, pp. 20–50.

——, The mountain Arapesh I. an importing culture, *Anthr. Pap. American Museum Natural History*, 1940, *36*, Pt. 3.

——, The mountain Arapesh II. supernaturalism, *Anthr. Pap. American Museum Natural History*, 1940, 37, Pt. 3.

——, The mountain Arapesh III. socio-economic life. IV diary of event in Alitoa, *Anthr. Pap. American Museum Natural History*, 1947, *49*, Pt. 3.

——, The record of Unabelin with Rorschach analysis, *Anthr. Pap. American Museum Natural History*, 1949, *41*, Pt. 3.

——, *Sex and Temperament in Three Primitive Societies*, Part I: The Mountain Dwelling Arapesh, William Morrow & Co., 1935.

Oglala Dakota:

Black Elk Speaks. Being the Life Story of a Holy Man of the Oglala Sioux, as told to John G. Neihardt (Flaming Rainbow), William Morrow, 1932.

Brown, Joseph Epes, *The Sacred Pipe, Black Elk's Account of the Seven Rites of the Oglala Sioux*, University of Oklahoma, 1953.

Eastman, Charles A., *From the Deep Woods to Civilization; Chapters in the Autobiography of an Indian*, Little, Brown, 1916.

——, *An Indian Boyhood*, Little, Brown, 1902.

——, *The Soul of an Indian*, Houghton Mifflin, 1911.

Standing Bear, Luther, *Land of the Spotted Eagle*, Houghton Mifflin, 1932.

——, Luther, *My People the Sioux*, Houghton Mifflin, 1928.

Australia:

Elkin, A. P., *The Australian Aborigines,* Sydney, 1938.
Kaberry, Phyllis M., *Aboriginal Woman—Sacred and Profane,* Blakeston, 1939.

Navaho:

Reichard, Gladys A., *Prayer: The Compulsive Word,* J. J. Augustin, 1944.

Health as Value

KURT GOLDSTEIN

WE HAVE and shall read in this volume many interesting papers concerning value in relation to the great problems of the world. I do not consider it my task to write about that here; rather, I wish to bring the problem of value onto a more concrete level, and I consider that Mrs. Lee, in the preceding paper, prepared the ground, so to say, for such a consideration of the problem.

The profound difficulty in reaching a definite position pertaining to the problem of values seems to me to originate in the assumption that value is not inherent in objects, events, actions, persons, etc., but is a judgment determined by outside factors; by religious, metaphysical, scientific, or social convictions. The arbitrariness, uncertainty, ambiguity of these convictions is mirrored in value judgments, and all criticism and skepticism as to them is an expression of dissatisfaction with this relativity. It does not suffice that the differences in contents to which values are ascribed are considered as due to the differences in individuals or in cultural, environmental, or historical influences. Our inner experience, when we think of value, is in principle, a feeling of something definite, something absolute, something essential for man's life, for his existence. What do we signify by the word existence in this context? The word does not mean survival. Survival, as important as it is, is not really a value in itself. We observe survival particularly in situations of great threat to life or in abnormal conditions, in severe bodily and mental illness, as we shall show later. Existence means something much more than, one may say something essentially different from, mere survival. Existence means the realization of the individual, of the individual's *intrinsic nature*, the fulfillment of all his capacities in harmony with each other.

VALUES AND SELF-ACTUALIZATION

This intrinsic nature is not the sum of the physical and mental capacities; it is related to personality and is the essence which the individual presents. This is what man tries to actualize, or, in other words, from this point of view alone can man's behavior be understood. The tendency to actualize one's intrinsic nature sometimes so determines man's behavior that he gives up life when he feels that self-realization is no longer possible.

From this hypothesis, the different values of different individuals, groups, cultures, etc., would appear to be the means of assuring the self-realization of the individuals by the organization of the particular group. My viewpoint is the result not of deliberating about various values in various situations but rather of assimilating the experiences in the special field of my *professional activity as a physician*. It may well be that the consideration of concrete phenomena in the life of individuals from the point of view of this hypothesis can enable us to find a *criterion* for our assumption of something as a value; it may well be that by this procedure we can overcome the *uncertainty* in our concept of value, its accustomed character of relativity. It is my intention to show that this may be possible by discussing the *essential significance of the phenomenon of health for man's self-realization*.

Anticipating my results, I came, through the observation and treatment of sick people, to the conclusion that the behavior of patients could be understood only if it is considered as determined by a *definite value* and that *we can help the patient only when we take account of this value*.

To explain this I have to refer to the loss or impairment of *health* —to what we call *sickness*—and what this means in respect to human existence.

We must distinguish the condition of sickness from the phenomenon of *being sick,* which is the effect of sickness. We are here interested in the phenomenon of being sick as it manifests itself in the patient's *behavior* and *inner experience.*

Let me characterize this phenomenon by a simple example. Take an individual suffering from a "common cold." He may have various disturbing symptoms, such as headache, temperature, etc. In his everyday life he may not show any essential deviation from the norm. He may not feel well, but yet *not "sick."* If the same individual finds himself in a situation in which he has to do something very difficult and at the same time very important, for example, to take an examination the passing of which is essential for his whole future, we may find a totally different picture. The individual may display a number of unusual physical and mental symptoms, such as sweating, trembling, increase of pulse rate, etc. He may not be able to answer questions that under other conditions he could answer without any difficulty. He appears to be physically and mentally in a state of confusion and disorder, in a condition that we call *catastrophic.* This condition can be observed particularly in patients with chronic diseases, for instance, in those who are suffering from severe brain damage. Due to their mental defect, they are not able to fulfill many normal demands and therefore easily come into catastrophe and experience this subjectively as anxiety. In such cases particularly we can observe the characteristics of being sick.

From the analysis of my many observations, I concluded that the anxiety of the sick individual—as well as the anxiety of the normal individual—is not a reaction of the individual to the experience of failure and the anger involved as a result of it. It is rather the behavior expressive of disorder and anxiety, *i.e.,* the concomitant objective and subjective expressions of the danger in which the sick organism finds itself. The sick person comes into this condition when he is no longer able to actualize his "essential capacities," his essential nature. The danger to which disorder and anxiety belong is the danger of losing his existence in the sense in which we have defined it before.

After a certain time even the severely sick individual reveals a more ordered behavior and is no longer so stricken by catastrophe and anxiety. The pathological condition, however, is not improved, as examination shows. The new order is reached by a change in the environment produced by the people about him, an environment in which the patient is not so exposed to tasks that he cannot fulfill. Thus he is protected from the catastrophic condition. In this way he is better able to use his preserved capacities. He is not "normal" but can do what is required in order to realize his preserved personality. That this self-realization does not correspond to his premorbid condition he is unaware of, due to his mental defect.

ADEQUACY AND THE DEMANDS OF THE WORLD

Thus we can say he is in a state that corresponds in principle to the self-realization of the normal individual, *i.e.*, in a state of adequacy between the demands and the capacities of the individual. Thus a condition is achieved that is experienced as healthy and to which we can ascribe value. This shows that self-realization, and with it value, does not occur exclusively in the fulfillment of definite tasks but is present when an individual is able to do what is demanded of him by the world. Normally the individual is in a state of adequacy with the complicated world, which corresponds to normal human nature. Thus we can say that value is not related to a definite content but to the experience of adequacy between an individual's nature and his world.

Certainly normal healthy life is not always ordered and anxiety is not alien to it. Shocks and anxiety belong to normal life, but as a rule we are able to overcome anxiety by the use of our mental capacities, by foresight, by experiencing the hope that the situation may not be so dangerous, or that we can bear it, or that the danger belongs to life itself. This takes place with the help of one of the most important characteristics of man: *courage*. Courage ultimately reveals its enormous significance for man not in handling the simple difficulties of everyday life but in *overcoming the danger to existence* that the difficulties may bring about. It presupposes the highest capacity of man, his *abstract capacity* through which he differs essentially from all other living things.

CAPACITY TO ENDURE SUFFERING AND SELF-REALIZATION

In respect to the experience of health, the situation is the same as we have described in patients with brain damage or in patients with severe bodily diseases, such as severe heart failure. In the acute conditions they also experience frequent catastrophes and anxiety. Later they, too, can come into a state of order without improvement in the underlying disease. But there exists an essential difference between them and the brain-damaged patients due to the fact that they are aware of the restrictions in their activities and of the shrinkage of their world by the conditions of a regained order, and with that they are aware of their *diminished self-realization* due to *these restrictions* by the protections. They tend, as all mentally normal individuals do, to achieve a self-realization that corresponds to their unchanged personality, their intrinsic nature. They can achieve a higher self-realization only if they can *endure suffering*. They are in a dilemma that demands a *choice* between accepting and enduring suffering and getting fuller self-realization, or *the simultaneous diminution of suffering and of self-realization*.

Certainly we always try to eliminate suffering and especially pain. But it is not the task of therapy merely to reduce mental and physical suffering. One may be inclined to do this because one assumes that the elimination of suffering is an essential or even *the* essential drive of man, as psychoanalysis proclaims in the form of the pleasure principle. But placing this in the foreground would often *not* help the patient. The idea of the pleasure principle, particularly when applied to normal life, overlooks the enormous significance of tension for self-realization in its highest forms. Pleasure, in the sense of relief from tension, may be a necessary state of respite. But it is a phenomenon of "stand-still." It is understandable that one of its theoretical consequences should be the assumption of the "death instinct," the elimination of all tension. But this separates us from the world and therefore reduces the possibility of realizing ourselves.

One can achieve the right attitude toward the problem of the elimination of suffering in patients and in normal individuals only if one considers its significance for self-realization and its relationship to the value of health. If the patient is able to make the choice we have mentioned, he may still suffer but may *no longer feel sick; i.e.,* though somewhat disordered and stricken by a certain anxiety, he is able to realize his essential capacities at least to a considerable degree.

While stressing the significance of this *choice* for regaining "health," we admit that health is not an objective condition which can be understood by the methods of natural science alone. It is, rather, a condition related to a mental attitude by which the individual has to value what is essential for his life. "Health" appears thus as a value; its value consists in the individual's capacity to actualize his nature to the degree that, for him at least, it is essential. "Being sick" appears as a loss or diminution of value, the value of self-realization, of existence. The central aim of "therapy"—in cases in which full restitution is not possible—appears to achieve transformation of the patient's personality in such a manner as to *enable him to make the right choice;* this choice must be capable of bringing about a new orientation, an orientation which is adequate enough to his nature to make life appear to be worth living again.

PSYCHOTHERAPY, VALUES, AND CHOICE

It has often been demanded that psychotherapy keep *free from values.* As far as the therapist's attitude towards the failures of the patient is concerned, this demand is correct. Furthermore the therapist is not supposed to impose his own values upon the patient; but that does not mean that the problem of value has to be, or even can be, totally avoided. Freud as a typical positivist believes that therapy should be based on scientific concepts and methods alone. "All that is outside of science is delusion, particularly religion." Whether or not Freud's own attitude is free of value judgments is debatable. In my opinion the belief in science alone is also based on a value judgment. Freud's emphasis on the significance of pleasure as a driving force in man is certainly based on his special estimation of it for normal life, on the value he sees in the relief of tension.

It would not be helpful if the new orientation of the patient were determined by the values of the therapist. The patient must find his own values, *i.e.*, come to an ordered condition which permits his self-realization to the extent that it satisfies him. The degree of self-realization he attains will depend upon the extent to which he is able to make the choice. This depends upon his previous personality and his mental capacities. Choice is a decision based on the consideration and evaluation of the whole situation, which in turn presupposes a definite mental capacity, the capacity to abstract, particularly in the sense of being able to assume the category of possibility. Patients—such as severely brain-damaged ones—who are impaired in this capacity cannot make the choice. They can achieve, as we said above, some degree of self-realization only if the people around them make the choice for them, arrange the world in such a way that the patient can realize his preserved capacities, as we have explained before. The catastrophic effect of incapacitation here is not eliminated by the patient. The order is achieved by the activity of "others."

All that the individual considers important for a worthwhile life can be of the same significance, for example, religious beliefs or other ideas, that the particular culture considers valuable. But this will be helpful only if it is not used as a simple means for mere relief, but rather represents experiences which belong to the intrinsic nature of the individual, the essentials for his self-realization.

When demands are forced on the individual under the guise of value, this is often a cause of breakdown, as, for instance, in neurotic patients. The restriction involved may be accepted with resentment and the ensuing conflict thus produces anxiety. Something negative cannot be a value. I am aware that the demands issuing from a value may have a negative character in the form of sacrifice of self-realization, etc. But as long as these demands are experienced as something negative, they have little effect and are always debatable. Restriction, sacrifice, is not a real value. Restriction is, as Whitehead has said, the price of value. It becomes valuable only in relation to some real value, *i.e.*, a particular form of self-realization, and acquires a positive character through this relation. Restriction means lack of "being" as long as it is not accepted as a necessity for achieving the best form of self-realization possible for the individual.

We have seen before that the sick patient with the impairment of abstraction can achieve a condition in which his life may have a value for him when he is protected by the people around him. However, the value of his life will then consist of nothing more than survival. He is incapable of full self-realization due to his mental defect, to his impairment of the abstract attitude which is the presupposition for his full self-realization. The sick individual (with an unimpaired abstract capacity) will achieve the latter only by accepting the necessary restriction without resentment. In this respect therapy is of particular significance. The patient learns that he is in principle in a situation not different from the condition in which the healthy individual finds himself.

All human beings have to suffer and to endure suffering. This is due to our difficulty in relation to nature, particularly in relation to other living things and especially to other human beings. As with the patients, so normal individuals can live only if they are helped by others and others are helped by them. The help we give patients in therapy is not an external, merely practical, activity but something that originates in the most characteristic property of man, the tendency to help and the desire to be helped. This is the expression of the original unity of men, which man has lost and must try to regain. Only if he achieves this is he able to realize himself. Man can be an individual only in this unity with the other. Thus self-restriction is the price for being an individual. It has been said that individuality as such is no end in itself, is no value. This is true, but only if one does not see that self-realization is impossible unless the self-realization of the other is guaranteed. What appears in the behavior of severely sick people—that self-realization is possible only with the help of the "other"—is also valid in normal human beings.

Only in a unity with the "other" is the self-realization of the individual guaranteed. Indeed, unity will be effective only if it is not a pseudo-unity, a merely external relationship, but if it is a real renewing of a lost communion. This is ultimately the value which guarantees human existence, *i.e.*, its essential nature.

VALUE AND COMMUNION

From this point of view we must consider all the empirical relationships of the individual when we wish to determine whether we are justified in ascribing to them the character of value. Thus, for instance, there is no doubt that the social organization is a very important factor in man's existence, but not simply, as is often said, because it brings about man's security. Security in itself is no value. Value demands self-restriction. It will help in the process of self-realization not when it arises in an external way, but only when it is based on a communion or when it has at least intrinsic characteristics which permit us to assume that it will develop into a communion.

Social organization itself is not a value, though it may also be a successful means of guaranteeing a certain degree of self-realization. It will never—if it is not communion—satisfy the individual's tendency toward self-realization; it may even bring the individual closer to the breaking point. Only an "adequate" social organization is a value and will be experienced as such. And this requires freedom for individuals to follow the fundamental tendency of man's nature. Indeed, the term organization may then no longer apply. Living in the communion does not mean that one must be like the other; the situation must be such that the individuality of both is assured through living together. Only then will the self-restriction be taken without resentment, which is the basis of all living together. This is the basis not only of social life but of friendship and particularly of *love*.

This living in communion guarantees, on the one hand, the uniqueness of the individual; on the other hand, it makes possible the feeling of responsibility for the other's actions in the attempt to realize oneself. This may appear to justify even the encroachment upon the "other" in the interest of *his* self-realization. The distinction between this behavior and *aggression* cannot be taken too seriously. Aggression never has a positive value, neither for the aggressor nor for those aggressed against. It is essentially a reaction to those situations in which the individual cannot come to terms with the demands of self-realization. Clarity about the phenomenon of aggression is of the greatest significance for any concept of value.

Only in such a situation of communion can *loneliness* be overcome, the isolation of the individual which is a basic hindrance to self-realization. Kant's moral postulate, "We should not do to another what we would not have him do to us," is too abstract, too regulative and negative. The concern about the other's self-realization is a positive tendency of man; when it exists it is an experience, not a demand.

This is not the place to discuss how such a communion may develop. I would like only to stress that it is based on man's highest mental capacity, by which the world is considered from the symbolic point of view. The symbolic aspect is not only the basis—as is often stressed—of the intellectual interpretation of the world; at the same time it communicates the immediate relationship of people to each other. The basic significance of this relationship is often overlooked; or the way it occurs is erroneously considered as irrational and therefore as a dubious guarantee for man's existence.

I would like to summarize my discussion in the following way:

Value is not a characteristic which is secondarily ascribed to something from judgments based on concepts externally determined. Value is a characteristic of the true being of man, of his essence which manifests itself in reality mostly in a somewhat distorted form. It is "being" as it appears in man's self-realization. Man's self-realization is based on the condition of adequacy between the individual's behavior and the "world," the world which is ultimately given in the totality of all individuals but which becomes apparent in the greater or smaller contact with individuals. If it were not an intrinsic potentiality of man's nature to acquire such a state of adequacy, man as we see him, his culture, religion, the problem of value itself would not exist.

We have reached our conclusion through an analysis of health and sickness. Health appears thus as the prototype of value. It may even be considered *the* value, from which all other values experienced under special conditions become comprehensible. It acquires this significance because it guarantees man's self-realization. Because value is *being* as it appears in man, the study of man's intrinsic nature is of the greatest importance for the determination of the nature of value.

I should like to conclude with some words from Immanuel Kant, written in the introduction to his work on logic. These words stress essentially the same significance of the evaluation of man's nature in respect to all human endeavor, *i.e.*, to value:

"What can I know?
"What should I do?
"What may I hope?
"What is man?"

BIBLIOGRAPHY

Goldstein, K., *Human Nature*, Harvard University, 1951.
———, The idea of disease and therapy, *Review of Religion*, March 1949, 229–240.
———, *The Organism, A Holistic Approach to Biology*, American Book, 1939.
———, The smiling of the infant and the problem of understanding the "Other," *J. Psychol.*, 1957, *44*, 175–191.

Is a Science of Human Values Possible?

—————————————————————————— PAUL TILLICH

WHEN I accepted the invitation to address the Conference on New Knowledge in Human Values, I hesitated, because from my early student years on up to the present day I have been an outspoken critic of the philosophy of values. But the tolerant assurance of the organizers of the meeting that they consider the criticism of value theory in itself as a value convinced me that I should express the reasons for my attitude precisely in the frame of such a meeting— and now, in this paper.

THE RISE OF THE PHILOSOPHY OF VALUES

Since I am a victim of the European vice of being unable to think any thought without seeing it in the light of its history, I want to start with a short retrospective analysis of the rise of the philosophy of values in modern thought and a short description of the point where I myself encountered this philosophy.

By some historians Lotze is called the heir of classical German philosophy. This is true insofar as you can call a general, who after a lost battle gathers the battered army into the last possible position of resistance, the successor of formerly victorious generals of that same army. It was Lotze who did just this in the middle of the nineteenth century by introducing the concept of value prominently into the current philosophical discussion. In doing so, he tried to save human dignity from the onslaught of a reductionist, materialistic naturalism. Here he succeeded, and for this he deserves a

189

higher place in the history of philosophy than he is usually accorded. Many schools of value philosophy took over his principle, and more than a hundred years have not annihilated his influence. But Lotze and all those who followed him had to pay a high price: they had to separate the world that we encounter from the world of values in a radical way. Being and value have nothing in common for them: value has no being and being has no value. There is a gap between what is and what ought to be, between what is and what is good. The assumed catastrophe of metaphysics has shown, so they argued, that any attempt to bridge the gap by trying to discover value in being must fail. The leaders of the defeated philosophical army gave up any attempt to regain the lost positions.

They were exclusively defensive; and in all fairness, one must say that their defense of human dignity was their greatness. In my student years, the German philosopher Münsterberg was called to Harvard and became the most influential mediator of the philosophy of values to this country.

But the way in which I personally encountered and passionately rejected the philosophy of values was in the theological realm. The greatest systematic theologian of the nineteenth century after Schleiermacher—Albrecht Ritschl—had reduced the assertions of classical theology to value judgments. In doing this he did in theology what Lotze, upon whom he was dependent, had done in philosophy: he fought a battle of retreat and defense. Before him, and partly during his time, a philosophical theology dependent on Schelling and Hegel controlled the European universities. With the so-called breakdown of the Hegelian system, more precisely with the turning away of the Western mind to scientific, political, and religious positivism, these theologians lost their control, and on most European faculties and later in many American Protestant theological schools, they were replaced by Ritschlians—meaning theologians representing a theory of values as the foundation of theology. When I started my theological studies in 1904, they were the masters in all important theological faculties. But we students and younger people revolted for theoretical as well as emotional reasons. We did not accept the defeat of metaphysics and the flight into the defenses of the value theory as final. *We wanted being.* And the experience of being as the power of being became the existential experience out of which most of my later thinking grew. And today there are almost no traces of the old value theory in European philosophical or theological faculties.

THE SUBJECTIVITY OF VALUE

But now I must leave the historical and autobiographical reports and come to the arguments. It is almost pathetic to see how the philosophers of value tried to overcome one of the main weaknesses of the value theory—its subjective and relative character. They are aware of the fact that the concept of value in its original meaning is related to a valuating subject, and it becomes impossible to escape the conclusion that a theory of values cannot be more than a theory of actual valuations. In order to escape this consequence, they speak of basic values as criteria of a hierarchy of values, or they speak of the *a priori* and absolute character of the ultimate values. They interpret the psychological and sociological conditions of valuating as mere channels through which the objective values enforce our acknowledgment. By this interpretation, values are not invented but discovered.

According to Münsterberg, the value of the world as such is absolute. All valuations can be derived from the demand that there is reality at all. Most instructive in this respect are Max Scheler and Nicolai Hartmann by whom the philosophy of values was driven toward a point at which the ontological question could not be avoided any longer. Neither of them denied the anthropological conditions of the feeling for values and their hierarchies. But both of them insist that this feeling and the human being in whom it occurs is not their cause, but the place and the occasion for their manifestation and for the manifestation of their hierarchical order. Neither should one make the truth of values dependent on their relation to life (*e.g.*, Nietzsche); for life itself stands within the hierarchy of values and not even on the top of it. A higher value may demand the sacrifice of life. According to Hartmann, values are powers with laws of their own. They have a character of being, standing against the desires and interests of the subject who experiences them as values. They have an ideal being in themselves.

Looking at these endeavors of the philosophers of values, I come to the conclusion that the whole theory is wrecked by the necessity of distinguishing between relative values, which can be reduced to valuations, and absolute values, which require another foundation because they command valuations.

Obviously, pragmatism cannot give such a foundation. Consistent pragmatism cannot accept the concept of absolute values at all because it subjects every value to the never-ending test of experience —whatever "test of experience" may mean. But, fortunately, most pragmatism is inconsistent and indulges in a hidden metaphysics, e.g., that of life as growth (citing Dewey) or that of an almost mystical realm above subjectivity and objectivity (citing James), or that of a universal self-affirmation of the will (citing Nietzsche). If I say that they indulged in a metaphysics, this is somehow unfair. For they could not avoid it because it is unavoidable.

There is no way to distinguish valid values from mere valuations other than to show the root of a value in the structure of being itself. Pragmatic tests lead into a vicious circle if the criteria of the texts themselves shall be tested pragmatically. But they lead into ontology if the criteria are derived nonpragmatically. The question we are asked, "Is a science of human values possible?" is identical with the other question: Is an ontological approach to values possible?

My answer is that it is, and even more, it always has been done successfully within the limits of ontology as such. It may be inopportune to call such an approach science, and it might well be that in this semantic question the material question is implied. Therefore, I want to expand a little on this point. If science is understood, as it is being more frequently in recent discussions, in the sense of the German word *Wissenschaft*, a science of values is possible in the sense in which ontology is a science. If, however, science is understood as a cognitive approach according to the pattern of physics, only a science of actual valuation is possible, not a science of values.

ONTOLOGICAL FOUNDATION OF VALUES

What then, we ask, is the ontological foundation of values? Where must we look within encountered reality to discover the source of the ought-to-be in being? The first answer must be a negative one: values cannot be derived from existence. This was the abortive attempt of pragmatism. Values must be derived from essential structures of being which appear within existence, though in a state of distortion.

If we judge the value of a tree not from the point of view of its wood or shade value for us but from the point of view of its potentialities as a tree for itself, we compare its actual state with an image, an *eidos* or an idea that we have of its essential nature. We call it a poor or sick or mutilated exemplar of what, for instance, a pine tree could be. The way in which this *eidos* or essence of tree-hood—which is more than concept—is attained and tested is identical with the way in which an *objective* value in this realm can be known, namely, the value of a tree for itself. This approach combines an ideating and an empirical element. The ideating element, the intuition of the essence within some existing exemplars, has been rediscovered by the phenomenological school; it had controlled most of the ancient and medieval philosophy but had later been lost in the positivistic type of nominalism. The ideating method as rediscovered had limited success in official philosophy (although in practice even the hostile philosophers used it all the time) because it was not able or willing to relate the ideating to the empirical-scientific method. The essential nature of a tree can become the problem of research in which the biological conditions of a perfect tree are imagined and in which the result of this research may change the intuitive picture of the essential nature of such a tree. But the empirical analysis cannot create the image of the perfect tree.

Leaving this example, we turn to man and the realm of ethical values. Man is the valuating subject. But from our presuppositions it follows that man also must become the place where special values receive their ontological foundation. Ethical values are commands derived from the essential nature of man. Human nature is their ontological locus. Therefore, I would say: our knowledge of values is identical with our knowledge of man, of man not in his existential, but in his essential, nature.

If this is true, the ethical value theory is reduced to anthropology in the sense of a philosophical doctrine of man. The ought-to-be which is implied in the objective value is rooted in the essential nature of man. Some examples will illuminate this. If one says that man is a composite of soul and body and that this composition is incidental both for the soul and the body, an ascetic system of values follows. For the soul—considered always as the higher one in this composite—must exercise its role by suppressing an independent development of the bodily values. The historical significance of such an understanding of man's essential nature is immense and well known to every student of ethics and history. If, on the other hand, one says that man is a soul-body unity, as does the Old Testament and genuine Protestantism, a system of values with the emphasis on vitality and the liberation of man from the puritan system of repressing values becomes a necessary consequence. Or, if the function of the unconscious in the dynamics of the personality is stressed, the valuation of his intellectual and will power is reduced in favor of a high valuation of a life in symbols which influence the unconscious. In the opposite view, the conscious center is ultimately responsible for everything and the intellectual values become predominant, disregarding the dynamics of the unconscious.

One cannot compare the validity of values of individuality with values of society without having an image of what man is in both directions. That is, the value of individual uniqueness, which is valid in some respects, is restricted by the way in which the individual person becomes a person only through the encounter with other persons. The tension of these trends becomes manifest in such conflicts as the present one between anticonformist and conformist solutions of the problem individuality-and-society.

No value theory without ontological foundation can solve the conflict between love and justice as it appears in ethics as well as in theology. If one asks the question—Which value is higher, love or justice?—one destroys the authentic meaning of both. If, however, one asks—What is the root of both of them in being-itself?—one can answer: the dynamics of love and the form of justice condition each other. If love is understood as the universal dynamics of life driving toward the reunion of the separated, justice can be understood as the form in which the reunion occurs. This kind of justice, of course, transcends the proportional type of justice which gives retribution positively and negatively in reward and punishment. It is creative justice which transforms by accepting the unacceptable. And creative justice *is* love. Of course, this also presupposes that the idea of love is liberated from its emotional connotations and its merely subjective character. Only if love has ontological roots is its union with justice possible.

The ontological foundation of values guarantees the autonomous process in which they are discovered. Value is man's essential being, put as an imperative against him. The moral imperatives are not arbitrary ordinances of a transcendent tyrant; neither are they determined by utilitarian calculations or group conventions. They are determined by what man essentially is. The moral law is man's own essential nature appearing as commanding authority. If man were united with himself and his essential being there would be no command. But man is estranged from himself, and the values he experiences appear as laws, natural and positive laws, demanding, threatening, promising. Nevertheless, it is not a strange, heteronomous power which gives authority to the law; it is man's own essential being. And because this is the ultimate source of the law, the law has unconditional validity in spite of its changing contents.

From this follows a last consideration about the way in which values can be known: the knowledge of values is identical with the knowledge of one's essential being. And this occurs in two complementary ways, the intuitive and the experiential. Intuitively, man sees the contrast between what he is essentially and what he is actually. This awareness has a predominantly negative character: the basic function of the conscience is to judge, and it applauds and confirms only indirectly. But the intuitive side of the knowledge of values, including the "voice of conscience," is open to error and must be subjected to the continuous criticism of experience, not only the individual experience but the experiences of mankind as they are embodied in its ethical traditions. They are the manifestations of wisdom, the wisdom mankind has acquired in positive and negative experiences. There is no external criterion for the validity of norms that can be applied at will. But there is a continuous tension between the intuitive and the experiential element in the cognition of values. No calculating and measuring method will overcome this situation. One cannot escape the existential risk in the knowing of values. There is no safe place outside the risk that characterizes life in all its dimensions.

BIBLIOGRAPHY

Tillich, P., "Being and Love," in Ruth Nanda Anshen (ed.), *Moral Principles of Action*, Harper, 1952, 661–762.
——, *Love, Power and Justice*, Oxford, 1954.
——, *The Protestant Era*, University of Chicago, 1948.

PART II. COMMENT AND REPLIES

Comment

_____ WALTER A. WEISSKOPF

THE INVITATION to the Conference on New Knowledge in Human Values expressed the "hope *that a science of values is possible.*" With few exceptions, the preceding papers give an affirmative answer. Almost all contributors presuppose—explicitly or implicitly —that an antinomy exists between the dimension of values and the dimension of facts, of life, of existence; but all of them try to establish an interrelation, a union, a harmony between the two dimensions.

There are three different avenues of approach to values in modern thought which are also reflected in the preceding papers. They are based on three different models of thought or images of man which can be called the naturalist, the humanist, and the ontological approach. These three models differ in their methods of acquiring knowledge and in their concepts of reality.

The *naturalist* image emerges from the application of the natural sciences, especially of physics, to the study of man. Its implicit concept of reality is limited to the facts of the world as presented to us by the five senses. Inner experiences, emotions, products of the imagination, thought constructs, values, are considered as a lower type of reality and require factual verification by the senses in order to be acknowledged as real. The method used in arriving at this image of man is the application of logic to observed facts. In terms of the trinitarian schema developed by Weisskopf, the naturalist approach deals with the level of antinomies where the differences between things and dimensions appear given and insuperable in the bright light of logic and factual observation.

The *humanist* image is based on a different method of acquiring knowledge, which can be called a holistic one. It takes into account the totality of human experience, including not only the facts of the sensory order but the inner experiences, the results of imagination, fantasy, and thought. They attempt to grasp the total human situation with its transcendence, consciousness, self-awareness, and freedom. To establish knowledge, the humanists use not only logic and factual observation but empathy and intuition. The humanist image of man tries to include the polar interrelation of the antinomies of human existence which point toward ultimate unity.

The *ontological* image goes one step further. It seeks to transcend the facts of sensory observation and of intuitive experience. It derives its image of man from the analysis of being as such and of the place of human existence in the totality of being. Its concept of reality starts and ends with being itself, to which it attributes the highest reality. It tries to grasp the unity of all polar antinomies within being itself.

The preceding papers cannot all be strait jacketed into one or the other of these models which should be considered as typological classifications, However, they show preponderant traits which relate them to these types of thought. Bronowski and Margenau are mainly naturalists. The psychologists among the contributors (Allport, Fromm, Goldstein, and Maslow) are mainly humanists although they show naturalistic traits in their reasoning; the same applies to the social scientists (Lee, Sorokin, and, to some extent, Weisskopf).

Bertalanffy and Dobzhansky form a link between the naturalists and the humanists. Weisskopf mediates between the humanists and the ontologists. The latter are represented by Tillich and Suzuki.[1]

---

[1] By choosing some of the papers as "ideal types" and others as intermediate links between ideal or prototypes, no evaluation is intended. "Ideal" is used here not with a normative but with a typological meaning; some papers present

THE NATURALISTS

Bronowski goes farthest in the direction of deriving values directly from science. He interrelates science, society, and values. For him, our society is a scientific society. He identifies science with empiricism, and empiricism with society. Our society "more and more commits itself to seeking the truth of its concepts by the correspondence of their consequences with the facts."[2] The scientific method is successful if the consequences derived from the concepts are borne out by the facts. The pattern is taken mostly from classical physics and astronomy. It was calculated that a planet must exist at such and such a point of the planetary system and then the planet was discovered at that place. This is represented as the basic pattern of science and of all knowledge. No doubt is raised as to the certainty of the results of the verification and their unshakeable truth value. All this is tied in with a social situation; society is built on this scientific procedure. Socially, it is success which decides about truth value. An empirical society is one "in which the relation between concept and action is held to be governed wholly by the successful factual outcome."[3] Thus, not only science and society are identified; the modern Western attitude of striving toward success in terms of prediction and control of external events is tied in with science. Science is defined very much in the same terms as technology, and the two are closely linked to society.

Values are derived directly from this social and scientific process. Values are at the same time scientific and social virtues: being committed and seeking the truth, independence of thought and observation, originality, the virtues of tolerating and accepting dissent. All these virtues are directly derived from the scientific process and from the rules governing a society in which the empirical scientific attitude is predominant.

---

the types in greater purity, whereas others contain elements of several models; that does not make any of them better or worse than the others. Neither can the space devoted to the presentation of any one of the contributors be taken as a symptom of preference, or positive or negative evaluation.

[2] In this quotation Dr. Weisskopf refers to Dr. Bronowski's spoken address.
[3] *Ibid.*

Truth is defined entirely in empirical terms and finding the empirical truth is a commitment of society. The commitment to factual truth is a virtue.

The term "empirical" is not defined by Bronowski; it is too well known to require definition. Empirical is the world as presented to us by our senses, even if our senses are helped by instruments. Only what can be seen, heard, touched, smelled, and tasted is empirical. Thinking, concepts, ideas, inner experiences are excluded from this world. Inner experiences, thoughts, ideas, concepts have to be empirically verified—that is, confirmed by factual observation of the senses; otherwise they are revealed as errors and illusions. I may do injustice to Bronowski by thus defining his use of the term empirical; but it is obvious that he assumes empirical, factual verification to be of such an unequivocal, secure, certain nature as routine statements about the sensory world; thus he considers further elaboration unnecessary. This is the usual approach of empiricists, naturalists, and positivists, and it seems appropriate to interpret his use of the term empirical, factual verificaion along the lines of thought of these schools.

The ultimate validation of values is for Bronowski *survival*. "A fundamental value system must fit the society which hopes to live and *survive* by it."[4] Also, values are an instrument of *evolution*. "This set of values has been generated by the single command of truth and has shown itself as a most powerful *instrument of evolution* . . . Values are an instrument of *social* evolution."[5] Thus, values are again derived from facts; *survival*, and whatever is meant by *evolution*, become the supreme values. The idea of survival as such, without any more precise definition, can only be understood in a physiological way, as protection from premature death. It can apply to individuals and society. Individuals have often cherished values which are not at all conducive to individual survival. Dying for one's ideals, sacrificing life for something that is considered of higher value than life, has been a value attitude frequently found

4 *Ibid.*
5 *Ibid.*

in human history. This fact alone does not, of course, prove that survival cannot be the supreme value; the mere fact that it has not always been considered to be the supreme value does not prove anything as to its value character. However, Bronowski and those who consider survival as a supreme value will have to prove and to explain the reasons for this commitment. If the facts are the supreme criterion for the verification of values, the facts of history show that survival has often been rejected as supreme value. Would Bronowski deny that the Christian martyrs who chose death in the arena instead of denying their faith have put the value of faith above the value of survival? And how about those who believe that dying in the service of one's country is a higher value than trying to stay alive at all costs?

If it is the survival of society which is considered as the supreme value, there can be a conflict between individual and social survival. Should the individual survive or die for his country in order to insure the survival of his society? How can this conflict be solved on the basis of a purely factual verification of values? And what is meant by the survival of society? Has Austria survived because there still is a country called Austria? Has the Russia of the Czars survived in the form of the U.S.S.R.? And could there not be higher values than the survival of a group in mere name and form?

Values are undoubtedly an instrument of *evolution*, however evolution is defined. The term evolution is in itself a value concept unless one means by it mere change.

Few people would assert that mere change is a value. It depends upon the direction in which change takes place. If we need a criterion as to how to evaluate change, we need a higher value concept by which we can ascertain whether the direction of change is good or bad. If evolution means change in some direction, this direction would represent such a value concept by which we could evaluate change. That requires a concept different from that of evolution itself. Some describe evolution as a change toward more complexity, refinement, diversification, consciousness, domination of nature, and the like. But are these necessarily positive values? We may all agree that they are; but in this case it is not social evolution which is the highest value but the specific element toward which society evolves and which we evaluate in a positive way.

Margenau is also a naturalist; but whereas Bronowski could be called an empirical realist, Margenau is a hypothetical nominalist who uses an "as if" epistemology. Margenau clearly adheres to a dualism which juxtaposes facts to postulates, theorems, and laws and also to norms. He finds this dichotomy between a conceptual and a factual dimension within the field of science and of values. In the latter field he distinguishes between *factual* and *normative* values. In the field of science, there exists a corresponding dichotomy between the *descriptive* and the *theoretical* sciences.

Factual values are "observable preferences, appraisals, and desires of concrete people. . . . are neither right nor wrong but are facts of observation" (p. 39). "Normative values are the ratings . . . which people *ought* to give to value objects. . . . [normative value claims] . . . . validity, presumes to have suasive force and regulative power. . . . [it] is like a law of nature, idealized, lofty, and universal."

What Margenau distinguishes here as two kinds of values represents perhaps two different approaches to values. Values are norms. A factual or logical statement interconnects two data in the form of an "is"; values and norms interconnect data in the form of an "ought to" or "ought not to" (thou shalt not kill, people ought to love each other, etc.).

These two modes of statements or judgments represent two different realms which can be juxtaposed as values and fact, the "ought to" and the "is," values and nature. The realm of nature is the realm of causality in which one fact is the condition and the cause of another fact. The realm of values is the realm of normative judgments in which a condition is connected with its effect by a "should be." (If a person murders another person, he *should* be punished. If one person is a human being, he *should* love another human being as he loves himself.)

Both the realm of nature and the realm of values refer to the same reality. The statements, "A person loves his neighbor," and "A person should love his neighbor," refer to a world in which people live and coexist. Values belong to one realm and facts to another; but both realms are interrelated insofar as the realm of values points to the realm of facts.

Hartman, quoting G. E. Moore, has called this situation "the root of the naturalistic fallacy." It consists in a confusion between goodness as such, and things that are good. Goodness is of an autonomous nature, *sui generis,* or of a normative character. It refers to a norm which can be applied to natural, factual things. Goodness "is not a natural property . . . though . . . it depends entirely on the natural properties of that which has [goodness]" (p. 18). Thus, values can be said to have a factual and a normative aspect: their content refers to the facts but their special value character points to a specific normative interrelationship between facts.

This enables Margenau to make his distinction between factual and normative values. One can observe, describe, measure the degree of realization of values in the world of facts; one can make statements about the degree to which a moral law is actually conformed to. But it may be misleading to consider the factual and the normative aspects of values as two kinds of *values.* The norm "Love thy neighbor as thyself" *could* be a valid norm even if no single human being were convinced that it is a valid norm and even if nobody conforms to it in his behavior. Its *validity* has nothing to do with its *realization,* although the very content of the norm requires its realization. Statements about the degree of the realization of a norm are not statements about values at all; they are statements about facts related to, pointing to, a norm, a value. Only what Margenau calls normative values can be called values as such.

Margenau compares the two types of values with two types of sciences. "A factual value is like an observation, primary, ubiquitous, and particular" (p. 39); it is ascertained by the same methods as used in the *descriptive* or *classificatory* sciences such as geography. They observe, describe, tabulate, use induction. "A *normative* value is like a law of nature," which is discovered by the theoretical sciences, such as physics. These theoretical sciences aim to "predict"; they "proceed deductively from general premises and . . . arrive at relatively certain knowledge by methods sometimes characterized as casual . . ." (p. 40).

It is doubtful whether the parallel between these two types of sciences and values can be maintained. The two types of sciences are distinguished from each other merely by the degree of precision and ability to predict future events. It may not be quite appropriate to choose as an example for the descriptive sciences, geography, which, as Margenau himself states, becomes a theoretical science in cooperation with geology, astronomy, and nuclear physics. There are also areas in physics which are descriptive. If meteorology is chosen as an example of a descriptive science of lesser precision and certainty, the similarity with a theoretical science is obvious. All sciences, descriptive and theoretical, try to discover regularities which can serve as a basis for prediction. Some have been less successful than others, perhaps because of the multiplicity of variables and the impossibility of laboratory experiments. The common link among all of them is that the validity of their findings must be confirmed by the observed facts, whether derived by deduction or induction.

The dichotomy that Margenau wants to establish exists rather between the objects of all the natural sciences and the facts related to values on the one hand and "normative values" on the other hand. This dichotomy cannot be denied; disagreement exists merely as to where the dividing line should be drawn.

Margenau tries to prove that the methods of derivation of laws and of verification are the same in the field of values and in the natural sciences. Scientific laws are based on the postulates which are to some extent arbitrarily chosen. Scientific propositions are not "universally valid . . . testable by everyone, 'objective,' unrelated to commands or commitments . . ." (p. 45). They are based on formulae to which the scientist commits himself. The scientific process "starts with a *postulate,* spins out by analytic means the consequences of the postulate in the form of *theorems* (sometimes called laws) and finally checks these against immediate experience through *verification*" or confirmation (p. 47). This verification or confirmation is not a simple "look and see" procedure; it entails an element of choice, agreement within the possible error of the measurement, and other conventions.

The value process contains similar elements; the postulate is a command, an imperative, an exhortation, a directive to which a person is committed. The command gives content to a value, the commitment makes it effective. Margenau makes it very clear that the command and the commitment cannot be derived by the methods of science. Science cannot prove that happiness, evolution, progress are values; it cannot deduce values from human nature and drives because its findings do not imply any commitment such as fulfill your nature, "follow your drives." (p. 44).

According to Margenau, commands originate with heteronomous authorities such as God, a monarch, legislative bodies, any authority of "a known and specifiable origin" so that "the commands must engage commitment" (p. 44). These sources of values are outmoded today. Therefore, we must again look at science and transplant "into value theory that formal feature which imparts universal acceptance and persuasive power to science" (p. 45).

Both scientific laws and values can be verified, confirmed, validated by the observed facts. In science, prediction—based on laws, derived from postulates—is checked by factual observation. In the fields of values, the validation of such ethical norms as the ten commandments, *the principle of verification which becomes a principle of validation* can be found in the *survival* of the group which observed the ten commandments. Not only can the validation take place through the test of survival of the group, but this test, "can be replaced by others such as *maximum happiness* for all members of the group, certain kinds of *utilitarian* requirements, the acquisition of *material wealth*, and so on . . ." (p. 49, ITALICS MINE).[6]

---

[6] *Allport* agrees with *Margenau* that "although moral values cannot be derived from natural data nor from science, they can in some sense be validated (confirmed or disconfirmed) by the activity of science" (*Allport*, p. 137).

This procedure of establishing an interrelation between values and facts through the principle of verification is difficult to maintain in the light of Margenau's previous discussion. He points out with great lucidity that there is an antinomy between facts and laws and facts and values and that the normative commands and the commitment to these commands cannot rest on the findings of science. Thus, he asserts that the *validity* of values is *not* dependent on the facts to which values are related. The ten commandments are valid values if one believes in God who has promulgated them on Mount Sinai; and not because they insured the survival of the tribe of Israel (assuming that they did). In contrast to the laws of science whose validity depends on factual confirmation, normative laws can be valid in the logical sense regardless of confirmation by facts. Or, the "facts" which confirm normative laws are the facts of their origin, the source of the command; whereas the facts which confirm scientific laws are the facts to which they are being applied. Values are confirmed in their validity by the "facts" of their promulgation; scientific laws are confirmed by the facts of their realization. This is the essence of Margenau's own argument.

By searching for a factual principle of verification for values, Margenau actually hypostatizes such ideas as survival, maximum happiness, utilitarian principles, and the laboratory of human history as values. He commits himself to these values and attributes to them the character of a comamnd. Thus, he does not confirm values by facts but derives values from ideas which he has invested with a value character, that is, from "higher" values. Much of this is confirmed by other contributors, some of them natural scientists. *Goldstein* explicitly rejects survival as a supreme value. His concept of self-realization transcends mere survival. He likewise rejects security, which may be said to be part of survival values. Goldstein's ideas of self-realization as a supreme value do not imply the avoidance of tension, anxiety, and suffering.

Dobzhansky sees clearly that man is not merely an animal but has the ability to transcend himself. Therefore, values cannot be derived from biological processes and from evolution. Evolution is utilitarian, opportunistic, not planned in advance and appallingly myopic. The genes invest man with abilities implanted under conditions very different from those under which he lives. It is his ability to think in terms of symbols and abstractions, his ability to have a culture, which makes man what he is. His values are an instrument of adaptation but cannot be derived from his natural conditions. "The origin of human values through natural selection is an over-simplification which can hardly be sustained" (p. 79).

Bertalanffy asks explicitly the question: Can human values be derived from and reduced to biological values?—and answers it with a resounding "No." Thus, a majority of scientists in this symposium rejects the derivation of values from facts—which is the object of the natural sciences. Even Margenau (like *Allport*) belongs to this group because he does not derive but merely tries to confirm values through facts and ultimately rejects eudemonistic, hedonistic, and utilitarian confirmation of derivation of values.

The preceding analysis of the naturalist approach leads to the conclusion that, on the level at which their discussion moves, a relation between science and values is difficult to establish. The naturalist discussion takes place on the level of antinomies; facts and logic are kings; here the differences between things, ideas, concepts, and dimensions form discordant antinomies, and no degree of refinement and sophistication seems to be able to bring them together. There is one escape from this negative conclusion. If the *source* of the command and of the commitment is the basis of the validity of values, is that not also a "fact" from which values can be derived? The answer is, at the same time, yes and no. Logically, it is not the "fact" that God issued the ten commandments that makes them valid but the belief in God and the investment of his command with a binding value character. A unity of fact and value in the source of the command could only be established if God is conceived as a form of reality in which facts and values, actualities and potentialities, existence and essence are combined in harmony. The conception of such a unity seems to be impossible to antinomic naturalist thought, with its self-chosen confinement to the instruments of factual observation and logic.

THE HUMANISTS

The humanist approach to values forms a link between the naturalists and the ontologists. They share with the naturalists the belief that values are, in some way, derived from life, from nature, from human existence. But they differ somewhat from the naturalists in the way they view the human situation; their point of view resembles that of the ontologists because they include elements of transcendence in their image of human existence. And the main difference between naturalists and humanists is that the latter have found a unifying principle in the human self.

The ideas of values centering around mental health and self-realization may serve as a guide to unravel the naturalist and the humanist trend. Maslow puts self-realization in the center of his argument. He sides squarely with those who consider a scientific ethic possible. At the outset, he derives value principles from the "wisdom of the body" and the physiological trends towards homeostasis (pp. 120 ff.). In this respect he is in disagreement with Bertalanffy and Dobzhansky, who clearly state that moral values cannot be derived from biological ones; also with Allport and Margenau who merely confirm but do not derive moral values from biological facts. Maslow gets into a logical difficulty when, after pointing to the wisdom of the body, he ascertains that there are good and bad choosers not only among people but even among chickens. If the wisdom of the body cannot even guide a chicken to the good life, how about human beings?

In Maslow's concept of self-realization, however, more is included than the wisdom of the body and physiological instincts. Maslow describes self-realization in terms of the tendency of an organ system to express itself, to function. It accomplishes the subjective feeling of harmonious, integrated, uninhibited, satisfying functioning that Maslow equates with psychological health. Self-actualization is identified with integration, psychological health, individuation, autonomy, creativity, productivity; it is the ultimate human goal. Self-actualization is propelled by the innate tendency toward growth. There is within the human being "a pressure toward unity of personality, toward spontaneous expressiveness, toward full individuality and identity, toward seeing the truth rather than be blind, toward being creative, toward being good, . . ." (p. 126). All these forms of self-actualization imply "good values . . . serenity, kindness, courage, . . . honesty, love, unselfishness, and goodness" (p. 126).

It is obvious that the concepts of self-actualization and psychological health contain value elements. What is good functioning? What is creativity and productivity? Why are such generally recognized virtues as kindness, love, unselfishness the result of self-actualization and why does Maslow exclude such obvious phenomena of "self-realization" as aggression, destruction, hostility, domination, egotism? Are productivity and creativity in an anti-social direction, are crime, exploitation, and war, a part of self-actualization? We need a criterion of a higher logical order to separate the positive from the negative strands in self-actualization. Maslow does not use the term self-actualization to mean simply living out any and all tendencies in the human person; he discriminates between good and bad tendencies.

Maslow insists that his goals of self-actualization are derived from the scientific observation of self-actualizing people. "I do not say 'He *ought* to choose this or that' but only 'Healthy people, permitted to choose, are *observed* to choose this or that'" (p. 128). He is thus referring to what Margenau calls "factual values" and not to any normative values. How did Maslow choose his healthy people? Some normative criterion for health must have been behind his choice, consciously or unconsciously, explicitly or implicitly. Any distinction between healthy, self-actualizing people, and neurotic, sick people requires a normative criterion for health in the same way as a distinction between good and bad choosers requires such a criterion. Maslow points to the fact that the good choosers among the chickens become "stronger, larger, more dominant" (p. 121).

In this case, Maslow considers strength, large size, dominance, as a value and as the normative criterion on the basis of which he calls the chickens who attained these goals "good choosers." This is perfectly legitimate procedure; but the choice of "good chickens" is derived from the implicit normative value judgment and not vice versa. The concepts of health and self-actualization, like the concept of "good choosers," imply normative value judgments, without which they would not have any meaning. To sum up: neither the concept of mental or psychological health nor the concept of self-actualization in itself seems to be an appropriate scientific basis for values because these concepts are based on implicit value judgments which are not derived from the scientifically observed facts. The concept of health used by Maslow and other psychologists (*e.g.*, Allport and Goldstein) is a normative concept. Thus, it still leaves open a gap between facts and values. It seems, then, that the psychologists who center their value theories on the concept of self-actualization seem to be caught in the same antinomic predicament as the naturalists.

However, there is a basis of difference. The naturalists and the humanists differ in the scope of their views on human reality. The humanists include elements which cannot be grasped by the purely logical and factual methods of the naturalists. The picture of man arrived at by the humanists with the help of introspection, intuition, and empathy is all-inclusive, not partial, as the one of the naturalists. This can be seen in Fromm's analysis of the human situation. He describes it as a state of distortion and separation. "Man is torn away from the primary union with nature . . . Having at the same time reason and imagination, he is aware of his aloneness and separatedness" (p. 151). He needs ties with his fellow men. He needs love and union. He has "the urge to transcend the role of the creature . . . by becoming a 'creator' (p. 153). "Man can be defined as the animal that can say 'I,' that can be aware of himself as a separate entity . . . man needs . . . a sense of identity" (p. 157). "The fact that man has reason and imagination leads . . . to the necessity . . . for *orienting himself in the world intellectually"* (p. 159).

Here, the concept of reality has been enlarged to include not only nature but man. It is recognized that man is partly nature and partly more than nature. Through his memory, his imagination, his consciousness, self-awarenesses, and reason, man transcends the conditioned, finite realm of nature, although he is part of this conditioned, finite realm. This is recognized by the humanists.

In a way, humanists and naturalists have the same premises: values can be confirmed by reality. They differ, however, in respect to their definition of reality. The naturalists include only the non-human reality, or, insofar as they include human reality, they include only those aspects of it which are isomorphic with the reality of nature, the finite, the conditioned, the realm of necessity. The humanists include those aspects of human reality which cannot be subsumed under the finite, the conditioned, the necessary, such as memory, imagination, fantasy, consciousness, self-awareness, and reason and the human ability to transcend the given, conditioned, finite situation.

The difference between the reality concept of the naturalists and of the humanists stems perhaps from the difference in their backgrounds. The naturalists, being natural scientists, are not accustomed to deal with all the "facts" of human existence. They deal habitually with phenomena without consciousness, self-awareness, and reason. Therefore, they are somewhat inclined to neglect these aspects of human existence.[7]

The difference is often one in style rather than in the results of thought. Both, naturalists and humanists, try to derive values from reality; but they use different methods of knowledge and arrive, therefore, at a different concept of reality.

This different conception of reality of the humanists is reflected

[7] This does not apply to some of the natural scientists among the contributors. Bertalanffy and Dobzhansky, for instance, make a clear-cut distinction between nature and man and emphasize man's reason and ability for symbolic expression as his distinguishing characteristic.

in their ideas on self-actualization and growth. Their outlook is geared to *man in his totality*. Psychological health and self-actualization is tied in with the *human person*. The human person forms a unity which is different from the entities found in nonhuman nature. All organisms are centered wholes; but man is a centered entity with self-awareness and the ability to transcend his environment and himself. In his person, man at the same time includes the given situation and transcends the given situation. In the human person, antinomies are in polar interrelation; factually and logically different dimensions are united within the entity of the human self. Man in his person, his centered, self-conscious self, forms that *unity of opposites* which is sought for by all those who are trying to interrelate facts and values. In man, facts and values are one. There is a difference between relating values to the human person as a whole and relating values to partial aspects of human existence. If values are rooted in this totality, the arguments based on the different dimension of facts and values do not apply.

Within the human person values and facts are united even if the individual suffers from inner conflicts of values. The very conflict, the very antinomy, is a part of the entity that we call a person. C. G. Jung has shown how personalities often balance within themselves one tendency by another one: an unconsciously emotional person may balance this aspect of his personality by an extremely rational, logical philosophy and mode of action.[8]

The person itself is the unity within which such antinomic tendencies as facts and values are united.

The term self-actualization should not be interpreted in a naturalistic fashion to mean the living out of a variety of innate instincts. It means the existential realization of a unity which is potentially pre-existent in the human person. It implies balance and integration and points to the union of opposites, the essence of ultimate values. The theme of union recurs again and again in the preceding papers. When Allport considers values as formulae for the handling of con-

[8] C. G. Jung, *Psychological Types*, H. G. Baynes, Jr., Harcourt, Brace & Co., 1924. See Jung's analysis of Tertullian and Origines, *op. cit.*, pp. 15–29.

flicts through the harmonious integration of interests, when he advocates the principle of inclusion, he has in mind such a union of opposites. All the supreme values that Fromm derives from the human situation, such as love, creativity, rootedness, and the tying together of the universe in form of a frame of orientation and an object of devotion, imply union and harmonization. Goldstein talks about communion with others as a prerequisite of well being, about self-realization in terms of wholeness and communion with nature. In Lee's opinion the open self is a prerequisite for the reunion with the other.

Self-realization implies the rejection of any repressive value system which completely rejects one aspect of human existence in favor of another. Allport also rejects value systems of renunciation or negation. Self-actualization as used by Maslow, Goldstein, Kepes, and others implies an integrative value system which synthesizes opposites and affirms individuality. The supreme value is the "high nirvana" (Maslow), the union of opposites on a higher plane than on the level of the antinomies.

This is also confirmed by Hartman's definition of a good thing as one which fulfills its concept applied to the human person. The concept, the idea, the essence of the human person is a composite of natural traits and of tendencies which transcend the natural. A good person then is one in which all these elements are balanced. This leads to the important conclusion that human tendencies should not be repressed but counterbalanced by and unified with opposite tendencies. As Sorokin points out, the counterbalancing amalgamating force is love. It is the unifying element within the human person. Sorokin gathers together all the strands of knowledge which emphasize the unifying power of love. Love is a driving element even in biological evolution. It is a countervailing power against suicidal tendencies, against anomic loneliness. It is a life-sustaining factor, a support for growth and human strength. The "deficiency of . . . love is . . . responsible for . . . mental disorders" (*Sorokin*, p. 8). It is the tie that holds societies together. Love is union: union with oneself, with the other, union with the universe. It is the force that

operates within the individual to harmonize the opposing tendencies and to heal and overcome the split inherent in human existence. Love means acceptance of oneself and of others in the totality
of their being. Love embraces all; it does not mean that we accept
only partial aspects of ourselves, of others, of the world, but that
we accept the whole and find it good. *Hartman's* logical derivation
of the world as good leads to the same conclusion. "Badness . . . is
. . . the incompatibility of things . . ." (p. 25). The concept of the
world is the unity of the whole. Unity is good and unity is established by love. The function of love is to purify the "bad" by counterbalancing and uniting it with the good. If aggression is bad, it is
purified by channeling it into the productive channels of work and
creative action. This is the result of love because aggressive action
becomes creative action if one unites oneself in love with the object
of action. The Freudians have called this "sublimation." This is
another term for the amalgamation of opposing tendencies with the
help of love. The murderous, aggressive, dominating, hostility-
charged forces of the personal unconscious become fused with the
loving, creative, altruistic ones by loving union. And self-realization
refers to this process of love and union. (For Kepes, as for Maslow
and Hartman, not only love but also art is a way to union.)

All human needs distinguished by Fromm imply love and union.
Man needs new ties with his fellow man; they can only be established by love, that is, by union with something outside the self, but
without impairing the integrity of one's own self. The need for
creativity and transcendence should be satisfied positively by
creation and not negatively by destruction, although destruction of
life is also a form of transcendence. The need for rootedness again
is satisfied by love and work, and not by a regressive craving for the
mother womb inspired by fear of life. The need for a sense of
identity can only be positively satisfied by individuation which
involves love of oneself, union with oneself, and not by passive
identification with clan, group, class, society or by automaton conformity. The need for intellectual orientation is satisfied by an objective realistic frame of reference which includes the whole of

reality and an object of devotion which gives meaning to his existence and position in the world; it implies re-unification of self and world. Thus from an analysis of the human situation and the needs created by this situation emerge the ultimate values of love, creativeness, participation without impairment of individuation in the value system of the humanists.

THE ONTOLOGISTS

Tillich, an ideal-type representative of the ontological approach, rejects at the outset the naturalistic separation between the world we encounter and the realm of values. He answers in the affirmative the question that this symposium set out to answer: a science of values is possible. This, however, requires a redefinition of science; the affirmative answer is valid only if ontology is considered as science. *Values are derived from the essential structure of being.* In human existence the essence of being is found in its *distorted form;* but being itself contains the *eidos,* the essence of things and persons. This *eidos* is more than a mere logical concept. The ideatic element of being cannot be grasped merely through factual observation, nor through logical conceptualization, but only through intuition of the essence (the *Wissenschaft* of the phenomenologists). The ideational grasping of essences is a rational process. It is related to, but not identical with, the empirical scientific method: "The essential nature of a tree can become the problem of research in which the biological conditions of a perfect tree are imagined and in which the result of this research may change the intuitive picture of the essential nature of such a tree. But the empirical analysis cannot create the image of a perfect tree" (p. 193).

One could relate this statement with Hartman's thesis that *"a thing is good when it fulfills the definition of its concept"* (p. 00). Tillich states explicitly that the essence, the *eidos,* is more than a concept. It seems to me that *Hartman's* definition of the good as the fulfillment of a concept comes very near to this derivation of values from the essence of things. The difference lies perhaps mainly in the method of apprehension and the objective reality value attributed to the *eidos*. *Hartman* refrains from investigating how concepts are formed and how they come into existence. The way concepts arise lies outside of his frame of reference. He sees the formation of concepts as an accidental, naturalistic, conditioned process, caused by historical, social, psychological factors. It seems also that he considers the grasping of the definition of a concept as a purely logical process, carried out with the help of analytical, logical intelligence. For *Tillich*, the *eidos* is part of the essential nature of being; it is rooted in being itself; it has an objective, unconditional existence; it "is," independent of natural and conditioning factors. It can be grasped, not by logic and factual observation alone, but by intuition, by ontological reason which grasps being itself. Thus, the difference lies in the reality character of this *eidos* and in the method of its apprehension. There is, however, a similarity between the concept of Hartman and the *eidos* of Tillich. Both refer to an essence, to something that is different from the actuality of a thing; it has a normative, a transcendent character.

Tillich answers the question posed by Margenau: What is the source of the commanding character of values? Margenau uses the philosophical armament of the nominalist and of the philosopher—the "as if." The moral commands are more or less arbitrary assumptions, postulates, hypotheses, in the same way as the presuppositions of scientific theories are arbitrary; to validate them, factual verification is necessary. Margenau's theory requires the command of an heteronomous authority such as God, a monarch, etc., and utilitarian verification on the basis of utilitarian principles such as survival, greatest happiness of the greatest number, maximum of wealth, etc. Tillich rejects both the heteronomous derivation of values from "the arbitrary ordinances of a transcendent tyrant," and values as "determined by utilitarian calculations or group conventions" (p. 195). Values are autonomous because they are *rooted in man's essential being*. They have a command and imperative character because "the moral law is man's . . . essential nature appearing as commanding authority" (p. 195). The imperative, command nature of values stems from the estranged state of existence in which man finds himself: "If man were united with himself and his essential being, there would be no command. But man is estranged from himself and the values he experiences appear as laws, natural and positive laws, demanding, threatening, promising" (p. 195). The ontologists explain the imperative, commanding form of moral values by the existential split between essence and existence. This line of thought refers to the trinitarian structure of antinomy, polarity, and ultimate unity. On the antinomic level, man's exisence is distorted, estranged, separated from his essence; a conflict exists between values and facts, values and human reality, human essence and human existence. An ontologically oriented anthropology will recognize the polar interrelations of essence and existence, of values and being; and it will also understand that the normative character of values stems from this existential situation. Thus, the seemingly inseparable gulf between the "ought to" and the "is" is ultimately derived from a factual situation, namely, the estrangement, the distortion of human existence in relation to its essence. Ultimately, values are part of the facts of reality, of being; only through the existential distortion are they made to appear as separated. The separation of fact and value is a special case of an ontological separation, the separation of human existence from ontological essence. And ultimate unity is seen in being itself, in that realm, in that sphere in which all estrangement is dissolved, in which essence and existence, fact and value, being and potentiality are united and harmonized. In that final ultimate sphere and realm, the conflict is dissolved; everything "is," and values and facts are not part of being, but they are being itself.

This does not mean that the conflict, the antinomy, the dichotomy is shifted from the one between fact and value to the one between essence and existence. In the dichotomy of fact and value the two spheres are qualitatively different. Facts are phenomena of the sensory world and values are thought concepts with a qualitatively normative character. The dichotomy of existence and essence is antinomic but polar and harmonized, embraced in an ultimate unity. The formulation of the antinomy in terms of existence and essence makes both realms, the dimension of existence and the dimension of essence, in a way homogeneous and unified; they are both dimensions of being.

However, the humanist formulation and the ontological formulation both lead to the conclusion that values are based on anthropological knowledge, on knowledge about man. Only a correct image of man will lead to a correct knowledge of man's essential goodness which is the basis of values. Tillich presents a few examples as to how the right and the wrong image of man can influence our knowledge of ultimate values. An image of man as a mechanical composite of soul and body will lead to a repressive, puritanical, ascetic value system in which the soul will have to dominate and repress the body. An image of man as a body-soul unity will lead to a value system "with the emphasis on vitality and the liberation of man from the puritan system of repressing values. . . ." (p. 194). A mechanistic picture of man as a mechanistic composite of conscious and unconscious mind will lead again to a value system in which the unconscious is repressed and dominated by the conscious center. A unitarian image of man as a union of conscious and unconscious elements will lead to an acknowledgment of the importance of unconscious factors and symbols. It will stress not merely the importance of conscious control but also the necessity of opening up the mind to the influences of the unconscious, which is a source not only of demonic distortions but also of all creativity, of all symbols, and the entering door to the unconditional and the absolute. A purely individualistic image of man as a purely autonomous person will derive all values of participation, cooperation, altruism, and love from the self-interest of the individual. In such an image participation encounter with others is not an essential element of human existence. The basis is removed for all cooperative, participating, altruistic values and for love. An image of man in which the formal elements of existence are completely separated from the dynamic elements will never grasp the interrelations between love and justice; for on the basis of such an image the two will be in eternal conflict with each other. Only the understanding that, in human existence, form and dynamics are mutually interdependent and stand to each other in polar interrelation can lead to the recognition that "the dynamics of love and the form of justice condition each other" (p. 195). In all these examples the union of opposites plays a decisive role.

It may not be too far-fetched to identify essence as used by the ontologists with the self-actualization of the psychological humanists. What is being actualized is not certain isolated trends of the human organism but a well-rounded entity, a Gestalt, an essence. This entity does not include any and every drive and tendency present in human beings. It encompasses only those traits that are *essentially* human. Human existence and human essence are not identical, but human existence is related to human essence *in being*, and not only in the form of the hypothetical connection of an "ought to." Human essence forms a holistic Gestalt in which the totality of what is human is included, but without its distortion in actual existence. It has the character of a Platonic idea and is related to existence in the same way in which the *eidos* is related to its specific realizations— e.g., the *eidos* of a circle to actually drawn circles. The striving for self-realization can be interpreted as the striving for the realization of human essence.

The concepts of self-realization and of essence have also in common the holistic, balancing, integrating, harmonizing character. All of Tillich's examples in which he shows the way towards a derivation of values from a correct image of man point in this direction. Union between dynamics and form, between individualization and participation, between love and justice is the ultimate goal. And here we find the focal point of general agreement between all contributors, in spite of the many differences in detail and method: union established through love emerges as an ultimate value in all the approaches of the naturalists, the humanists, and the ontologists.

To bring the difference and similarities between the three approaches to the problem of values down to one somewhat over-simplifying formula: the naturalists move on the level of the antinomies; the humanists stress the polarity of the antinomies and their unity on a purely human level; and the ontologists attribute a higher reality value to the dimension of unity. They all strive for unity through love but within different dimensions.

To those who believe in cultural relativity it may come as a surprise to see how well a non-Western philosophy of values fits into this over-all pattern. Suzuki rejects science and technology. He definitely denies that science with its precision can be the source of values. However, he joins the other contributors in the final conclusion that values and being are interrelated. They are not only interrelated but one. His approach is definitely ontological, and not very different from the one of a Western ontologist such as Tillich. "The good is just-so-ness." "The 'good' is the isness of things. . . . When a thing is genuinely in its isness, it is valuable" (p. 95). All this means that values are rooted in being itself, in the just-so-ness, in the isness of things. Underlying is the idea that there is a dimension of being in which all differentiations are negated and harmonized, in which essence and existence "the human and the divine are one . . ." (p. 96).

There is obvious agreement between the ontologists (Tillich, Suzuki, and Weisskopf) about the dialectical structure of existence, In line with Western tradition, Tillich and Weisskopf stress the rational character of this dialectical structure, whereas Suzuki as an Easterner, does not hesitate to reject rationality insofar as it implies precision, definability, and verifiability. In order to tell about the experiences belonging to ultimate reality, we will have to resort to those extraordinary expressions which are "paradoxical or contradictory or non-sensical or full of absurdities" (p. 102). This, however, may be nothing but a different style of talking about the dialectical structure which can only be understood if one leaves aside certain laws of logic. On the level of the antinomies the "law of the excluded middle term"—and the "law of contradiction" do apply; but one could maintain that on the level of polarity and ultimate union these laws are repealed. That does not mean that one cannot talk rationally about these dimensions and especially about being itself. Dialectics is a form of rationality; and Suzuki himself states that the language of the apparently "non-sensical" Zen stories will tell more *precisely* or more *definitely* about ultimate reality.

Love is union; and, at the same time, surrender and salvation of individuality. The Western humanists and ontologists stress the salvation and the maintenance of individuality; Suzuki stresses the surrender. He is, however, in agreement with such a typical Western philosopher as William James when he talks about the necessity of being "twice born," of being crucified and then regenerated, of the paradise that must be lost and regained—we must die once while living and live a new life.

Death and rebirth in a spiritual sense, individualization and participation in amalgamated harmony, are the essence of love. From the deliberations of this symposium emerges union through love as the ultimate value. And there may be no more fitting ending for this book than the saying from the Zen story: "Have a cup of tea, O my brother-Monk."

Reply to Professor Weisskopf

DR. WEISSKOPF's three different approaches to values—*the naturalist, the humanist,* and *the ontological*—do not cover the fourth, *the integral theory of values.* This integral theory appears to me to be in itself unifying all the other three approaches, and as such it may be more adequate than any of the three conceptions. Since, in my paper, I hardly touched upon the integral theory of values, developed in several of my works,[1] it may be advisable to give here its terse outline in the form of the black-and-white theses.

1. *The concept of value presupposes the concept of reality* in the sense that only what is real can be valuable, and what is nonreal (in any sense, form, and mode of Being) is not a value. "The nonreal value" is self-contradictory and is equivalent to "pseudo-value" or "no value" at all.

2. On the other hand, *the concept of reality is somewhat broader than that of value* because analytically we can think of "the value-less reality" as a genuine reality, whereas it is hardly possible to think of "the nonreal value" as a true value. This means that the category of value is superimposed upon, covers, and can be applied

---

[1] Cf. P. Sorokin, *Social and Cultural Dynamics*, vol. II, chaps. 1–12; vol. IV, Chap. 16; in the abridged, one-volume edition of this work, Chaps. 13, 14, 24, 41; "Integralism Is My Philosophy," in Whit Burnett (ed.), *This Is My Philosophy*, Harper, 1951; *Fads and Foibles in Modern Sociology and Related Sciences* (Henry Regnery Co., 1956).

only to a part of reality. This part can be designated by the term *reality-value*.

3. The integral theory views *the total reality* and *the total value* as the infinite X and X*a* of numberless qualities, quantities, and modes of being: spiritual and material, eternal and temporal, unchangeable and ever-changing, personal and superpersonal, one and many, spatial and spaceless, the littlest than the little, and the greatest of the great. In this sense it is the veritable *mysterium tremendum* and the *coincidentia oppositorum* (reconciliation of the opposites). In their infinite plenitude, the total reality and the total value cannot be adequately defined by any concept or described by any words or signs. In their inexhaustible plenitude they are unutterable, undefinable, and unthinkable by the finite human mind.

4. However, in their main aspects they can roughly be grasped by us because we are also an important part of the total reality and the total value. Of their innumerable modes of being, four differentiated forms appear to be most important: *a*) empirical-sensory; *b*) rational-mindful (or logico-mathematical); *c*) supersensory-superrational; *d*) the fourth—the integral-mode of being of reality-value—represents a harmonious unification of these three modes of being into one consistent whole—richer, fuller, and nearer to the infinite plenitude of the total reality-value than each of these single differentiations.

5. *The empirical form of reality* is perceived by us through our sense organs and their extensions: microscopes, telescopes, etc. The *empirical kind of reality-values* becomes a part of our sensory life and of its values not so much through rational intellection as much as through the actual experience of them as a stream of diverse pains and pleasures, sensations and perceptions, images and memories, emotions and feelings, biological tensions and relaxations. These reality-values are partly reflexological-instinctive, partly acquired; partly unconscious and partly conscious; they are neither rational nor irrational (but arational). Empirical science, including the empirical science of values, is largely preoccupied with cognition of the sensory reality-value.

6. *The rational realm of reality-value* consists of the phenomena and relationships—in the cosmic and the man-made universe—which display the tangible marks of rationality, are understandable and justifiable rationally, that is, by rational-logical and mathematical thought. In the physical and biological fields all the phenomena and relationships that exhibit cosmic harmony, natural order, causal or probabilistic uniformity, cosmic beauty (such as a sunset or a starry night), and rational utility—in brief, all the reality-values that appear as though created by the rational creator (by God-the Mathematician, to use Jeans' expression) belong to the rational reality-values.

In the human universe the rational reality-values are represented by all the rational phenomena discovered and created by the rational or a consistent logico-mathematical thought of man. Such are: a large part of logically consistent science, especially mathematics and logic; all forms of rational philosophy, rational religion, rational ethics, law and fine arts, rational economics and politics, rational applied arts: sports, medicine, agriculture, technology, rational human conduct, and forms of social and cultural organizations. All these cultural reality-values exist and function not only as a system of meaningful propositions but also as objectified and socialized "sensory" reality-values in the form of books, libraries, instruments, pictures, sculptures, buildings, funds, and human groups of scientists, philosophers, artists, politicians, etc., who create, use, react to and act upon these reality-values. And a large part of all these cultural systems—of all truly great scientific, philosophical, religious, aesthetic, ethical, legal, and other meaningful systems—are logically or aesthetically consistent in their propositions or style. A large part of these rational cultural reality-values have been discovered, cognized, and created by the rational, *i.e.*, logico-mathematical, thought in all forms of logic and mathematics.

7. Finally, *the suprasensory-suprarational form of reality-values* is the least known mode of being. The glimpses of this class of reality-values are given to us by true suprasensory-suprarational "intuition," "divine inspiration," or "flash of enlightenment" of all

the great seers, sages, and creative geniuses in all fields of cultural creativity. This realm of reality-values is the least susceptible to definition or description by words or signs. Very symbolically and vaguely it has been designated by such terms as Tao, Yen, Zen, "the Kingdom of God," Plato's realm of "ideas-forms," or by the terms "the ineffable," "the supreme," "the highest," "the divine" forms of reality-value. Quite generally this class of reality-values is viewed as the center or the source of the highest creativity known to man. Even more, *it is creativity at its highest, purest, and best.* Being infinitely finer and greater than the merely rational and sensory creativity, the suprasensory-suprarational creativity ranges all the way from that of the infinitely supreme, passing all human understanding, creativeness of the Cosmic Creator, up to the creativity of the greatest human geniuses in all fields of cultural activities. Even within the range of human creativity, it is as much the superior of the sensory and the rational creativity, as are Bach's, Mozart's, or Beethoven's masterpieces in comparison with the fourth-class compositions of professors who know all the *rational* rules of composition of great musical *chef-d'oeuvres;* or as are the masterpieces of Homer and Shakespeare, of Plato and Aristotle, of Phidias and Michelangelo, of Galileo and Newton, of Jesus and Buddha in comparison with the submediocre achievements of the pedestrian, rational fiction writers, rational and empirically minded professors of philosophy, rational sculptors and architects, rational scientists and missionaries. A mere sensory experience and rational knowledge of how to create the great masterpieces is not enough for becoming their creator. To be such a creator one must be a genius; and genius is another name for the suprasensory-suprarational creative grace. Only those who are blessed by this grace in abundance become the "few chosen and anointed" creators. These geniuses unanimously testify to the fact that their discoveries, inventions, or masterpieces have been started and guided by the suprarational-suprasensory intuition, and that they have been but a mere instrumentality of this creative force far transcending their sensory and rational capacity. In a limited way, now and then, for a moment, almost every one of us is visited by this grace of "the supreme enlightenment" and "creative *élan*."[2] As mentioned, this realm of reality-values is cognized not so much through sensory perception, or through logico-mathematical thought as through the unpredictable, momentary flash of the suprasensory-suprarational "enlightenment" (in the sense of the Buddhist *jnana*), "intuition," "inspiration," "divine madness," "divine revelation," "mystic union with the Absolute," when one reaches the state of the Zen-Buddhist *satori* or the Yoga's *samadhi* or the Sufist "divine ecstasy."

8. Finally, the *integral reality-value* represents the harmonious, organic, and consistent unification of all these forms of reality-value into one meaningful whole. Like the Christian conception of one God, differentiated into the God-Father, Son, and Holy Ghost, the integral reality-value is one with the three main aspects, different from, but inseparable from, each other. Containing in itself all the other three forms of reality-value as its "components," it is fuller, richer, and nearer to the plenitude of the total reality-value than each of its differentiations.

The integral reality-value is cognized and experienced through the combined three "channels of cognition and experience": senses, reason, and intuition. The truth obtained through integral use of these three channels of cognition is a fuller and more valid truth than that received through only the senses or the rational reason or the suprasensory-suprarational intuition. The integral theory of reality-value does not overlook any important mode of being, as the sensory, the rationalist, the intuitional theories do. It gives *suum quique* to each mode of reality-value. It does not declare any of its three forms as a mere mirage or illusion, and it fairly clearly defines the nature, the position, and the relationship of all four forms of reality-value in regard to one another and in reference to the total reality and the total value.

9. In the integral conception of the total reality-value *man* is

---

[2] See a more detailed analysis and a vast body of empirical evidence confirming these characteristics of the suprasensory-suprarational reality-value in the works referred to, particularly in *The Ways and Power of Love*, Chaps. 5, 6.

also conceived as a *marvelous integral being.* He is not only an empirical organism of the *homo sapiens* species, and not only rational thinker and doer; he is also a supersensory and superrational being, an active participant in the supreme, creative forces of the total cosmos. In other terms, man is not only an unconscious, conscious, and rational creature or reality-value; he is also a supraconscious-suprarational master-creator capable of transcending his unconscious and rational energies, and actually doing so in the moments of his "divine inspiration," in the periods of his intensest and best creativity. Man's greatest creative achievements and man's highest moments of the *summum bonum* have been due largely to the integral man as the supraconscious master-creator assisted by man as a rational thinker and doer and by man as an empirical observer, and biosensory creature. This integral nature of man as reality-value allows him to live, to know, and to create amidst the cosmic, integral universe of reality-value.

10. In the infinite universe of the total reality-value, there is *the supreme integral value-reality*—the veritable *summum bonum.* It is unnamable and undefinable in its inexhaustible plenitude. Most often it has been called by the term God or its equivalents.

Its highest manifestation in the human universe is the supreme Trinity of the greatest reality-values: Truth, Goodness, and Beauty. Each of these value-realities has an individuality different from that of the other two. Each has its own hierarchical gradation from the smallest, least significant, impure, parochial, and temporary semi-truths, semigoodnesses, and semibeauties up to the greatest, purest, universal, immortal, and most significant Truth, Beauty, and Goodness.

At their lower grades these (cognitive, moral, and aesthetic) reality-values appear to be fairly separate from, and even contradictory with, one another, if and when each of them is evaluated in the terms of the other two reality-values. Thus, a "little beauty" such as a sexually charged dance of Salome or "rock and roll" music may be found, from the cognitive or moral standpoint, to be "a false" or "evil" sham-beauty. A correct statistical study of the number of datings by the students of a small college in October and November of 1957—this little informational truth is fairly indifferent morally and aesthetically. An invention of a new mass-destructive means of warfare and its successful use against the enemy turns out to be an "ugly" and "demoralizing" scientific truth. From a tribal standpoint, a good action, such as a patriotic, preventive nuclear attack against an enemy for the purposes of establishment of peace, may easily appear to be "the ugliest" and superstitious or ignorant action, so far as the establishment of peace is concerned. In other words, on the low level of the sham-values, the semivalues, and the little values of truth, beauty, and goodness, each of these reality-values may often exert either no tangible—or even negative—effects upon the other two reality-values. On this low level a progress of the small cognitive values does not necessarily lead to the progress of moral and aesthetic values; and the moral or aesthetic progress does not necessarily entail the progress of the other two values.

11. As we move on to the progressively greater truths, goodnesses, and beauties—more universal, perennial, and significant—their separateness and contradiction tend to decrease. When we reach the highest Truth, Beauty, and Goodness, they merge into one supreme, integral reality-value, into the veritable *summum bonum* most frequently called by the term God. At this highest level the genuine—universal and perennial—Truth is always good and beautiful; the sublime Goodness is invariably true and beautiful; and the pure Beauty is always true and good. At this level these three value-realities are not only inseparable from one another but are transformable into one another, as one form of physical energy, say, heat, is transformable into electricity or light or mechanical motion. Each newly discovered great truth contributes also to the values of beauty and goodness. Each act of unselfish creative love enriches the realm of truth and beauty; and each masterpiece of beauty morally ennobles and mentally enlightens the members of the human universe. On this level a great mathematical formula becomes an aesthetic masterpiece and a moral reality-value; and the masterpiece of Bach or Mozart mentally enlightens and morally ennobles us more effec-

tively than many a scientific text or a moral sermon could. This means that the criterion of the integral reality-value is a more reliable "measure of all the reality-values" than the criterion of one of the three reality-values.

12. The preceding gives a fairly adequate criterion for evaluation of all the values, and especially of the total value of the life-process of every person. *The more reality-values of Truths, Goodness, and Beauty, especially in their highest forms, a person cognizes, experiences, deals with, lives through, and creates, the happier, the richer, the more significant and more valuable is his or her life-adventure.* With a slight modification, the same criterion can be applied for the evaluation of the life-process of human society and of the whole mankind. The main historical mission of mankind consists in an unbounded creation, accumulation, refinement, and actualization of Truth, Beauty, and Goodness in the nature of man himself, in man's mind and behavior, in man's sociocultural universe and beyond it, and in man's relationships to all human beings, to all living creatures, and to the total cosmos. By discharging this task man is fulfilling in the best and most faithful way his duty of master-creator toward the Supreme Cosmic Creator.

13. A careful study of the history of each of the four outlined systems of reality-values shows that these systems fluctuate in their rise and decline in various societies and cultures. For instance, in the history of the Graeco-Roman and Western cultures, in the centuries from the ninth to the sixth before Christ, the fairly primitive variation of the suprasensory-suprarational system of reality-values (the Ideational system) was dominant in the Greek mentality and culture; from the sixth to the fourth century before Christ a splendid variation of partly the rational, but mainly the integral, system of reality-values (Idealistic-Integral system) dominated the mind, the soul, and the culture of Greece; from the fourth century before Christ to the fourth century anno Domini a variation of the sensory-empirical system of reality-values (Sensate) was dominant in the Graeco-Roman mentality and culture; the centuries from the fifth to the end of the twelfth in the Western culture were dominated by the

Christian (mediaeval) suprasensory-suprarational system of reality-values (Christian-Ideational system); from the end of the twelfth to that of the fourteenth century partly the rational but mainly the integral system of reality-values (Idealistic-Integral) was the main cultural system in the total culture of the West; from the fifteenth to the twentieth century a new splendid variation of the sensory-empirical system of reality-values has been dominant in Western culture, society, and man. At the present time this sensory-empirical system is rapidly disintegrating. This disintegration is the real cause of the greatest crisis of our age, with its world wars, endless local wars, revolutions, revolts, mental, moral, and social anarchy, its destruction and insanity, its liberation in man of "the worst of beasts," and the feverish preparations for the next suicidal thermonuclear wars.[3] The building of this new integral-system of reality-values is the best and most powerful antidote against the continuation of man's present moral anarchy. A realization of this task means an opening of a magnificent era in the creative history of mankind.

[3] See a detailed analysis and corroboration of the fluctuation of the four systems of reality-values and of the crisis of our age in P. Sorokin, *Social and Cultural Dynamics,* and in P. Sorokin, *Crisis of our Age,* E. P. Dutton & Co., 1941, and 1957.

Reply to Professor Weisskopf

————————————— ROBERT S. HARTMAN

I SHALL supplement Weisskopf's summary with an óbservation which seems to me crucial for the aims of the Conference. Almost all the participants share in the conviction that "a science of value is possible." Yet, as Weisskopf's summary makes clear, very few of them discuss the conditions of such a science. Rather, they deal with items which, without examination, they suppose to be *subjects of* such a science—evolution, self, Being, and the like—to which Weisskopf's three categories, the naturalistic, the humanistic, and the ontological, are relevant. These categories, however, are not relevant to the question whether, and in which respect, these items and indeed the categories themselves, *are* values. To answer this question presupposes a definition of value itself.

Thus, while most of the contributions more or less fit into Weisskopf's categories, it confuses the issue my own contribution raises to try to fit it, even tentatively, into these categories. My paper is concerned with science rather than with value. Its tenor is that a science of value is impossible unless and until the question of what to understand by such a science is first examined. Weisskopf himself uses this Moorean procedure when he says with respect to Maslow: "Neither the concept of mental or psychological health, nor the concept of self-actualization in itself seems to be an appropriate scientific basis for values because these concepts are based on implicit value judgments which are not derived from the scientifically observed fact" (p. 212). This argument is applicable *universally:* to assume of anything that it is valuable implies a previous value judgment. And this goes also for something so universal and supposedly so valuable as Being. Yet Weisskopf believes that the ontological view is exempted from his objection—that it provides the solution of the value question because it finds value in Being itself. Actually, to attribute value to being presupposes an implicit value judgment, as does any attribution of value. There are many, such as Heidegger, who find no value at all in Being. There is, then, no difference, logically, between attributing the predicate "good" to chickens or to Being. In both cases, if I want to be *scientific,* I must logically justify such attribution. This, in turn, presupposes clarity about the notion of value itself, and such clarity can be had only by a science the subject of which is value and nothing else. The science of value, thus, is logicaly necessary if we want to account for value judgments.

Those who obstruct such a science today and regard it as impossible are the positivists. If the participants of the Conference share in the conviction that a science of value is possible, they cannot be positivists. Actually, however, all of them, insofar as they fit into Weisskopf's three categories, affirm the positivistic position. This position is that value, such as love, is irrational; and that what is rational is not value but fact. Weisskopf's ontologists affirm the irrationality of value and thus confirm the positivistic position even though they profess to deny it. Obviously, one does not deny a position by affirming its tenets. The ontologists affirm the positivistic *irrationality* of value; Weisskopf's "naturalists" and "humanists," on the other hand, affirm the positivistic irrationality of *value*—for the phenomena they call rational are not those the positivists call value but those they call fact. Thus, *all* of Weisskopf's categories are positivistic; and only insofar as one does *not* fit into them is one on the way to a science of value.

The only way to deny the positivistic position is to *deny what it affirms,* namely, the irrationality of value, including love; and to *affirm what it denies,* namely, the rationality of value, including love. This, to my mind, is the only basis of a *science* of value. Hence, formal axiology shows love as the epitome of rationality—a rationality, to be sure, fundamentally different, yet no less rational, than that of any phenomenon of science. And the definition of intrinsic value in formal axiology happens to be literally the same as Suzuki's of good, "the isness of things." Only, axiological isness is a formal and not a material concept, and it means something systematically and in detail.[1]

Thus, if, as Weisskopf says, the consensus of the Conference is *"union through love,"* and if it also is a *science of value,* then it can only be *union through love axiologically understood.* For this reason Weisskopf's three categories—the naturalist, the humanist, and the ontological—must be supplemented by a fourth, the category of the *logical,* as a model of thought not only about *human* value but about value *itself.*[2]

---

[1] The notion that the mystic experience is extralogical is based on one of those fallacies of Aristotle, for which Bertrand Russell called him one of the great disasters to befall humanity. The fallacy is to assume that the unique individual is not logically accessible, because thinking is based on abstraction, and if unique things had something in common they would not be unique. The fallacy is resolved by understanding that the uniqueness of a thing means the thing's having all the properties it has, but that "having all the properties it has" is not one of the properties it is said to have. It is a property *of* these properties; and it is, precisely, the property that all unique things have in common. Thus, the axiologist can scientifically deal with the mystic experience. This does not mean that he is a mystic—as little as the entomologist's dealing with worms means that he is a worm. Or that "having a cup of tea" means to be a tea expert. To be a mystic and to be an expert in mysticism are two different things.

[2] Value *itself,* as I tried to expound in my own essay, is the *concept* of value by which the *phenomena* of value are to be understood. It is "value" rather than value. In terms of the present book it is part of *"knowledge"* rather than of *"human values."* In addition to my own essay, Professor Margenau's essay deals, in part, with the concept "value." The other essays of this book, including Professor Tillich's and Weisskopf's, deal with value phenomena.

Reply to Professor Weisskopf

HENRY MARGENAU

It is my understanding that a naturalist in ethics is a person who derives ethical values from the facts of natural science, and the term has furthermore come to suggest the stigma of the "naturalistic fallacy" in the bearer of that name. The proposal that a careful distinction be made between *de facto* preferences and normative values (and it is completely irrelevant whether the former are *called* values so long as they are not mistaken for the sort of thing that matters in ethics), followed by the outline of a method whereby the ought can be seen to arise from principled scientific procedures rather than the facts of science, is hardly an appeal to naturalism. I think, therefore, that my endeavor has been incorrectly classified in Weisskopf's otherwise very perceptive postscript.

Neither had I supposed that I am a nominalist, except perhaps in the simple sense that I cannot accept naive realism. Other writings (see my *Nature of Physical Reality*) which search for and propose ways whereby concepts are reified will surely exempt me from the charge of nominalism.

Weisskopf's criticism, suggesting that the distinction between descriptive science and theoretical science is a doubtful one because "all sciences, descriptive and theoretical, try to discover regularities which can serve as a basis for prediction," is not acceptable to me. The quoted sentence is true, of course, but the manner in which prediction is achieved is different in the two kinds of science. One

236

relies mainly on induction; the other uses constructs together with a complex interplay between inductive and deductive procedures. No nameable science is wholly one or the other, but a given theory can be designated as belonging primarily to the descriptive or the theoretical category.

Further discussion of this problem may also be found in the book cited above. There, too, I have endeavored to show that the Humean view of causality, according to which "one fact is the condition or cause of another fact" is not compatible with modern physics.

But perhaps Weisskopf's use of the word "fact" differs from the one I advocate. For he says that "the source of the command and the commitment" are themselves facts. Would it not be better to restrict that word to the more immediate, tangible, primary, sensory aspects of experience, and employ such terms as postulate, regulative principle, for the commands in question? This, at any rate, is a distinction which underlies my discussion, and I am grateful to Dr. Weisskopf for evidence that the word "fact" is often used in other ways.

Reply to Professor Weisskopf

_____ JACOB BRONOWSKI

A SUMMARY of a discussion made by one of the protagonists in it is not likely to please the others. It is therefore natural that I, and no doubt other participants, find Dr. Weisskopf's summary unsatisfactory. I am particularly puzzled by the questions he puts to me in his version of what I said. My speech must surely, and in the nature of things, have raised several questions that it did not answer. But Dr. Weisskopf surprises me by asking again only those questions (Can truth to fact be defined without some act of judgment? What is meant by the evolution of society? Are there other values than those which I sketched? and so on) to which I myself drew attention in my speech, and which I specifically answered there.

Clearly, therefore, we shall get no further by using these pages to argue matters of detail. Instead, I will turn to a matter of principle: it is this. Under Dr. Weisskopf's view, there runs always the assumption that values are already known, in their essentials, once and for all—that, for example, Buddha and Christ at bottom said all that will ever be said about values. For my part, I find this assumption pointless, but not because I think it untrue; on the contrary, I find it pointless because I think it is a truism. I think that we all know the essential values, when we can think about them abstractly. But one cannot build a theory of values on this abstract knowledge, this lip-service that men pay to their nature when they are alone.

The business of a theory of values is to find and to elucidate those values which in fact are expressed by the way that men act and live in their age. These deep and unspoken values in action are no less human than the precepts of sages; and my speech was a practical study to uncover some of them in our age.

Reply to Professor Weisskopf

——————— LUDWIG VON BERTALANFFY

I HAVE read with much interest the essay by Dr. Weisskopf attempting to systematize the diverse approaches toward the problem of human values that are possible and reflected in the present Conference. I believe his classification into "naturalistic," "humanistic," and "ontological" theories is essentially correct. It is my opinion, however, that the concept (or to use a fashionable term, the model) of man as a builder of symbolic universes is, in principle, capable of bringing these different approaches under a common denominator.

So far as the naturalistic and humanistic approaches are concerned, the viewpoints expressed all too sketchily in the present author's paper, embrace both of them. The roots of man and his behavior in the biological realm are taken as self-evident and granted; on the other hand, that unique characteristic which appears to distinguish him profoundly from other beings is emphasized against a purely naturalistic and biological "model" of man. Naturally, the question remains how man has become an *animal symbolicum* different, in this respect, from his animal forebears. Present science does not offer an easy answer, and the positions of the naturalist biologist referring to some process of natural selection leading to the evolution of man's brain and symbolic activities, and of the believer claiming the supernatural position of man, both are an act of faith inaccessible to proof as this term is used in natural and experimental science. "Self-actualization," "psychological health," "creativity,"

240

and similar notions used to characterize a "humanistic" definition of human values are, however, well within the model proposed; it being understood that such notions not only mean fulfillment of man's biological nature and fullness of experience, but that man's most characteristic activities are in the symbolic field, that this is more than a means of adaptation and survival and follows its own autonomous laws.

The contrast between the first two and the "ontological" approach pivots upon the age-old problem of nominalism and realism in the scholastic sense. In its pure form, ontology presupposes the existence of Platonic ideas in some supercelestial space, to be intuited by the adept. This obviously is beyond the realm of science even though it is worth mentioning that Plato's problem of "ideas"—of the lion, the cooking-pot, or man is not obsolete but persists in somewhat modi- fied form in the question of the meaning of laws of nature. Are these only means for a stenographic description of natural phenomena, or do they represent "reality"? The view of the old-fashioned physicist believing in inexorable "laws of nature" is not essentially different from that of the Platonic believing in the "reality" of ideas of the lion, man, and all the rest. A "perspectivist" evaluation of the sym- bolic universe[1] appears to present an answer. A "law of nature," such as Newton's law or, for that matter, the "idea" of man does mirror a certain aspect of reality; otherwise it would be worse than useless, and there would be neither a practicable technology nor morals. None of these aspects, however, exhausts or fully embraces reality, whatever this may mean. The nearest approach to the latter seems to be the statement that reality can only be experienced, not told; what can be told in conceptual symbols are aspects concerning certain of its formal relationships; and, so far as its representation in discursive symbols is concerned, *"coincidentia oppositorum"*[2] is the nearest description of the Ineffable.

---

[1] Cf. L. von Bertalanffy, "An Essay on the Relativity of Categories," *Phi- losophy of Science* 22, 243–263, 1955.

[2] Cf. L. von Bertalanffy, *Nikolaus von Kues,* George Mueller, 1928.

Reply to Professor Weisskopf

_____ DAISETZ SUZUKI

AFTER reading Dr. Weisskopf's Summary I am reminded of the last of the three Zen *mondo* ("question and answer") given in my paper which concerns the world and man living in it. I will give my conceptual interpretation of the *mondo* as follows:

The whole transaction between the monk and the master may sound to the outsider utterly enigmatic or altogether too symbolic beyond the ordinary human intelligence. But after some reflection the meaning will grow clearer, and the Zen view of the world or reality and value may dawn upon us.

"The temple" referred to in the *mondo* is really the garden or grove where the monks congregate for study or rest, and means the world or the objective world facing us as an irreducible fact. We now ask, "What is it?" The Zen master answers, "Just this." (Or "Just so.") Neither more nor less. It is the given. We are born into it and face it. If we do not take it as it is in its suchness or isness, we are doomed.

We then go on to the second question, "Who is the 'I' or the subject who asks?" The master answers, "What?! What?!" This is the most significant response. "What" here is at once interrogative and exclamatory. It is a question and at the same time an assertion. Ever since the awakening of consciousness we have been constantly asking such questions as, "What is this world where we have been ushered without our knowledge or consent and where we are to eke

242

out our existence willy-nilly, talking about the value or meaning of all this?"

The animals and vegetables go on living, even thriving, without raising any questions whatever and for this reason without torment-ing themselves as we do. We boast ourselves to be human beings, but I often wonder if there is anything in us that really deserves this distinction. The intellect prompts questions of various natures, but the solutions it gives are never final. We thus are destined to en-counter an *aporia* or run into a blind alley. However hard we may struggle, we cannot escape this so long as we follow the way of intellection. Zen is fully conscious of this.

Zen, therefore, stops at the question and turns the question into the answer. "What?" thus becomes "What!" "What!" may be re-garded as the synthesis of "What?" and "That!" or "This!" Instead of a period, "That" has an exclamation mark after it. For when "What" finds its own solution in "That" (or "This"), it is completely taken aback to become conscious of the fact that the solution has not come from the plane of intellection itself which raised the question, but from a higher and a more basic order. And it is this order where Zen has its abode.

In "What?!" fact and value coalesce, or rather, it is in "What?!" where science and the humanities are grounded. When the "What?!" of the Zen master is understood, the doors open to Zen and to the mystery of being.

"What will you do when a visitor comes?" This is where the objective world of brute facts comes in relationship with the sub-ject, "I." The object is "Just this!" or "Just so!" whereas the subject is "What?!" If the object is a brute fact, the subject is also of the same nature, but it is the subject that raises the question. It is not, how-ever, really the subject or the intellect, though superficially it may so look. The question-raising comes from a very much deeply rooted source. It points to the moment when God willed to give his fiat, "Let there be light." The question is already implied in the fiat, and therefore the answer is also there.

When you and I, subject and object, man and the world, "take a cup of tea," there is "union of love," and the question of fact and value is satisfactorily solved here without much ado. Zen is anxious to have us see into this moment. It is left to philosophers to argue, to discuss, to quibble, or to do whatever they like about the Zen solution.

Reply to Professor Weisskopf

_____ ABRAHAM H. MASLOW

WHILE agreeing in general with Dr. Weisskopf's brilliant analysis, I think it desirable to point out that, even though the naturalist, the humanistic, and the ontological approaches are in fact different from each other at this time, they *need* not be. Weisskopf himself indicates how the humanistic and ontological approaches can be very much alike. I would maintain that my studies (and others) have been empirical and naturalistic in the broad sense even though dealing with "being." For instance, I have demonstrated that both dichotomies and the resolution of dichotomies at a higher level of human development ("union upward") can be studied and described empirically.

Weisskopf states that "It (the ontological image) seeks to transcend the facts of sensory observation and of intuitive experience." I would deny that this leap is necessary in order to study being and the "unity of all polar antinomies within being itself." Science, defined broadly enough, can and has managed this job too. Of course, Weisskopf is quite correct in assuming that many (most?) scientists do not *now* define science broadly enough to measure up to its new tasks. Sooner or later, however, they will have to.

As for Weisskopf's specific critique of my paper, I agree that with great perspicuity, he has selected out the crucial points at which further research and clarification are necessary. I feel, however, that a closer reading of what was necessarily an extremely condensed

245

presentation can resolve his doubts. For instance, I think I have shown that the concepts of psychological health and of self-actualization need *not* be based on implicit value judgments. When properly defined, they *are* derived from scientifically observed facts. They are descriptive concepts in about the same sense that physical health is a descriptive concept. I agree that we urgently need more knowledge of what "humanness" and "human capacities" are before we can be unequivocal or avoid the appearance of circular reasoning when we define self-actualization as the fuller use of human capacities, or as being more fully human. As the defining and differentiating charactristics of humanness become better known, it will be easier and easier to select out people who are "more fully human" and to describe *their* values (rather than the covert values of the investigator). These must then be considered to be the ultimate values for all mankind (since all men press toward being more fully human). In principle, this kind of descriptive study could be done by robots or by Martians or by other entities that do not share human values. Also, in principle, we human beings may one day be faced with the task of discovering the values of some other kind of nonhuman species on some other planet. This too we shall be able to do.

Finally, I should like to point out that love, of which Weisskopf speaks almost exclusively, is not the only path to unity within the person, between persons, or with the world. The arts, in both their creating and enjoying aspects, should have been more stressed. And so also should the human intellect (properly defined) be more properly appreciated as an integrating and unifying tool. I should like to suggest two books which demonstrate what I mean by these statements. One is *The New Landscape* by G. Kepes, and the other is *On Not Being Able to Paint* by M. Milner.

Reply to Professor Weisskopf

_____ KURT GOLDSTEIN

I AM sorry that I am not quite in agreement with Professor Weiss-kopf's characterization of my standpoint concerning value. In his attempt to distinguish among the concepts of the various speakers three different approaches which differ in their methods of acquiring knowledge and their concept of reality, he places me among the "humanists," "although their viewpoint shows naturalistic traits in their reasoning." If one is a humanist, according to Professor Weiss-kopf, when one tries to get knowledge which can be called a holistic one, and attempts to grasp the total human situation with its transcendence, consciousness, self-awareness, and freedom and establish knowledge by using not only logic and factual observation but empathy and intuition, then I could consider myself a humanist; only, however, with some reservations, insofar as my standpoint is not simply holistic but tries to bring what is called value in relation to the *"existence"* of the organism expressed in its trend to *realize its intrinsic nature.* Value is not secondarily ascribed to something; it is not a norm. It is a *characteristic of the true being of man,* the essence of which manifests itself in reality mostly in a somewhat distorted form, which is the expression of the particular nature of man. It represents the conditions of adequacy between the individual and the world, which means *health.* Health appears as value, *the* prototype of value because it guarantees self-realization. I can further not agree that I show *naturalistic traits in reasoning.* If one means by the term naturalist (as is usually meant) someone who applies the method of natural science to biology, then I am not a biologist. I am a sudent of living beings who tries to understand them in their intrinsic nature and considers the phenomena revealed by the method of natural science not as part processes of the functioning of the organism but as expressions of its nature as it appears under special conditions and application of a special method of investigation and interpretation. The "empirical" facts have, from this point of view, to be evaluated as to their significance for the organism in its totality and unity and insofar as they contribute to its existence. How this approach differs essentially from that of natural science appears in the fact that many of the findings of this method are irrelevant—and others become relevant which do not find even a mention in the usual biology. The laws by which the behavior of the organism becomes understandable represent themselves as such which guarantee the organism's existence.

Thus, my viewpoint in respect to my concept of the nature of man and of value in particular I would rather term humanist with an ontological attitude. Thereby ontology would mean ontology in respect to living beings, which makes *understandable* the phenomena that natural science and biology bring to the fore, and the particular form and its existence under special conditions in man, naturally in accordance with the special form of his intrinsic nature.

My approach to value—at least in principle—corresponds somewhat to that of Paul Tillich. I agree with him when he rejects heteronomous derivation of value "from the arbitrary awareness of a transcendant tyrant" or as determined by utilitarian calculations, and considers *value as derived from the essential structure of being.* I would add only, of living beings in their different intrinsic nature. Therefore it is not accidental that I reject as values—as he does—survival, greatest happiness of the greatest number, or similar concepts. In my opinion also, for instance, security has to be rejected as value. I tried to show that man's behavior *cannot* be understood as determined by a *trend for security,* by a *pleasure principle, simply* by *avoidance of tension,* anxiety, and suffering. All these and other

trends may under special conditions come to the fore as determinants of behavior and may appear thus as values, but they have to be
considered as *expressions of reduction of the nature of man* and can
be correctly evaluated only in relation to the trend of self-realization
or, more precisely, as expression of the fact *that the individual is,
under the given conditions, not able to realize himself fully*. Therefore, a special behavior, for example, survival, may be accepted as a
compromise evaluated as the next best form of self-realization.

Biographical Notes on the Contributors

GORDON W. ALLPORT, Professor of Psychology, Department of Social Relations, and Chairman of the Committee on Higher Degrees, Harvard University, was born in Indiana. Dr. Allport attended public schools in Cleveland and took both his bachelor's and doctor's degree at Harvard. In 1919–1920 he taught English and Sociology at Robert College, Istanbul, Turkey. He held a Sheldon Traveling Fellowship between 1922 and 1924 and studied in Berlin, Hamburg, and Cambridge. In the following two years he was Instructor in Social Ethics at Harvard and for four years thereafter Assistant Professor of Psychology at Dartmouth College. Dr. Allport was appointed to the Harvard faculty in 1930. During World War II he served on the Emergency Committee in Psychology and specialized in problems of civilian morale and rumor. He was President of the American Psychological Association in 1937, of the Eastern Psychological Association in 1943, and of the Society for the Study of Social Issues in 1944. His books include *The Psychology of Radio* (with Hadley Cantril); *Personality: A Psychological Interpretation; The Psychology of Rumor* (with Leo Postman); *The Individual and His Religion; The Nature of Prejudice;* and *Becoming: Basic Considerations for a Psychology of Personality.* During 1956 Mr. Allport served as Consultant to the Institute for Social Research, University of Natal, South Africa.

LUDWIG VON BERTALANFFY, Director, Biological Research, Mount Sinai Hospital, and Visiting Professor of Physiology, University of Southern California, Los Angeles, was a professor of the University of Vienna until 1948 and subsequently Professor at the University of Ottawa and Senior Fellow of the Center for Advanced Study in the Behavioral Sciences at Stanford, California. His scientific contributions include the foundation

251

of organismic biology which, in contrast to the then-dominating mechanistic view, emphasized the necessity of investigating the organism and its laws as a whole; the development of a quantitative theory of organic growth; the theory of open systems and steady state; a recently introduced method for the detection of cancer by way of fluorescence microscopy; and the introduction of General Systems Theory, an interdisciplinary field aimed at integration of the various branches of science. Mr. Bertalanffy's ten books (partly published in the English, German, Spanish, and Japanese languages) include *Modern Theories of Development; Theoretical Biology;* and *Problems of Life; An Evaluation of Modern Biological Thought.*

JACOB BRONOWSKI, Director of the Coal Research Establishment, National Coal Board, Cheltenham, England, was born in Poland. As a child, he spent World War I in Germany. He went to England in 1920 and was trained as a mathematician, being a Wrangler in the University of Cambridge in 1930 and M.A. and Ph.D. in 1933. In 1942 he left university teaching and became head of a number of mathematical units dealing with the statistical and economic effects of bombing. He was a pioneer in the development of operational research methods. In 1945 Dr. Bronowski was Scientific Deputy to the British Chiefs of Staff Mission to Japan and wrote the British report, *The Effects of the Atomic Bombs at Hiroshima and Nagasaki.* He was Carnegie Visiting Professor at Massachusetts Institute of Technology in 1953. His recent work has been in the philosophy of science and has been concerned with the place science should occupy in a modern culture. This problem is discussed in his book *The Common Sense of Science* and will be the theme of his most recent book, based on his Massachusetts Institute of Technology lectures, *Science and Human Values.*

THEODOSIUS DOBZHANSKY, Professor of Zoology, Columbia University, was born in Russia. He graduated from the University of Kiev in 1921, and became Lecturer in Genetics at University of Leningrad 1924–27. Coming to the United States in 1927, he was a Fellow of the International Education Board 1928–29 and in 1930 was appointed Assistant Professor of Genetics at the California Institute of Technology. In 1936 he became a professor and was invited to Columbia University in 1940. He was exchange professor at the University of Sao Paulo, Brazil in 1943, 1948–1949, and 1955–1956.

A member of the National Academy of Sciences, he has been elected a foreign member of the Danish, Swedish, and Brazilian academies of sciences. Dr. Dobzhansky is the author of *Genetics and Origin of Species; Evolution, Genetics, and Man; Biological Basis of Human Freedom; Heredity, Race, and Society.*

ERICH FROMM, Psychoanalyst and Professor, Michigan State University and University of Mexico, was born in Frankfurt-am-Main, Germany. He studied psychology, sociology, and philosophy at the University of Heidelberg, from which he received his Ph.D. degree in 1922. He also studied at the University of Munich and the Berlin Institute of Psychoanalysis, of which he is a graduate. He has been Guest Lecturer at Columbia University and Lecturer at the New School of Social Research, and he delivered the Terry Lectures at Yale University. He is a member of the faculty of the William Alanson White Institute of Psychiatry, Psychoanalysis and Psychology, and has been a member of the faculty of Michigan State University. He is also a Diplomate of the American Psychological Association and is presently head of the Department of Psychoanalysis of the Medical School of the National University of Mexico. His books include *Man for Himself; Escape from Freedom; The Forgotten Language; Psychoanalysis and Religion; The Sane Society;* and *The Art of Loving.*

KURT GOLDSTEIN, Jacob Ziskind Professor of Psychology, Brandeis University, was born in Germany and received his M.D. degree from Breslau State University in 1903. He served in various German institutions as a psychiatric assistant and instructor until he was named Professor of Neurology and Psychiatry at the Medical School of Frankfurt-am-Main and Director of the Neurology Institute in 1914, a post which he held until 1930. During World War I, he was Director of the Military Hospital for Brain-Injured Soldiers. From 1930 he was Director of the Neurological and Psychiatric Division of City Hospital, Moabit, Berlin, and was Professor of Neurology and Psychiatry at the University of Berlin. He came to the United States in 1935, as Clinical Professor of Neurology at Columbia University. From 1940 to 1945 he was Clinical Professor of Neurology at Tufts Medical School. He returned to New

York in 1946 as Visiting Professor of Psychology at City College and entered private practice. During 1955–1957, Dr. Goldstein was Visiting Professor of Psychology at the New School of Social Research, New York City, and at Columbia University. He was Visiting Professor of Psychology at Brandeis in 1955, returned in 1957 to lecture at the Brandeis Summer School, and was appointed for the following academic year. He is the author of *The Organism.*

ROBERT S. HARTMAN, State Department Exchange Professor of Philosophy and Research Professor, Center for Philosophical Research, National University of Mexico, studied at the German College of Political Science, University of Paris, London School of Economics and Political Science, and the University of Berlin, from which he received an LL.B. degree. Leaving Germany, he was representative of Walt Disney Productions in Scandinavia, Mexico and Central America from 1934 until 1941, when he studied at the University of Mexico. He was a master at Lake Forest Academy 1942–1945 and received his Ph.D. degree from Northwestern University in 1946. Since then he has taught at the College of Wooster, Ohio State University, and, as a visiting professor, at Massachusetts Institute of Technology. He has been Chairman of the Commission on Peace, International Council of Community Churches. Among his publications are the report on Value Theory for the Institut International de Philosophie 1949–1955, and their quinquennial *Chronique de Philosophie,* published for UNESCO. Others include *Profit Sharing Manual; The Language of Value; The Partnership of Capital and Labor: Theory and Practice of a New Economic System;* and the forthcoming *The Structure of Value: Foundations of Scientific Axiology.*

GYORGY KEPES, Professor of Visual Design, Massachusetts Institute of Technology, was born in Hungary and graduated from the Royal Academy of Fine Arts in Budapest in 1928. He came to the United States in 1937 to become head of the light and color department of the New Bauhaus, Chicago (later to be called the Institute of Design), until 1943. He worked in film and theatre designs in Berlin and London and designed a number of major exhibitions in the United States. In 1944 he designed the Exhibition of the Arts of the United Nations, Art Institute in Chicago and, in 1945, the introductory room of the *Exposition des techniques Americaines de l'habitation et de l'urbanisme,* in Paris.

He designed mosaic walls, stained glass and porcelain enamel murals, etc., for such buildings as the Harvard Graduate Center, Fitchburg Children's Library.

His works have been exhibited at the Art Institute of Chicago, San Francisco Museum of Art, Museum of Modern Art, New York, Whitney Museum of American Art, New York, Carnegie International, Pittsburgh, Stedelijk Museum, Amsterdam, Royal Academy of Arts, Copenhagen, L'Obelisco Gallery, Rome, Syracuse Museum of Art, Institute of Contemporary Art, Boston, etc.

Mr. Kepes is the author of *The Language of Vision* and *The New Landscape*. At present he is working on a major study of the perceptual form of our urban environment.

DOROTHY LEE, Leader of the Cultural Anthropology Program, The Merrill-Palmer School, Detroit, was born in Constantinople, attended schools there, in Smyrna and in Athens. She came to the United States in 1924 and studied at Vassar College and the University of California, where she received her Ph.D. degree in anthropology. She has been a member of the Faculties of the University of Washington, Sarah Lawrence College, Pomona College, and Vassar. She was Consultant in Anthropology to the fact-finding staff for the White House Conference for Children and Youth in 1950. Mrs. Lee has done field work among the Wintu Indians. She has been giving special interest to the study of values and of the conceptual framework of experience in different cultures.

HENRY MARGENAU, Eugene Higgins Professor of Physics and Natural Philosophy, Yale University, began his education in Germany and continued it in the United States, after he came to this country in 1923. He attended Midland College and the University of Nebraska and received the Ph.D. degree from Yale in 1929. During World War II he worked in micro-wave theory, particularly duplexing systems, which made possible the use of the same antenna in a radar set for both sending and receiving. He has been consultant to the Atomic Energy Commission, Brookhaven National Laboratory, the National Bureau of Standards, the Argonne National Laboratory, the Rand Corporation, and numerous industrial laboratories, a staff member of the Institute for Advanced Study at Princeton, New Jersey, and the Radiation Laboratory at Massachusetts Institute of Technology. Mr. Margenau is president of the American

Philosophy of Science Association and has been an Associate Editor of *The Journal of the Philosophy of Science*, of *The American Journal of Science*, *The Reviews of Modern Physics* and the *Journal of Chemical Physics*. He is the author of *The Mathematics of Physics and Chemistry* and *The Nature of Physical Reality*, co-author of *Foundations of Physics* and *The Nature of Concepts*.

ABRAHAM H. MASLOW, Philip Meyers Professor of Psychology and Chairman of the Department of Psychology, Brandeis University, received his A.B., M.A., and Ph.D. degrees from the University of Wisconsin, where he was Research Assistant in Social Psychology, Assistant Instructor, and Teaching Fellow until 1935. Then he became a Carnegie Fellow at Columbia University from 1935 to 1937, after which he joined the faculty of Brooklyn College. Dr. Maslow was a member of the board of directors of the Massachusetts State Psychological Association and of the Society of Psychological Study of Social Issues. As a member of the American Psychological Association, he was elected a fellow in the Association's Division of Abnormal and Clinical Psychology and the Division of Esthetics; also in the Division of Personality and Social Psychology, of which he served as President. Mr. Maslow is on the Board of Editors of the *Journal of Nervous and Mental Diseases* and *Social Problems*, and has contributed articles in many professional journals and chapters in a number of books. With B. Mittelmann, he is author of *Principles of Abnormal Psychology*. His most recent book, published in 1955, is *Motivation and Personality*.

PITIRIM A. SOROKIN, Director of Harvard Research Center in Creative Altruism, Professor of Sociology, Emeritus, Harvard University, was born and educated in Russia and became the first Professor and Chairman of Sociology of the University of St. Petersburg. He was imprisoned by both the Czarist and Communist regimes, once condemned to death by the Communists, pardoned by Lenin, and finally banished by the Soviet government in 1922. In November 1923 he came to the United States and was appointed to the faculty of the University of Minnesota in 1924. Harvard invited Mr. Sorokin to be its first Professor of Sociology and chairman of the department in 1930. He became Director of the Harvard Research Center in Creative Altruism, established by a grant from Mr. Eli Lilly and the Lilly Endowment in 1949.

From among some thirty volumes, Mr. Sorokin has published most recently *The Ways and Power of Love, Forms and Techniques of Altruistic and Spiritual Growth, Fads and Foibles in Modern Sociology,* and *American Sex Revolution,* and, abridged, a one-volume edition of *Social and Cultural Dynamics.* His volumes are translated into all the main languages, and, besides hundreds of papers, a score of books is already written about Sorokin's books.

Daisetz Teitaro Suzuki, Philosopher and Professor Emeritus, Otani University, Kyoto, Japan, was born in 1870 in Kanazawa, Japan. He attended Imperial University in Tokyo, but did not officially graduate, spending his spare time in this period as a novice in a Zen monastery in Kamakura. In 1897 he came to the United States as translator for the Open Court Publishing Co., La Salle, Illinois, which was devoted to religious and scientific books and periodicals, including the *Monist.* In his eleven years there he helped Paul Carus translate Tao Te Ching from Chinese into English and wrote his first book in English, *Outlines of Mahayana Buddhism.* He returned to Japan to resume his studies in Zen Buddhism, traveled to Europe through Russia in 1910, and was again back in Japan in 1911. During World War I he taught at the Peers' School and the Imperial University of Tokyo. In 1921, he accepted a position at Otani University, Kyoto, where he spent twenty years. In 1936 he attended the World Congress of Faiths in London, and was in Japan during World War II. In 1949, he attended the East-West Philosophers' Conference in Honolulu. In the same year he was decorated by the Emperor with the Cultural Medal, and was also elected a member of the Academy of Japan. Since 1951, he has made New York his headquarters and has lectured at Columbia University during the past six years.

The scores of books he has written, besides his works on Zen, include annotations of Chinese and Sanskrit Buddhist texts, translations into Japanese of writings by Swedenborg. His most recent work is *Mysticism: Christian and Buddhist.*

Paul Tillich, Professor, Harvard University, was born in Germany, the son of a Protestant minister. He studied at several European universities, including the University of Berlin, and received his Ph.D. degree from the University of Breslau in 1911. He held teaching posts in leading German universities from 1924 to 1933. In World War I he was a chaplain in the German army. He came to the United States in 1933 at the invitation of Union Theological Seminary, where he was Professor of Philosophical Theology. Upon his retirement from Union, he joined the faculty of Harvard Divinity School. From his early German writing to the present, he has been mainly interested in the boundary line between theology and philosophy. Earlier, his interest was in the relation between religion and depth psychology, and in recent years in relating religion and the philosophical movement of existentialism and religion and the visual arts. Among his numerous books are *The Courage To Be; Love, Power and Justice; Dynamics of Faith;* and *Systematic Theology,* the third and final volume of which he is currently writing. His theology is built "on the method of correlation between questions arising out of the human predicament and the answers given in the classical symbols of religion."

WALTER A. WEISSKOPF, Professor of Economics and Chairman of the Department, Roosevelt University, Chicago, Illinois. Born in Vienna, Dr. Weisskopf studied at the university there and received a J.D. degree in 1927. He also studied at the Universities of Cambridge and Geneva. He was a lawyer in Vienna until 1938, when he came to the United States, where he studied at the American University in Washington. From 1939 to 1943 he taught economics at the University of Omaha, from 1943 to 1945 at the Central YMCA College in Chicago until, in 1945, he assumed his present position at Roosevelt College. Dr. Weisskopf's publications include *Social Anxieties and Human Conflicts; Cultural Conflicts in the Political Community; Hidden Value Conflicts in Economic Thought; Modern Industrialism and Human Values; The Ethical Role of Psychodynamics; Christian Criticism of the Economic Order; The Socialization of Psychoanalysis; The Psychology of Economics* (London and Chicago, 1955). He is currently engaged in a project on the relations between ontological and social thought.

Index

Absolute, the, mystic union with, 228
Acquisition, of knowledge, humanist image of, 200; of material wealth, 49, 207, 218
Acquisitiveness, competitive, 116
Adaptation, methods of, 83–85; to environment, 76–85, 241; symbolic universes and, 68
Aesthetics and principle of validation, 49
Affect and intellect, split between, 163–64
Agape, as distinguished from eros, 97
Age of Enlightenment, 77, 79
Allport, Gordon W., 8, 137, 200, 209, 212, 214–15; biographical note on, 251
Altruism, creative, 98–100, 105; effect of evangelistic conversion on, 4–5
Analytic concept, fulfillment of, 25
Anatman, 97–99
Anatta, 97
Angell, R. C., 145
Animal symbolicum, man as, 75, 240
Animals, constitutional differences in, 122; diets of, homeostasis and, 83, 120–21
Anthropology, emphasis on love in, 5–6; ontologically oriented, 191, 194, 219, 220; valuation as phenomenon of, 16
Antinomies, level of, 199–200, 209, 215, 221, 222; polar, unity of, 108–10, 115, 118, 200, 209, 214, 221–22, 245
Anxiety, avoidance of, 208, 248; overcoming of, 181–82; resistance

against consciousness as cause of, 111; sickness as factor in, 180–81
Appel, K. E., 8
Arapesh, culture of, 167–73
Aristotle, 21, 40, 41, 91, 128, 227
Art, as factor in union, 87–92, 113, 216, 246; and self-realization, 87–92; as symbol system, 70
Asceticism, theories of, 138, 215
Asoka, securing of peace by, 10
Assagioli, R., 8
Attraction, inverse-square law of, 46–47
Automation, 66, 117, 118
Axiology, see Science of value
Axiom, implications of, 22–25

Babies, importance of love to, 6, 7
Badness, see also Goodness; calculus of value and, 28–29; heredity as factor in, 80, 84; humanist definition of, 216
Basic needs, 122, 129; hierarchical arrangement of, 123–25
Beautiful and divine, Buddhist valuation of, 96–97
Being, ontological view of, 109, 234; unity of polar antinomies within, 108–10, 115, 118, 200, 209, 214, 221–22, 245; value derived from essential structure of, 193, 195–96, 200, 248
Being and Becoming, 124–25, 130
Benedict, Ruth, 70
Berkeley, George, 15
Bertalanffy, von, Ludwig, 65, 200, 209,

259

Intuition, 17, 103, 200, 226, 247; suprasensory-suprarational, 226, 228

Intuitive experience, 245; ontological image of, 200

Inverse-square law of attraction, 46–47

Irrationality of value, positivistic, 234–35

Isness, 95, 221, 235, 242

James, William, 223

Jeans, Sir James Hopwood, 226

Jesus Christ, 10–11, 69, 227

Jnana, 228

Jung, Carl Gustav, 111, 125, 214

Justice, and love, conflict between, 195, 220, 221; creative, 195

Juvenile delinquency, increase in, 72; lack of love as factor in, 7, 8, 11; Chinese communities, low rate of, in 7–8; Hutterite communities, low rate of, in, 7–8; Mennonite communities, low rate of, in, 7–8; Quaker communities, low rate of, in, 7–8

Kant, Immanuel, 15–16, 50, 107, 149

Kepes, Gyorgy, 86, 215, 216, 246

Kepler, Johannes, 47

Kwakiutls, moral values of, 70

Lao-Tze, 10–11, 69, 95

Lee, Dorothy, 165, 178, 200, 215; biographical note on, 255

Legalistic theories of morality, 138, 146

Leibnitz, Gottfried Wilhelm, 15

Leibnizian metaphysics, 25

Life, value of, 42; Buddhist definition of, 100–102

Likert, Rensis, 139

Locke, John, 15, 79–80, 82–83

Logic, application of, to factual observation, 107, 199–200, 209–10, 218, 247; as basis of normative value, 41; explication of value in terms of, 21; universal, calculus of, 15; of value, 22, 26–28, 118

Longevity, of ethico-religious organizations. 9–10; goodness as factor in,

43; increase in, 66; of saints, love as factor in, 6–7

Lotus Gospel, 100

Lotze, Rudolf F., 189, 190

Love, as antidote against suicide, 6, 11, 215; Buddhist valuation of, 97–99; curative power, 8; death as essence of, 223; emphasis on, in disciplines, 5–6; as epitome of rationality, 234–35; as factor in longevity, 6–7, 9–10; importance of, to health and survival, 6–7, 11, 122; influence of, on delinquency, 7–8, 11; influence of, on human history, 10–11; and justice, conflict between, 195, 220–21; lack of, as cause of mental illness, 7–8, 11, 215; longing for, 44, 123–24; need for, 6, 7, 212; parental, 6, 7, 79; power of, in abolishment of war, 9–11; power of, in mitigation of hatred, 8–11; rebirth as essence of, 223; sexual, 113; as surrender and salvation of individuality, 223; transcendence of isolation by, 6; unifying powers, 5–12, 113, 152–53, 215–17, 223, 235, 246; as weapon against sin, 12

Low Nirvana, 125, 134

Malthus, Thomas R., 80

Malthusian theory, 66

Man, as animal symbolicum, 75, 240; body-soul image of, 194, 217, 220; economic, 116–17; equality of, 82–83; estrangement of, 111; evolution of, 43, 75–85, 233, 240; extinction of, negligibility of, 77; integral nature of, as reality-value, 228–29; unitarian, image of, 220

Margenau, Henry, 38, 53–56, 200, 204–9, 211, 218; biographical note on, 255–56; reply by, 236–37

Martyrdom, Christian, 203; of saints, 6–7

Maslow, Abraham H., 32, 73, 119, 137, 147–48, 200, 210–12, 215, 216, 233; biographical note on, 256; reply by, 245–46

Material wealth, acquisition of, 49, 207

Date Due			
MAR 5 1969			
MAY 5 1969			
OCT. 1 3 1972			
APR 8 1977			
JAN 2 6 2000			
MAR 0 5 2006			
APR 07 2005			
APR 28 2017			

Demco 293-5